EDITH WHARTON'S INNER CIRCLE

Literary Modernism Series
Thomas F. Staley, Editor

Edith Wharton's Inner Circle

SUSAN GOODMAN

UNIVERSITY OF TEXAS PRESS
AUSTIN

First edition, 1994

Requests for permission to reproduce material from this work should
be sent to Permissions, University of Texas Press, Box 7819, Austin,
TX 78713-7819.

Excerpts from Edith Wharton's writings reprinted by permission of
the Watkins/Loomis Agency, including quotations from *The Custom of
the Country* (© 1985), *The House of Mirth* (© 1964), *French Ways and
Their Meaning* (© 1919), *A Backward Glance* (© 1985), *The Reef*
(© 1965), *The Writing of Fiction* (© 1925), *Italian Backgrounds* (© 1905),
The Age of Innocence (© 1987), *A Motor-Flight through France* (© 1908),
Summer (© 1989), *Twilight Sleep* (© 1927), *Hudson River Bracketed*
(© 1985), and *The Fruit of the Tree* (© 1907).
    Quotations from letters and papers of Edith Wharton and Percy
Lubbock in the Edith Wharton Collection published by permission of
the Beinecke Rare Book and Manuscript Library, Yale University.
    Excerpts from letters of Henry James published by permission of
the Houghton Library, Harvard University.
    Notes on Edith Wharton by G. T. Lapsley published by permission
of Trinity College Library, Cambridge.

⊗The paper used in this publication meets the minimum require-
ments of American National Standard for Information Sciences—
Permanence of Paper for Printed Library Materials, ANSI Z39.48-1984.

Library of Congress Cataloging-in-Publication Data

Goodman, Susan, date
      Edith Wharton's inner circle / by Susan Goodman.
          p.   cm. — (Literary modernism series)
      Includes bibliographical references and index.
      ISBN 0-292-72771-2
      1. Wharton, Edith, 1862–1937—Friends and associates.
    2. James, Henry, 1843–1916—Friends and associates.   3. Authors,
    American—20th century—Biography.   4. Americans—Europe—
    History—20th century.   5. Europe—Intellectual life—20th
    century.   6. United States—Intellectual life—20th century.
    7. Modernism (Literature)   I. Title.   II. Series.
    PS3545.H16Z654   1994
    810.9′0052—dc20   93-39606
    [B]

To my parents, Rhoda and Ralph Rudnick,
and the memory of Ada Cohen

Contents

Preface

Edith Wharton and Henry James were intensely private people who valued friendship second only to art. "What is one's personality," Wharton asked in her memoir, *A Backward Glance* (1934), "detached from that of the friends with whom fate happens to have linked one?"[1] Writing Wharton in 1910, James concurred: "We always tumble together . . . for that happy exercise & sweet coincidence of agility we may trust ourselves & each other to the end of time." Growing—to quote James—"more & more never apart,"[2] they brought together other friends whom Wharton called "the inner circle" or "the happy few." The coterie, which started to form about 1904 and lasted until Wharton's death in 1937, included Howard Sturgis, Walter Berry, Percy Lubbock, Robert Norton, John Hugh Smith, and Gaillard Lapsley. Margaret Chanler, a lifelong friend of Wharton, wrote that the privilege of being admitted to this group "was indeed flattering for many were called on but few were chosen."[3]

As with Bloomsbury, who was or was not "chosen" is subject to debate. Paul Bourget, the French playwright, critic, and novelist, and Bernard Berenson, the controversial Renaissance art critic, are cases in point. Although he introduced Wharton to an international world of letters, Bourget had, with the exception of James, only casual social encounters with the other friends. Berenson, whom Wharton considered an intimate around 1912, did not know Robert Norton until five years later. For the purposes of this study, I have defined the members of the inner circle not only in relation to Wharton but also to one another, referring to someone like Berenson, for example, when the discussion focuses on aesthetics.

The "happy few" considered themselves selected and selective. Bound by the particular problems self-imposed exile presented, the group envisioned itself—to use Wharton's ironic description from *The Custom of the Country* (1913)—as the last of the "aborigines," those vanishing denizens of civilization "doomed to rapid extinction" by the material and political advance of philistine invaders from the Midwest.[4] In truth, they were a small circle of confreres surrounded by a larger concentric circle of peers, such as Bourget and Berenson, who held the same convictions. They did not fear that science's denial of immutable truths about reality would necessarily end in the chaos Henry Adams predicted, yet, surveying the use and misuse of national and personal energies, they believed far more in the Virgin than the dynamo.

For those of the inner circle who were American—Lapsley, Berry, Sturgis, James, and Wharton—Europe seemed to offer a sense of history and definition, a richness and complexity, that the United States lacked. Expatriation legitimized a natural inclination for detached observation. As self-styled citizens of the world, they belonged nowhere and elsewhere. They lived less in their chosen communities than in another, composite country whose separate states included bits of eighteenth-century Italy, nineteenth-century America and Great Britain, and twentieth-century France. Perhaps most they lived in those elective countries Wharton thought contained within "the Urwald" of the self.[5]

Historians and sociologists, as Raymond Williams notes, remain uneasy with intellectual and artistic groups that have small numbers and sometimes hazy principles. But who can deny the achievements and influence of the Lake Poets, the Pre-Raphaelites, or Brook Farm? Statistically insignificant as it was, the group surrounding James and Wharton suggests larger patterns of social and cultural life. Its identity and sense of election, what constituted its distinguishable ethos and beliefs, rested on and were reflected in its exclusivity or selection. Less famous than other groups, and in certain ways less of a group, the inner circle defined itself against the society its principle founders left in the United States, while criticizing and accommodating the one it found in Europe. Providing a model of literary expatriation, it also represents a period of literature. Because of size, rather than in spite of it, the inner circle has—like its contemporary Bloomsbury—greater historical significance than its numbers would promise.

The stories of the individual members of the inner circle are grounded in time and place, consistent with themselves and consonant with one another. They form, as R. G. Collingwood terms it, a history.[6] James, Sturgis, Lapsley, and Berry did visit The Mount, Wharton's home in Lenox, Massachusetts, one late October weekend in 1904. What each felt, what magic occurred that linked these people for the rest of their lives, remains less tangible. We do know that Wharton created an imaginative construct which explained her connection to a particular group of male friends, who in turn mythologized her. *A Backward Glance* presents Wharton's interpretation of that history; Percy Lubbock's *Portrait of Edith Wharton* (1948) presents another. The discrepancies between these accounts and the gaps they leave hold rival, though no less valid, versions of the past. History is, after all, a conglomeration of stories, and the same events may engender a different reading or a different plot.

Each member of the inner circle has an individual narrative; collectively they negotiated, if not collaboratively authored, another. The writing of letters allowed them to sustain personas that eventually became inseparable from their definitions of themselves. With Bloomsbury in mind, Virginia Woolf explained the process this way: "we are the words; we are the music; we are the thing itself."[7] Facts may be characterized as "past" through the process of being registered and voiced in the past tense, but history, like all narrations, cannot free itself from the devices or inventions of discourse that Wharton and her friends consciously or unconsciously manipulated. Berenson recognized this when he observed that every biography or history must ultimately live on its quality as myth, "that is on an assimilable and inspiring ideated personality."[8] For the happy few, James and Wharton shared that function, ending—as Berenson wrote of himself—"as a myth whose *saga* I can scarcely recognize having any resemblance or even relation to what I feel or think I know about myself" (*BBT*, 392).

Always dangerously close to myth, history is still determined by the nature of the experience itself, which gives us a sense of "truth" being something concrete. In trying to relate and analyze a shared past, I have looked at those intersections between fact and imagination, knowing that what I offer is itself a kind of embroidery, a piecing together of separate appliqués. Commenting on history, I cannot wholly escape making it. Living as we all do, in both real and fictive worlds, both inside and outside history, I echo Alain Besançon in arguing that historical research, indeed all writing, is a form of introspection, "la recherche de soi-même."[9] The relationship between writer and subject is an exchange that evolves in its various stages. How much so is illustrated by a dream I had at the beginning of my project: Wharton had invited me for a motor-flight, after which I elatedly skipped down a hill, secure in the knowledge that she trusted me. Since then I have read a letter she wrote to her sister-in-law which stated that women scholars would be better off staying home and having babies.

Illustrating the danger of filtering another's story through one's own, my dream also gave me permission to explore Wharton's life. In much the same way, her dream of the inner circle gave that life form. As any writer must, Wharton used her specific narrative, based on the early vision of herself as a poetical child trapped in a prosaic universe, to enter her friends' worlds and admit them to hers. There were, to Wharton's thinking, those happy few, harassed by the Furies but blessed through suffering. *A Backward Glance* introduces us to these men, who successively testify to its author's double genius: an artist, yes, but no less a woman. Fact, fiction, dream? To a large extent, narratives, built on cultural assumptions and personal desires, themselves transform signifiers into signs, or, as Woolf suggests, markers into things.

This book is both biographical and critical. It aims to present an intimate view into the workings of an American expatriate community as well as the larger transatlantic culture it mirrored. The design of the chapters is largely chronological. The first chapter deals with the history of the group and the relationships of its individual members. Chapter 2 addresses the inner circle's competition with and connections to Bloomsbury, a group which differed from it politically but occupied a similar emotional and intellectual territory. Because James and Wharton were at the heart of the group, their friendship forms the center of my study and is considered in Chapter 3. Chapter 4 examines the dynamics of influence, and by necessity focuses on those besides James and Wharton who were published writers: Howard Sturgis, Percy Lubbock, and Bernard Berenson. The final chapter shows how Wharton's vision of the inner circle informs her fiction, and the Conclusion offers a perspective on literary exile, a way of understanding how Bloomsbury and another generation of American writers—Gertrude Stein and F. Scott Fitzgerald, for example—positioned themselves in their inherited or chosen places.

Defined as much by their contradictions as by their common bonds, the inner circle contrived to live in dual worlds: the literal as well as the constructed world of exile and the separate, intensely private, imagined one of self and art. Neither of these worlds is wholly "true," yet perhaps in their interplay there is—as Hemingway writes in the preface to *A Moveable Feast* (1964)—a chance of fiction throwing "some light on what has been written as fact."[10]

Writing this book, I am indebted to the great biographers of Wharton and James, R. W. B. Lewis and Leon Edel. Lyall H. Powers's edition of Henry James's letters to Edith Wharton has been invaluable. I wish to thank Nora Smith, Elizabeth Hallowell, and Betty McCagg, who generously shared memories of their relative Gaillard Lapsley. For various forms of help—from providing references to reading drafts of the manuscript—I also wish to thank Arthur Balderacchi, Shari Benstock, Dottie Carroll, Clare Colquitt, Luis Costa, Rich Duggan, Richard Dunn, Jerome Loving, Nigel Nicolson, Alan Price, Miranda Seymour, Patricia Shaw, and Carol Singley. My task has been made possible by the librarians at Smith College; Trinity College, Cambridge University; the Beinecke Rare Book and Manuscript Library, Yale University; the Houghton and Pusey libraries, Harvard University; and the Henry Madden Library, California State University, Fresno. In particular, CSUF's Program of Graduate Studies and the Office of Affirmative Action have provided vital release time and funding. The Beinecke Library, the Gloria Loomis Agency, and Alex James have generously granted me copyright permission. Most of all, I am grateful to Carl Dawson, who has been involved in every stage of this project, from its conception to completion, and whose thinking has stimulated my own.

EDITH WHARTON'S INNER CIRCLE

Edith Wharton, Christmas 1905.
Courtesy of the Lilly Library, Indiana University, Bloomington, Indiana.

Henry James, 1905.
Photo by Katherine C. McClellan
Courtesy of Smith College Archives.

The Mount, 1904. In front, Cook, the Whartons' chauffeur,
and Teddy Wharton; in back, Edith Wharton and Henry James.
Courtesy of the Lilly Library, Indiana University, Bloomington, Indiana.

Walter Berry at The Mount.
Courtesy of the Yale Collection of American Literature,
Beinecke Rare Book and Manuscript Library, Yale University.

The Mount, 1905.
Courtesy of the Yale Collection of American Literature,
Beinecke Rare Book and Manuscript Library, Yale University.

William Morton Fullerton,
circa 1908. Courtesy of the
Yale Collection of American
Literature, Beinecke Rare
Book and Manuscript Library,
Yale University.

Teddy Wharton, circa 1898.
Courtesy of the Yale Collection
of American Literature,
Beinecke Rare Book and
Manuscript Library,
Yale University.

Gaillard Lapsley, 1908.
Courtesy of Master and Fellows of Trinity College, Cambridge University.

Pavillon Colombe.
Courtesy of the Lilly Library, Indiana University, Bloomington, Indiana.

Ste. Claire.
Courtesy of the Lilly Library, Indiana University, Bloomington, Indiana.

Left to right, Howard Sturgis and
William Haynes-Smith on the steps
of Qu'Acre. Courtesy of the Yale
Collection of American Literature,
Beinecke Rare Book and
Manuscript Library, Yale University.

Bernard Berenson.
Courtesy of the Yale Collection
of American Literature,
Beinecke Rare Book and
Manuscript Library,
Yale University.

Percy Lubbock, Howard Sturgis, and Arthur Christopher Benson, 1906.
From *On the Edge of Paradise: A. C. Benson: The Diarist*,
by David Newsome (Chicago: University of Chicago Press, 1980).

Robert Norton and Edith Wharton picnicking, early 1930s.
Courtesy of the Yale Collection of American Literature,
Beinecke Rare Book and Manuscript Library, Yale University.

Hyères, 1936: sitting, John Hugh Smith, Mme Homburg,
Edith Wharton; standing, Robert Norton and Gaillard Lapsley. Courtesy
of the Yale Collection of American Literature,
Beinecke Rare Book and Manuscript Library, Yale University.

Edith Wharton's Inner Circle

*One seems to need them both—America for mental
stimulation, and England for quietness and rest.*
(LETTER OF FRANCES HODGSON BURNETT)

*The years, after all, have a kind of emptiness when we spend
too many of them on a foreign shore. We defer the reality of
life, in such cases, until a future moment when we shall
again breathe our native air; but, by and by there are no
future moments; or, if we do return, we find that life has
shifted its reality to the spot where we have deemed ourselves
have none at all, or only that little space of either in which
we finally lay down our discontented bones.*
NATHANIEL HAWTHORNE,
THE MARBLE FAUN OR,
THE ROMANCE OF MONTE BENI

AN ACRE OF GREEN LAWN surrounded the house. In its center, facing Windsor Park, sat Howard Sturgis with his favorite dog, Misery. At teatime, he gathered his workbasket and prepared to meet his guests. Before crossing the threshold of Queen's Acre, he smiled. It was going splendidly.

Percy Lubbock was not so sure. Who was this woman his friend John Hugh Smith too openly admired? Each time she snapped one of her perpetual cigarettes out of its gold case, Howard started slightly and then fussed with the dogs lying on either side of his crossed ankles. Later he would rise from his tangle of embroidery silks to mimic the exact intensity of John's infatuated gaze. She was hardly what Percy had expected, "sitting very upright and straight-backed, but all alive, easy and active in repose."[1] Henry James and Howard had been talking about Edith Wharton for weeks, and here she was: one of Henry's own creations, an older Isabel Archer perhaps, still stylish at forty-four, her hair artfully arranged and her gown from the best house on the Rue de la Paix. Henry was inspired by her, spinning cobweb bridges from his mind to hers, extending every strand to its finest tip, ruthlessly plucking loose threads to weave another patch, until the whole collapsed and was washed by her tears and spilling laughter.

This was how Gaillard Lapsley liked her best: her mirth "ringing out of the shades" (*Portrait*, 76). "Funny she laughed that way," he thought, "hers was not really a humourous view of life, if humour is tolerant and contemplative; she was too quick and practical to give humour its time, and her irony was always brisker than it was deep" (*Portrait*, 76).

"Ask Percy what he thinks of that, Edith," Gaillard teased, but the talk swirled so fast and he was so shy, and she and Henry were so focused on each other and John on her and Howard on John, that it was easier for Percy to sink back into the chintz cushions and watch.

"Well, here it is at last," Wharton prophetically sighed, "'the distinguished thing.'"[2] Here were people who knew, as she had written years before in "The Fullness of Life" (1893), the feeling at sunset, the line in the third canto of the *Inferno*, the stooping Victory in the frieze of the Nike Apteros. There was, as the Spirit of Life informs her heroine, "compensation in store for such needs as you have expressed."[3]

Edith Wharton published her first book of short stories, *The Greater Inclination* (1899), when she was thirty-seven years old. In her own mind, the event produced two significant results: it marked her acquisition of a "real personality," and it "broke the chains" which had held her "so long in a kind of torpor" (*ABG*, 112, 122). For nearly twelve years she had tried to adjust herself to the life she had led since marrying her likeable but unintellectual husband, Edward ("Teddy") Wharton. Now she was "overmastered" by the longing to meet people who shared her interests. "What I wanted above all was to get to know other writers," she confesses in her autobiography, *A Backward Glance* (1934), "to be welcomed among people who lived for the things I had always secretly lived for" (*ABG*, 122). At Queen's Acre (abbreviated to Qu'Acre and pronounced "Quaker"), she may not have found writers in the sense the quotation implies, but she did find people with whom she could try to build something her fiction shows to be impossible: what one of her characters in *The House of Mirth* (1905) calls the Republic of the Spirit, a land free "from everything—from money, from poverty, from ease and anxiety, from all the material accidents."[4] In truth, this republic was open only to those with the power to choose the kinds of futures they desired to lead and the kinds of values they wished to uphold.

At the beginning of her career, Wharton identified Henry James as a citizen of this republic. Following the publication of *The Greater Inclination*, she recalls: "I felt like some homeless waif who, after trying for years to take out naturalization papers, and being rejected by every country, has finally acquired a nationality. The Land of Letters was henceforth to be my country, and I gloried in my new citizenship" (*ABG*, 119). Over the years, its features took shape in the letters that Wharton exchanged with her most intimate friends. Relying on group consensus, the correspondence produced a collaborative vision of both reality and identity that helped to make her feel "naturalized" or less alien.

Hoping to meet James in 1887, at the home of Edward Boit, the water-colorist, Wharton had tried to look her prettiest by donning a tea-rose pink Doucet dress embroidered with iridescent beads: "But, alas," she writes, "it neither gave me the courage to speak nor attracted the attention of the great man" (*ABG*, 172). Several years later, Ralph Curtis arranged a meeting in Rome. Despite a becoming hat (or perhaps because of it), the second introduction "fell as flat as the first" (*ABG*, 172). In 1902, Wharton's historical novel, *The Valley of Decision*, set in eighteenth-century Italy, accomplished what the new dress and the new hat had failed to do: it captured James's attention. "The first duty to a serious & achieved work of art is the duty of recognition *telle quelle*," he wrote before admonishing her in favor of an American Subject. "There it is round you. Don't pass it by—the immediate, the real, the ours, the yours, the novelist's that it waits for." [5] "And as for the date of the meeting which finally drew us together, without hesitations or preliminaries," Wharton explains, "we could neither of us ever recall when or where that happened. All we knew was that suddenly it was as if we had always been friends, and were to go on being (as he wrote to me in February 1910) 'more and more never apart'" (*ABG*, 173).

The friendship between Edith Wharton and Henry James brought together the group of people whom Wharton would refer to as "the inner circle" or—echoing the embattled and gallant Henry the Fifth—"the happy few": "We few, we happy few, we band of brothers" (*Henry V*, 4.3.28).

> In this group an almost immediate sympathy had established itself between the various members, so that our common stock of allusions, cross-references, pleasantries was always increasing, and new waves of interest in the same book or picture, or any sort of dramatic event in life or letters, would simultaneously flood through our minds. (*ABG*, 192)

The original group consisted of well-known people, such as James and Wharton, and people now totally forgotten. John Hugh Smith, who pursued a career in banking, also had a great interest in the latest archeological finds. Known for his expertise in international law, Walter Berry headed the American Chamber of Commerce in Paris. Gaillard Lapsley taught at Cambridge and wrote academic books and papers about medieval constitutional history. Robert Norton retired from business to devote himself to watercolor painting and exhibited in two well-received shows. Perhaps the success of the other members looks modest only in comparison to that of James and Wharton. Howard Sturgis wrote three books, *Tim* (1891), a sentimental story based on his Eton experiences, *All That Was Possible* (1894), an epistolary novel narrated by a comedic actress unlucky in love, and *Belchamber* (1904), a semiautobiographical novel that focuses on the trials of an English marquis named Sainty. Unpopular with the general public, *Belchamber* found admirers in Virginia Woolf, E. M. Forster, and Wharton, who tried to convince Scribner's to bring out an American edition. Percy Lubbock, best remembered for writing *The Craft of Fiction* (1921) and editing the letters of Henry James, published among other works the diaries of Arthur Christopher Benson, the letters of Elizabeth Barrett Browning, and two novels, *Roman Pictures* (1923), awarded the Fémina-Vie Heureuse Prize, and *The Region Cloud* (1925).

The inner circle was first and foremost a group of friends. The importance that they placed on affection, loyalty, and pure fun ("the farce of life in its wildest and subtlest surprises") cannot be overemphasized (*Portrait*, 76). "Everyone knew that it was no more possible to dazzle Howard [Sturgis] than to exhaust his indulgence," Lubbock wrote. "His place in friendship was ever a little apart from the rest, in a corner of his own—where nothing mattered but what you really were, and that was what he loved" (*Portrait*, 7). The observations that Desmond MacCarthy, a critic associated with Bloomsbury, made about James were true of them all:

> In conversation he could not help giving his best, the stereotyped and perfunctory being abhorrent to him. Each talk was thus a fresh adventure, an opportunity of discovering for himself what he thought about books and human beings. His respect for his subject was only equalled, one noticed, by his respect for that delicate instrument for recording and comparing impressions, his own mind.[6]

"How we lived on Henry in those days!" Lubbock recalled. "He had just then finished the vast triple monument of his full-wrought art . . . and the happy few who knew themselves earnest and attentive, tracking him up the winding staircase of his porcelain pagoda, were absorbed by the quest" (*Portrait*, 8).

The inner circle came together as adults; in 1908, for example, their average age was forty-three. To borrow Wharton's phrase, they had already acquired personalities of their own. What they liked and respected in one another they liked and respected in themselves, a blend of intellect and sensitivity. When misunderstandings occurred, as in the case of

Wharton's misguided attempt to ease James's financial anxieties by presenting him with a check from his American friends for his seventieth birthday, the parties involved could be ruthless: "Barrett Wendell writes indignantly . . . to tell me how every one was in sympathy with the plan," she informed Lapsley. "It is a blow to think that our great Henry should be, *au fond*, only a Howells!"[7] "It hurts to see great beautiful real minds hurting each other," Lubbock observed.[8] The next week, a day after James's birthday, he reported to Lapsley that James was "in the mood to forgive everybody & forget everything," but wondered, "will that satisfy *her*?"[9] As the controversy illustrates, any threats to identity—in this instance Wharton's view of herself as acting in good faith and good taste—were fiercely warded off. The group tolerated disparate opinions and behaviors that did not call their own into question.

Because these friends retained their independence, it seems in some ways impossible to speak of them as a group at all. Wharton herself might have agreed, for in bringing Henry James, Walter Berry, and Howard Sturgis to life in her memoir she presents each apart from the group in discrete, atomized portraits. The men orbited around Wharton (or in James's case hovered at a safe distance) without forming a salon in any ordinary meaning of the word. But, like those who sought conversation in the red-damask drawing room of the renowned Parisian hostess the Comtesse Rosa de Fitz-James, who belonged to the Viennese-Jewish banking family of the Gutmanns, they understood that houses, valued for the people associated with them and also for the order and history they represent, hold special meaning. James hated to leave his beloved Lamb House in Rye, England; Wharton bought Pavillon Colombe outside Paris after hearing its erotic history (two sisters had been kept there by lovers); and Gerard Hopkins found the tone of Howard Sturgis's Qu'Acre on the edge of Windsor Park—characterized by picture-strewn walls, dogs snoring in baskets, and piles of books everywhere—"symbolic of the civilized standards which made a visit there so new, so delightful an experience. . . . The point about Qu'Acre was that it was a *place* existing by individual right."[10] "It had a way, that house, of effecting the oddest transformations, making the fantastic real, the real fantastic" (Hopkins, vii). At Qu'Acre, Lubbock writes, Howard was always on the table "like a richly sugared cake . . . he didn't exactly rule the feast, for as Henry James put it he *was* the feast."[11] Harry Crosby details the space that his cousin Walter Berry created: "the prayer shell from Tibet and the Egyptian stone cat imperturbable upon her haunches, and the Aztec death mask and the Bible from Siena . . . and the Indian and Persian colored prints and the Gauguin landscape . . . and the Burne-Jones lent by Berenson and the books books books books books. . . . "[12] A gathering of intimates converted these places into ephemeral utopias: "My idea of society was (and still is)," Wharton wrote near the end of her life, "the daily companionship of the same five or six friends, and its pleasure is based on continuity" (*ABG*, 224).

Although its members cared passionately about literature, the inner circle was not ostensibly literary. Neither did it promote contemporary political and artistic movements in the manner or the spirit of Bloomsbury (1904–c.1956).[13] Unlike the Tuesday Lunch Club, which Wharton and Bernard Berenson helped to found, it had no set structure or agenda for discussing topical political, scholarly, or artistic subjects. It resembled more and had ties to the Five of Hearts, the group that included the Adamses, the Hays, and Clarence King. If the inner circle differed from the Five of Hearts in its larger numbers, it shared with them an apolitical social focus and, in their own opinion, "a genius for befriending everyone worth knowing."[14] Paul Bourget's membership in the French Academy and Berenson's court at I Tatti, his estate in Florence, provided the inner circle with a legion of powerful acquaintances. The literary figures surrounding the group—to give a cursory list—included Joseph Conrad, Ford Madox Ford, H. G. Wells, Stephen Crane, Edmund Gosse, Charles du Bos, André Gide, Marcel Proust, Virginia Woolf, Anna de Noailles (Claude Silve), Lytton Strachey, Sinclair Lewis, F. Scott Fitzgerald, and Jean Cocteau.

When Wharton describes the inner circle, she is remembering something that did and did not exist. Because remembering is a form of fictionalizing, readers of *A Backward Glance* must reconstruct some approximation of the truth, whether literal or metaphorical, both about Wharton and the happy few. The text presents two faces of the same woman, one modestly disinterested, the other fiercely intent on settling old scores with everyone from her mother to Henri Bergson. The reality of the inner circle is equally elusive. Wharton imagined that these friends naturally thought and felt the same as she, a vision that history belies. For example, John Hugh Smith and Walter Berry did not share Wharton's sense of almost divine connection to the group as an entity in itself. Attached to individuals by varying ties of intimacy, they lived their lives largely apart from the group yet connected to it through a relationship with Wharton.

The members of the inner circle usually met in pairs and were joined by one or more of the others when convenient. Rarely was there a full gathering. The pattern of visits in 1910, the year before Wharton published *Ethan Frome*, is typical of those before the war. In that year, Berry resigned from his 1909 appointment as a judge to the International Tribunal in Cairo and decided to search for a suitable position in Paris. (He eventually opened a law practice.) While he looked for an apartment, he was the Whartons' guest from July through December. Wharton introduced him to Bernard Berenson, with whom she had been friendly for a year. The men immediately liked each other and spent much time together despite Berenson's complaints about Wharton's devotion to Berry.

In late July of 1910, Lapsley arrived. August saw Wharton, Berry, and William and Alice James at Lamb House. Both of the James brothers were seriously ill, William suffering from heart disease and Henry from heartache after the critical and financial disappointment of the New York edition of his work. An outing to Qu'Acre did nothing to lift Henry James's spirits, and none of his friends seriously protested when he announced his plan to accompany his brother home to Chocorua, New Hampshire, where William died eight days later.

Wharton's life was at a similar point of crisis. For the last three years, 1907–1910, she had been the mistress of William Morton Fullerton, a Paris-based journalist for the *London Times* known for having affairs with prominent men and women. September saw her in New York to deliver her husband to a friend, Johnston Morton, who had consented to take him on a curative trip around the world. Wharton hoped that the tour would restore Teddy's emotional equilibrium, which had been deteriorating since 1903, about the time that she actively sought intellectual companionship. Fullerton and Berry were already in the United States on family business, and, on October 16, they and James all saw Wharton's boat off to Europe. The men then dined, probably regaling each other with stories of Wharton's last-minute changes in plans or demands for service. James and Fullerton, friends since the early 1890s, also visited that evening. As this litany suggests, it was not the actual frequency of the visits, often determined by circumstance, but "the secret quality of participation" (*ABG*, 192) that made them so meaningful.

This pattern did not change markedly over the years. Naturally, in times of crisis the inner circle could be counted on to rally, as when Robert Norton's sister had cancer or Henry James's health deteriorated. A fortnight was the usual length of a stay at Sainte Claire in Hyères, Wharton's winter retreat on the Riviera, or I Tatti, although Norton and Lubbock might spend a month or more. Wharton made a yearly four-to-six-week pilgrimage to England, and Christmas and the New Year always saw some gathering of the inner circle. In the late twenties and thirties, for example, Bernard Berenson and his secretary, Nicky Mariano, tried to spend part of the Christmas holiday at Hyères while his wife, Mary Berenson, performing what she called her "tribal rites," saw children and grandchildren. The late spring and summer months would usually find Wharton traveling with Lapsley to Salsomaggiore or accompanied by Berry on an extended sightseeing jaunt. With the latter, she took—to give a partial list—trips to Italy in 1913 and 1927, Spain in 1914 (the same year that she and Lubbock toured North Africa), and Morocco in 1917.

Wharton experienced the inner group in a way that the other members could only partly share. Like many of their contemporaries, the friends relied on the mail to keep track of one another's activities. Wharton commonly wrote to James and Lapsley several times a week. When Lapsley visited Lamb House or Lubbock Qu'Acre, the hosts addressed those not there, making them vicarious participants.

The group's correspondence provided a frame of reference in addition to fostering a kind of collective memory that for James at least was even more satisfying than the actual encounter. Wharton's strained relations with Teddy were known to all by 1912, but her affair with Fullerton, which adds a semiautobiographical element to *The Reef* (1912), had been revealed (as far as one can infer from the tone of the correspondences) to just Sturgis and James, who marveled: "And there is the intolerable pressure! her bed is so *made* & such a great big uncompromising 4-poster!"[15]

During this time, Lamb House functioned as a clearinghouse for information. James wrote Lapsley, a guest of the Whartons, requesting information about Teddy's condition: "I pant and ache for your news of 53 r. de V . . . I yearn to know if Teddy is *there*—and what this new (I can't make out your word . . . 'hellishness'?) *is*."[16] In February, the following month, James informed him "that Walter B. tells me his [Teddy's] outward seeming gives no colour to K-n-tt's [Kinnicutt's] theory of confinement; he's unconfinable on present *appearances*."[17] To Sturgis seven days later, he confided, "I can neither do anything, write to her or be written to, about it—and ask myself why therefore cultivate, in the connection, a mere platonic horror—which permits me neither to hold her hand nor to kick his tail."[18] James reported that Berry, installed for moral support in the Whartons' apartment, found Teddy "extraordinarily well and strong and normal—but only the more helplessly futile and arid and énervant, and that though it be true that with his restlessness he can't 'endure,' so on the other hand, and from the same cause, he can't *be endured*."[19] Each letter reveals the intimacy between the correspondents as well as a subtly different degree of knowledge concerning Wharton's personal affairs.

Not unexpectedly, the refuge that Wharton found in the inner circle grew from her own imagination. By presenting the inner group solely in relation to its author, *A Backward Glance* reveals the egocentricity inherent in any version of collective or, for that matter, collected memories. Her letters show her sustaining one particular myth, that the Furies had selected her friends for extraordinary suffering made bearable by its attendant vision: "if you'd been well these last two years," she told Lapsley, who was recovering from tuberculosis, "the Furies would have found some other joint in your armour, & perhaps have given another twist to the screw."[20] These avenging female divinities provided a reason for people to hold fast to one another, and Wharton always invoked them, as she did with John Hugh Smith, at the beginning of a relationship: "the

Furies do dance in hob-nailed shoes on the sensitive tracts at a rate that sometimes makes one wish for any form of anaesthesia."[21] "The Furies know their job," Wharton wrote Berenson after a cyclone uprooted his ancient cypresses, "& generally do it thoroughly."[22]

To shield themselves from the legacy of the Furies in "this loneliest of worlds,"[23] the happy few formed an insular community in which they bemoaned the passing of social and artistic reticence, the latter exemplified for Wharton by the "me-novels" of James Joyce.[24] Analyzing James's persona in his letters, she isolates the desolation that distinguished and alienated them:

> . . . Henry James lived in the intellectual loneliness that is the lot of
> all originators. He once wrote of himself that it was the fate of the
> Cosmopolitan to be lonely; but this was a superficial diagnosis. He
> was not lonely because he lived in a country not his own, and at
> heart he knew it; he was never as lonely as in America. His sense of
> solitude was founded on his fundamental *differentness*.[25]

The names Wharton chose for her friends, "the happy few" and the "inner circle," themselves emphasize a fundamental differentness, proclaiming a relationship to the world that is at once defensive, judgmental, and elitist. Never entirely free from the prejudices typical of their class, the group envisioned itself, especially after the First World War, as the last haven for the civilized.

The seemingly disparate personalities of the happy few were united by a shared sense of exile. Perhaps because the late nineteenth century contained so many competing and exclusionary visions, one did not have to be expatriated to feel exiled. Percy Lubbock grew up knowing that his family's tenancy of Earlham Hall, three miles outside Norwich, England, which had begun in 1786 and encompassed five generations, would end with the death of his maternal grandmother. As a boy he used to imagine a great hand descending to snatch up the house and its contents. Hummingbirds clustered under bell jars, Chinese cups, carpets with green roses, and souvenirs from the Great Exhibition would magically vanish into thin air. The family's actual exile in 1895 foreshadowed what George Santayana described as "the gradual obscuration, dispersion, and decline" of a class that had become as hybrid as he thought his British-born cousin Howard Sturgis to be.[26]

The inner circle experienced exile in multiple forms: geographical, intellectual, sexual, aesthetic, and—surprisingly—economic. They were not able to avoid those "material accidents" examined in *The House of Mirth*, for the freedoms and burdens of being or not being born to money or not having enough of it in the company of those who did created another source of difference. James partly equated financial rewards with literary success; Wharton helped to support her sister-in-law and niece, a childhood friend, various petitioners, and retired servants; Lubbock gratefully accepted vacations he could not otherwise afford; and Berenson's business arrangements with Joseph Duveen called his integrity into question.[27] Wharton's pattern of exile was similar to James's, yet the values which sustained it were shared by Lapsley, who identified with British culture more strongly than with his own, by Lubbock, who felt most at home in the world of his Quaker grandparents, by Smith, who was temperamentally at odds with his banking profession, and by Norton, who largely retired from the world after making a modest fortune in London.

The friendship between Wharton and James was reinforced by an additional bond. As children, they were literally exiled by family considerations. In 1866, Wharton's parents needed to live with their youngest child and only daughter less expensively and so moved to Europe. Eleven years before, Henry James Sr. had decided that his sons had need of a more "sensuous" education, and in search of it he had moved the family from New York to London to Paris to Geneva and back to Paris and London.[28] At twelve, James found his time in Europe unsettling. At four, Wharton found hers a respite. Her keen visual sensibility and her photographic memory of rooms and houses had from the earliest years been a source of "inarticulate misery" (*ABG*, 28). "Always vaguely frightened by ugliness" (*ABG*, 28), she was mindful of the fact that others did not share her anxious awareness of surroundings. For her, the Old World had one obvious advantage over the New World: it was breathtakingly beautiful. There she wandered between tombs on the Appian Way, spied beautiful women peeking from behind carriage curtains on the Champs Elysées, and played on the Monte Pincio with Daisy Terry, the half-sister of the historical novelist Marion Crawford. Her family left Paris at the outbreak of the Franco-Prussian War and returned to New York in 1872. Later she characterized herself as a wretched exotic "produced in a European glass-house, the most déplacé & useless class on earth."[29]

After two years in Europe, from 1855 to 1857, the James family settled in Newport, Rhode Island. Within a year and a half, James's father, concerned again about the boys' education and manners, uprooted the family, returning to Geneva and then moving to Bonn. In the spring of 1862, as James reports in *Notes of a Son and Brother* (1914), Newport "imposed itself . . . to so remarkable a degree as the one right residence, in all our great country, for those tainted, under whatever attenuations, with the quality and effect of detachment. The effect of detachment was the fact of the experience of Europe." "Without an absolute remedy,"[30] that detachment was the beginning of exile or what Lubbock calls "the dignity" of James's isolation (*Portrait*, 8).

In 1902, William Dean Howells felt compelled to defend not just his friend Henry James but his many compatriots living abroad. To an increasingly hostile audience at home Howells explained that "literary absenteeism . . . is not a peculiarly American vice or an American virtue. It is an expression and a proof of the modern sense which enlarges one's country to the bounds of civilization."[31] James and Wharton might have substituted "refined" for "modern" and added that expatriation contributed to their artistic authority as dispassionate observers. "I think that to be an American is an excellent preparation for culture," James had written at twenty-four. "To have no national stamp has hitherto been a regret and a drawback, but I think it not unlikely that American writers may yet indicate that a vast intellectual fusion and synthesis of the various National tendencies of the world is the condition of more important achievements than any we have seen."[32] Americans were turning to Europe, the Orient, or the Middle Ages searching for sometimes contradictory things: social stability, absolute standards, sexual freedom, lost spirituality, refined aestheticism, exotic primitives, antiquarian simplicity, sublime experiences, and psychic remedies. Often what travelers found was what they needed to find. On seeing his "first peasant," a woman field laborer, James experienced an epiphany: "Supremely, in that ecstatic vision was 'Europe,' sublime synthesis, expressed and guaranteed to me—as if by a mystic gage, which spread all through the summer air, that I should now, only now, never lose it, hold the whole consistency of it" (*Notes*, 161).

James and Wharton traced the origin of their nurture and the cure for chaos to a largely fancied though emblematically united Europe, and their cosmopolitan worldview was shared, as George W. Stocking writes, by Europeans like François Guizot who thought of civilization "in terms of a unified conception of European progress," reaching its apogee in France.[33] Analyzing Wharton's move to Paris in 1907, Lapsley articulates its historical context:

> she was to all appearance standing (in America) between two worlds, "one dead, the other powerless to be born." The old social organization was in dissolution, and the society in which she worked, still socially and economically well placed, was in process of being pushed eastward and across the Atlantic; and the time was not yet when anyone could dare to affirm that the old American tradition could maintain, even with notable modifications, its continuous American identity.
>
> (*Portrait*, 48)

Twenty years after settling in France, Wharton was still complaining that the trouble with Americans "is that they don't know what a gentleman is, & after all it was a useful standard to get one's perspective by."[34] Her statement also implies that Americans never did know how to respond to a "lady."

When Wharton set her first novel in eighteenth-century Italy, she was following the example of Charles Eliot Norton, a Dante scholar and the first Harvard fine arts professor, by hailing that country as "the home of the imagination."[35] She later identified France in *French Ways and Their Meaning* (1919) as the most civilized of countries. Her initial impulse was to posit and thereby contain societal boundaries even as she expanded them. For James, the state of expatriation duplicated the conditions that once seemed to him an American birthright: "We are ahead of the European races in the fact that more than either of them we can deal freely with forms of civilization not our own, can pick and choose and assimilate and in short (aesthetically etc.) claim our property wherever we find it."[36]

The American members of the inner circle differed in one crucial way from many other travelers: their self-imposed exile had profound personal origins.[37] The closeness of the James family, which conflated illness and revelation, made self-definition seem almost heretical;[38] Lapsley enjoyed his nieces and nephews without wanting to assume full emotional and financial responsibility for them; and Wharton did not want to become a younger version of her mother. Exile allowed them to keep families at a manageable distance, making it possible for them—like Vance Weston in Wharton's *The Gods Arrive* (1932)—to live their inner lives in their own ways. For people who were asexual, homosexual, or otherwise inclined not to wed, pressures to marry and have children were more easily handled through the post than in person. In fact, Lubbock was the only member of the group to marry during Wharton's lifetime (Smith married in 1941), and his marriage to Sybil Cutting hastened the decline, already underway, of his relationship with Wharton. Wharton disliked Cutting, who appeared invitingly soft and delicately vulnerable, for a variety of complex reasons that included sexual jealousy as well as her antipathy toward doll-like women.[39] Her decision to justify her aversion in terms of Lubbock's desertion shows how well she knew her audience disliked upheavals in their own family circle. At times, James, Wharton, Smith, and Lubbock resented the nephew who shared Sturgis's home ("too much devotion & so little imagination" is how Lubbock described him); Wharton in particular mistrusted the "baleful influence" of James's family,[40] especially his brother William; and all the members of the inner circle supported Wharton's decision in 1913 to divorce her husband of twenty-eight years. The group's conspiracy to control the publication of James's correspondence after his death, which in a sense would wrest him finally from his family, indicates just how fierce and yet unresolved were many of the inner circle's primary relationships.

"There was in me," Wharton admits in *A Backward Glance*, "a secret retreat where I wished no one to intrude, or at least no one whom I had yet encountered" (*ABG*, 70). Exile is always more a state of mind than locale, and the innermost space that Wharton defines matches the literal space an exile inhabits. She believed that any change in one's surroundings made the self more accessible by throwing it into relief against a foreign backdrop. Expatriation provided an artificial country because it conferred more freedom than either the native or adopted land. For those who did not conform (socially, sexually, politically), a foreign theater promised a different script, one which gave them—because they were not expected to fully understand it—more latitude. Citizens of both nations and of neither, they were not bound by localized customs or thinking. In *Notes of a Son and Brother*, James describes the comfort of exile: "I have not, for myself, forgotten, or even now outlived, the particular shade of satisfaction to be taken in one's thus being in New England without being of it. To have originally been of it, or still to have had to be, affected me, I recall, as a case I should have regretted—unless it be more exact to say that I thought of the condition as a danger after all escaped" (305).

Lubbock thought that Wharton chose to settle in Paris rather than London because she found England too staid and dowdy for her tastes. The visionary landscape and the institutionalized standards of an imagined latter-day Italy and present-day France were precisely what she fictionally relied upon as foil and measure. In a sense, Wharton had no option but to follow the last traces of old New York to the shores of Europe. There she could recover the best the past had to offer without its rules and regulations threatening her identity as woman or author. Instead of escaping home, Wharton came home to Europe. The remains of an earlier world she tried to trace with the art historian Vernon Lee in Italy, the fashionable house parties she attended at Hill Hall in England, and the aristocratic atmosphere of the old Faubourg in France replicated to a large extent the one she later recalled in *The Age of Innocence* (1920). While no one can probably ever escape the home carried within, Wharton managed to reconstruct it according to her own design. When she entered Rosa de Fitz-James's Parisian drawing room, she saw the old New York of her youth Europeanized, and it now had room (to use Wharton's own phrase) for "a grown-up woman," one who "takes time to live, and has an extraordinarily clear and sound sense of what constitutes *real living*."[41] In Wharton's canon "real living" means no less than reigning with "a triple crown, as a business woman, as a mother, and above all as an artist" (*FW*, 111).

Wharton, who was childless, most achieved the ideal symbolized by the metaphor of the triple crown in her relationships with the members of the inner circle. However, the men's seriocomic sexualized references to her as a "devastating presence" sound a different note. Acknowledging her power, Wharton lamented to Lapsley: "If you knew how devastated is the devastatress."[42] Part cry, part plea, her words refer directly to the toll of both humoring and divorcing her emotionally disturbed husband. They also serve to underscore the paradoxical tension that underlay her relationship with her male coterie. No matter how individual the woman, she cannot—as Wharton knew—escape from being transformed into a type. To paraphrase Ellen Olenska in *The Age of Innocence*, "Where is the country, where is the world where categories like that won't exist?"[43]

Partly explained by her choice of vocation, Wharton's sensitivity to questions of gender grows from the fin-de-siècle debate about the nature of the sexes. In an era preoccupied with the scientific categorization of everything from plants to people, men and women shaped their own notions of themselves from the male and—as Martha Banta argues—the more frequently iconized female forms in the popular media: the American Girl, the Gibson Girl, the Western Girl, the Outdoors Girl, the Charmer, the New England Spinster, and the New Woman.[44] If women were to be felinely feminine, men were to be ruggedly masculine. The ideal male type, modeled after the illustrator Charles Dana Gibson or the reporter Richard Harding Davis, was white and European. Offering himself as an alternative to "the timid man, the lazy man, the man who distrusts his country, the over-civilized man,"[45] Theodore Roosevelt seemed to embody the forceful "masculinity" that was becoming an American archetype in the novels of Theodore Dreiser, Frank Norris, and Owen Wister. In *The American Scene* (1907), for example, James proposes "a recommittal to masculine hands of some share at least in the interests of civilization."[46] *The Bostonians* (1886) makes the same point.

The inner circle refused to categorize, prescribe, or judge behavior by gender. For them, gender worked in complex, fluid ways. George Santayana thought that Howard Sturgis's excessive reverence for his mother's memory and liberal humanitarian principles in politics and history made him a perfect young lady of the Victorian type;[47] Sturgis's friends found him candid, genuine, and serene—"Howard in his infinite Howardism," James used to say.[48]

Always conscious of and concerned with questions of gender, Wharton played with its parameters and privileges. When she called herself a "self-made man" (*Portrait*, 11), she was highlighting her femininity and asserting her equality in the company of men whom Geoffrey Scott dubbed "Edith Wharton's somewhat invertebrate friends."[49] "How it does agreeably titillate the author's vanity to have his pet phrases quoted to him!" she wrote Berenson after he praised *Summer* (1917). "You see I'm getting a little confused about my sex! A form of megalomania!"[50] Traveling with Lubbock or Lapsley, Wharton carefully diffused any potential embarrassments over money or accommodations by insisting that "confrères of the pen" should always attach a minimum of importance to such things.[51] Yet she partly encouraged John Hugh Smith's infatuation and—borrowing her own words from *The Reef* (1912)—acted like "a slave, and a goddess, and a girl in her teens" with Fullerton.[52]

Not without a degree of hypocrisy, the group tolerated behavior in its own members that it publicly deplored. James, for example, would not allow Violet Hunt to cross the threshold of Lamb House because he thought it would countenance her affair with Ford Madox Ford,[53] but he definitely encouraged and seems to have derived vicarious enjoyment from Wharton's adulterous relationship with Fullerton. Wharton saw nothing odd about Bernard Berenson's wife and mistress living amicably under one roof. Neither did she condemn Geoffrey Scott's marrying Sybil Cutting for the amenities she could provide. The inner circle itself was not free from the stresses that one would expect to find in any family or substitute family. Sturgis thought that he bored James. The older friends sometimes patronized the younger, as when James, with some degree of seriousness, wrote Wharton that she could administer "the great emotions & impressions" of Lubbock's "quivering young life."[54] Lubbock's novel *The Region Cloud* (1925), the story of a young man's homoerotic worship of a great painter and his eventual disillusionment, suggests that his relationship to James was at least as complex as that with Wharton.[55] Outlining an artist's need for a thinking but noncritical fellow watcher and the spectator's inability to suppress the seeing that establishes his own identity, Lubbock exposes the source of the inner circle's underlying tensions. Although James accepted Wharton on nearly equal terms as a fellow writer, her gender seemed to elicit a certain flirtatious indirectness missing when he conversed with male members of the group. Lubbock's attitude toward Walter Berry highlights some of the buried competitiveness: he was a man "of strong intelligence and ability—but also, I certainly know, of a dry and narrow and supercilious temper," whose influence on Wharton Lubbock thought "disastrous": he had "the harshness of a dogmatist, the bleakness of an egotist, and the pretentiousness . . . of a snob" (*Portrait*, 43–44).

To some degree, the inner circle exploited Wharton. Her life, summarized and parodied in letters, was their property. It provided imaginative stimulus for Sturgis and furnished James, the most gossipy of the friends, with kernels—what he called *les données*—for possible fictions. In return, the happy few gave her a model, most fully realized in *The Gods Arrive* (1932), for relationships that leave one independent while providing a necessary tether and connection. Each member had a distinct role in the functioning of the group. James was the acknowledged genius; Wharton, his successor, consort, cohort, and subject; Sturgis, mascot and host; Lapsley, the gate and record keeper; Berry, the adviser and (in Wharton's case) critic; Norton, the disinterested companion of Wharton's later years; and

Lubbock and Smith, the offspring and acolytes. Lubbock was so much the latter that Sturgis complained: "he is even *glad*" that Henry "died before he began in any way to decline."[56]

In *A Backward Glance* Wharton left posterity with an incomplete image of herself surrounded by a series of appreciative men. Where are the women whose friendships also sustained Wharton? Where are Sally Norton, Daisy Chanler, Mary Cadwalader Jones, Beatrix Farrand, and Elisina Tyler? Analyzing Wharton's friendship with Walter Berry, Leon Edel speculates that "she was in love, a little like Isabel Archer, with an image in the mirror, of herself, disguised as man."[57] More to the point, Wharton, who never had sexual relationships with any of the happy few, was in love with what the men of the memoir represent, what she would have thought of as a male birthright: power and authority. If Wharton had used her own sex as a mirror, the reflected image might have necessitated a restructuring of the self she fought so hard to win. Any absences in her life as a woman disappear when viewed in a masculine context. The unwomanly woman is transformed—to use Virginia Woolf's phrase—into an extraordinary one.

Wharton wanted to be remembered in two traditions: one of mostly male English and European prose masters, the other of fascinating women.[58] The men who inform the pages of her autobiography are there for a purpose: to testify to her femininity and artistry. Wharton wants her readers to know that she, unlike too many of her American counterparts who—in her words—were still in the kindergarten stage of development, cut off from real power and real living, is a woman who has had "close and interesting and important" relations with men (*FW*, 110). Her views of women and civilization in *French Ways and Their Meaning* parallel those of George Meredith. What constitutes real civilization is educated conversation between the sexes. Men may control civilization but women are its purveyors: "As life is an art in France, so woman is the artist" (*FW*, 112).

The cost of this vision is, of course, another form of exile. One of Wharton's first stories, "The Fullness of Life" (1893), articulates the isolation inherent for a woman conforming to the status quo; one of her last, "All Souls'" (1934), captures the loneliness of being the "extraordinary" woman. Set in a frozen landscape reminiscent of *Ethan Frome*, "All Souls'" is an allegory of self-analysis, told by an unnamed, androgynous narrator who tries rationally "to get at the facts" that cousin Sara herself does not want to confront.[59] Those facts concern the identity of Sara Clayburn.

Sara's adventure is ordinary enough. After turning her ankle, she spends a restless night waiting for the appearance of her maid, Agnes. When Agnes does not answer her mistress's summons, Sara goes in search of her. As she moves from room to room, she discovers that not another living soul occupies the house. If, as Wharton writes in "The Fullness of Life," "a woman's nature is like a great house of rooms: there is the hall, through which everyone passes in going in and out; the drawing room where one receives formal visits; the sitting room where the members of the family come and go as they list" ("Life," 14), then Sara's nature is like a great house of empty rooms kept in "scrupulous and undisturbed order" ("AS," 886). "Yes, that was what laid a chill on her: the feeling that there was no limit to this silence, no outer margin, nothing beyond it" ("AS," 887). Sara feels both formless and imprisoned in the sealed tomb of her own body.[60]

As Sara approaches the innermost room of her house, what Wharton in "The Fullness of Life" calls "the holy of holies," she hears a voice, "a man's voice, low but emphatic, and which she had never heard before" ("AS," 889). Even after she trips and crashes to the floor,

> the voice went on speaking. It was as though neither the speaker nor his listeners had heard her. The invisible stranger spoke so low that she could not make out what he was saying, but the tone was passionately earnest, almost threatening. The next moment she realized that he was speaking in a foreign language, a language unknown to her.
>
> ("AS," 889–890)

In "The Fullness of Life," the soul sits alone in the innermost room "and waits for a footstep that never comes." Here that space is already tenanted.

At the beginning of the story the narrator tells us that true terror resides in the ordinary, and as an allegory of both the woman writer and of women in a male world, "All Souls'" details a common enough experience, the appropriation of the female voice. Although the story criticizes the notion of a "universal" voice—the voice that Sara hears is mechanized and comes from a radio—it seems resigned to its use. The story summarizes the shadow side of being the one woman among the happy few. The group, which was crucially important to Wharton in defining herself as a novelist and a woman of the world, posed a potential threat. Wharton may have intellectually rejected James's view of the self as dependent upon others for definition,[61] but whenever identity is collaboratively constructed, the individual, who suspends judgment, compromises, or appeases for the sake of peace, is at risk.

The inner circle believed in the supremacy of art, its ability to bridge the limitations of time, history, and self. For all of Wharton's traveling, James's love of gossip, or Howard Sturgis's socializing, the happy few lived, paradoxically, intensely private lives. Wharton's commitment to a Republic of the Spirit or a Land of Letters lessened the isolation inherent in her vision of the self's intrinsic independence, while faith in art allowed James to transcend the powerlessness of a self relationally defined.

In a sense, the inner circle contrived to live in three separate worlds, none without its tax: the real world of their chosen places of exile; the "romantic" world, as Gertrude Stein was to call it, not so much "real" as "really there,"[62] realized perhaps in Wharton's wish for a Republic of the Spirit; and a separate world of work and personal struggle, sometimes shared but just as often kept inviolate. "There is something that holds one in one's place," James wrote, "makes it a standpoint in the universe which it is probably good not to forsake."[63] For the inner circle, as for most of us, the "something" that kept their often competing worlds in balance was friendship. Their importance lies most perhaps in their determined imagining of better and more satisfying lives, which they realized so determinedly.

CHAPTER ONE

The Land of Letters

Deep calleth unto deep.
(LETTER OF HENRY JAMES TO EDITH WHARTON)

Deep calls to deep.
(LETTER OF EDITH WHARTON TO GAILLARD LAPSLEY)

THE HILLS OF LENOX, Massachusetts, were a crazy quilt of oranges, reds, yellows, and greens when Henry James paid his first visit to The Mount in October 1904. Priding herself on being a "housekeeperish person," Edith Wharton surveyed the guest rooms one more time to make sure they had everything "conceivably needed for writing."[1] At the sound of the motor, she caught her breath and descended to greet her guests.

James (1843–1916) had arranged to meet his old friend Howard Sturgis (1855–1920) at Lenox. A short year before, Wharton and James had argued the merits of Sturgis's novel *Belchamber*, he seeing it as "feebly old-fashioned" and she as a minor masterpiece.[2] Now all three were under one roof. Originally James had been friendly with Sturgis's father, Russell, a transplanted Bostonian and senior partner in the London branch of the banking firm Baring Brothers. Wharton made the acquaintance of Sturgis in 1888, when he was visiting relatives in the United States after his mother's death. Sturgis soon discovered that "[n]obody could deny that to be a guest in a house of Mrs. Wharton's was a deeply, deliciously, delicately luxurious experience" (*Portrait*, 26)—motor trips every afternoon, picnics by the lake, tea in the garden, "evening talks on the moonlit terrace and readings around the library fire."[3] Following his stay at The Mount, Sturgis redefined his relationship with James as a joint guardianship shared with Wharton: "I am so glad to have that group of us all three together, & linked. Henry looks so delightfully frightened & in custody between us."[4]

Also present that weekend was Walter Berry (1859–1927), a tall, thin, mustached man with a heart-shaped face, high cheek bones, and deep-set eyes. Introduced to Wharton in 1883, he made a lifelong impression: "I never exchanged a word with a really intelligent human being until I was over twenty—& then, alas, I had only a short glimpse of what such a communion might be!"[5] That summer in the resort town of Bar Harbor, Maine, the pair had many talks about literature but none about marriage, no matter how much Wharton might have welcomed it. When they met again in Newport, Rhode Island, Wharton was collaborating with Ogden Codman on *The Decoration of Houses* (1897). Berry appeared as a muse, capable of drawing forth her instinct to write, shaping and setting it free (*ABG*, 116): "No critic was ever severer, but none had more respect for the artist's liberty. He taught me never to be satisfied with my own work, but never to let my inward conviction as to the rightness of anything I had done be affected by outside opinion" (*ABG*, 114). After her divorce from Teddy Wharton in 1913, their friendship resembled a companionate marriage. Nicky Mariano, who sometimes criticized Berry for pandering to the values and tastes of his "super-chic lady friends," recalls how happy he made Wharton during a 1926 stay at her home in Hyères:

> I found her in her bed in an elegant wrapper with a coquettish lace-cap on her head, books and writing things spread all around her, her pekinese doggies asleep at her feet and Walter Berry seated near her, in excellent spirits and she as happy as a young girl to have him all to herself and to let herself be teased by him.[6]

"I suppose there is one friend in the life of each of us," Wharton wrote of Berry, "who seems not a separate person, however dear and beloved, but an expansion, an interpretation, of one's self, the very meaning of one's soul" (*ABG*, 115). After his death, Wharton tried to console herself with the thought that "through all the coming & going of things in his eager ambitious life" she had remained for him "in the place he put me in so many years ago, the place of perfect understanding."[7]

Two months before the gathering at The Mount, Berry had introduced Wharton to her fourth guest, Gaillard Lapsley (1871–1949). When Lapsley told her she was taking a risk inviting him to her home, she answered, "I'm too old a bird not to calculate all the risks and only take those I'm prepared to face" (GL, 1). It was not much of one, for Lapsley already knew Sturgis and James, having called on James with a letter of introduction from Isabel Gardner in 1897. A master of elegant repartee sprinkled with allusions to nineteenth-century English and French literature, he was an expert on medieval constitutional history and a fellow and lecturer at Trinity College, Cambridge, where one wit described him as "the sincerest Englishman I have ever known—with the possible exception of Henry James."[8]

Lapsley's stiff manner concealed a deeply affectionate nature. He loved to entertain as much as Sturgis (though on a far more elaborate scale) in his paneled rooms in Neville's Court, and evenings always found him available to students, who were sometimes surprised that they were expected to have a cigar and later a whisky and soda. These eccentricities they thought "American." A great stickler for ritual, Lapsley was an autocratic disciplinarian in the Lecture Hall on behalf of good manners. Legend has it that when an unfortunate undergraduate distracted the audience by dropping some coins, Lapsley responded: "Gentlemen, I would ask you to note that there is wisdom in the saying 'A fool and his money are soon parted'" (Eley, 4). He disliked having women at his lectures, would actually have banned them if he could, and did his best to see that any who attended were segregated into a group on one side of the Hall.

The friendships cemented that fall weekend in Lenox, which ended only in death, led to others. By 1906, Wharton's inner circle also included Percy Lubbock (1879–1966), a companion of Lapsley's whom Sturgis had met on one of his frequent trips to Cambridge. All three—Lubbock, Lapsley, and Sturgis—had ties to Eton and the novelist Arthur Christopher Benson. Known for his beautiful voice, Lubbock loved to trade anecdotes into the morning hours. Bernard Berenson characterized him as "a Victorian Cambridge ultra-radical in thought, while conventional *au fond*, in the respect for the accepted rituals of his class."[9] When Wharton met him, she had published four books, *The Decoration of Houses* (1897), *The Greater Inclination* (1899), *The Valley of Decision* (1902), and *The House of Mirth* (1905). He was beginning his appointment as the librarian of the Samuel Pepys Collection at Magdalene College, Cambridge. Benson, who had recommended him for the position, observed in his diary that friendships "were for P.L. a series of deep thrills—exultations and agonies."[10] Moody and introspective, Lubbock was the opposite of Walter Berry, whom he disliked.

Initially, Lubbock reacted ambivalently to Wharton:

> So there she is—sitting very upright and straight-backed, but all
> alive, easy and active in repose; clothed with much elegance, expen-
> sive in her neatness . . . her head held high, and her red-brown hair,
> very pretty and fine, dressed with accurate art; and her face, not a
> young face at all, rather worn and reticulated. . . .
>
> (*Portrait*, 3)

Lubbock's response exposes the context that almost defeated Wharton. The flourish that begins the description, "So there she is," hardly prepares the reader for meeting Wharton face to face. She seems to emerge not only from the elegant trappings of dress, but from what dress represents in terms of gender and class. For Lubbock and for us, the face becomes its own text, "rather worn and reticulated." The dialectic between face and dress (or the book and its jacket) transforms the portrait of any society lady into a singular study. It also mirrors Wharton's own conflict by highlighting the larger cultural one between woman and "woman" as a category or a class marked by certain signs that determine value. If we accept, as the early semiologist Charles Sanders Peirce first postulated, that the assignment of meaning to an object determines how we behave toward that object,[11] then Lubbock's double vision prompted his initial ambivalence. The many friends who originally misread Wharton's character as "cold" or "overbearing" did so in part because they, like Lubbock, had difficulty placing her. Sharing some of Lubbock's ambivalence, the men of the inner circle found it freed them from the exactions of passion— allowing Lapsley, for example, to respect the individual, unclassifiable woman but not the sex.

John Hugh Smith (1881–1965) had none of these difficulties. "Ah, my dear young man," James hailed him in 1908, "you have made friends with Edith Wharton. I congratulate you. You will find nothing stupid in her and nothing small" (*Portrait*, 56). Lubbock describes his classmate, a compact, solidly built man, with a high brow, as

> the sort of young Englishman she needed, a most unusual sort; for the ideas that thronged in his brain weren't imprisoned there, they streamed out in lively order; and he knew so many books and so much life as well . . . that [he] could place her in her right position from many points of view—literary, social, racial, personal; and his range of illustration gave form and substance to a vision dazzling indeed.
>
> (*Portrait*, 69)

Smith characterized himself as a split personality, the Impulsive Idiot and the Prudent Prodigy. Wharton hoped that the latter would get hopelessly left behind in the race of life, and in 1925 asked: "I remember your saying, when I first knew you, that you meant to remain in business just long enough to make a modest competence, & then give the rest of your life to '*les choses de l'esprit.*' Isn't it almost time to hear Time's chariot-wheels, & carry out that resolution?"[12] Wharton thought that his talents would be better served writing literary criticism rather than directing the Hambros Bank or acting as treasurer of the executive committee of the National Art Collection Fund, for in him she met an equally omnivorous and discerning reader.

Smith's obvious infatuation with Wharton ("the more I saw of her, the more there was to learn and to enjoy—it seemed endless"[13]) realigned loyalties and made Lubbock feel excluded: she was "farther than ever beyond the reach of shyness (the real thing!) when she passed away into the world of her natural affinities. There might be little left that I didn't know about her now," he admits, "but I seemed no nearer to knowing Edith" (*Portrait*, 69). "Knowing Edith," was in some ways a kind of competitive sport that jocularly bound the men together.

Unlike Lubbock, Smith soon knew of Wharton's difficulties in caring for and coping with her emotionally ill husband: "I'm touched at your thinking so much of my worries, & understanding them & me as you do," she wrote him in 1912. "It's an effort of imagination that people of your age are usually too busy to make."[14] Passing on the advice that Sturgis offered after most likely learning of her affair (1907–c. 1910) with William Morton Fullerton (1865–1952), Wharton wrote: "'Keep it up—run your race—fly your flight—live your romances—drain the cup of pleasure to the dregs'—but when exhaustion sets in, think of your aff[ectiona]te friend."[15] In some respects, Smith's constancy of affection was an antidote to the vacillations of her lover. "Vanity came to my rescue, & assured me that your long silence could only be due to the fact that the things you wanted to say were not of a kind to be committed to paper by a cautious hand!" she confidently teased her young admirer;[16] whereas, two months earlier, in February 1909, she humbly petitioned Fullerton, "Are you coming to dine tonight? And am I not wrong in asking you, when I know how stupid, disappointing, altogether 'impossible' you found me yesterday?—Alas, the long isolation has made me inarticulate, & yet I wasn't meant to be! But that doesn't help now, I suppose. . . ."[17] With each of these men, Wharton self-consciously experimented with a variety of feminine personas that ranged from "wiser and older" to "lovesick." The composed quality of both her correspondence and the journal she kept during the affair make them seem like rehearsals for later fictions. Anna Leath of *The Reef* (1912), Charity Royall of *Summer* (1917), and Kate Clephane of *The Mother's Recompense* (1925) all echo their author's voice in the transformation of private letters for public consumption.[18]

If Robert Norton (1868–1939) sometimes found Wharton and "her damned Pekinese" impossible, his unflappable manner disguised it. In 1933, Wharton wrote Berenson that she and Norton had found their names in the visitors' book at Stanway, which they had signed twenty-five years before, and "kissed again with tears!"[19] Norton had begun his career as a clerk in the Foreign Office and later served as the private secretary of Lord Robert Salisbury, the conservative prime minister. According to Wharton, he belonged to the Society of Charm, Inc. Known as "Norts" (affectionately as "Beau Norts" or "Bob"), he had fine features, dark hair parted in the middle, and an acumen for business that allowed him to retire at forty and devote himself to landscape painting. His work is at once impressionistic in color and largely representational in detail. A painting of Wharton's garden at Sainte Claire in Hyères, for example, is clearly recognizable as such, though the autumnal trees appear to be weeping into the fountain reflecting their image. Wharton described his work as "quiet and strong studies of out of the way subjects." "I never thought he had anything but an amateur talent," she wrote Smith in 1919, "but I have changed my mind now, & think he will do something special."[20] For his part, Norton thought Wharton "a liberal education."[21]

Although Norton had known Wharton since 1904, their intimacy took on a new dimension after the First World War. Then Norton spent whole winters with her at Sainte Claire, involved in every stage of its founding and growth. When they were not traveling in the motor—outfitted with receptacles for maps and guidebooks, a book box, a net to hold sticks, umbrellas, capes, and rugs of different thicknesses—their days had a tranquil domestic quality. Each worked through the morning, she writing and he sketching. Afternoons tended to include a picnic, its spot supposedly chosen by Wharton "with the care and deliberation of a Roman general selecting the site of a fortified camp" (GL, 4). Following a typical lunch of eggs, cheese, olives, chicken, salads, chocolate, oranges, and coffee, they would take a long walk until teatime. In the evenings, he frequently read aloud from Hardy's *The Return of the Native* or Austen's *Sense and Sensibility,* to name two favorites. According to Lubbock, "this was one at any rate who enjoyed the society of the world and didn't fear solitude; and his presence, I can well imagine, might quiet the restlessness haunting a mind that isn't sure of its serenity in the company of itself" (*Portrait*, 179). Perhaps the most independent of the inner circle, Norton provided a model of steady, seldom-rewarded work, which enhanced rather than competed with daily life. At Christmas, Lapsley would routinely join them. In the dedication of *The Children* (1928), Wharton was most likely referring to these friends (and perhaps John Hugh Smith), her "patient listeners at Sainte Claire."

After 1912, Wharton considered Bernard Berenson (1865–1954) a confrere, and in 1913 the two traveled, somewhat testily, to Germany. The unspoken bond between the son of a Jewish peddler and the daughter of old New York grew out of their vastly different backgrounds. Berenson's metamorphosis had matched Wharton's own. He considered himself one of the "marginals," always on the ragged edge of any social body, including the inner circle, with nothing to offer but a "Pandora's box of personal gifts and characteristics."[22] Later he criticized himself for wasting too much of himself attempting to establish his position as a "monsieur," in much the same way that Wharton's fiction criticizes the process of making and maintaining a lady. "Seeing I had no roots in any of the countries I was living in," he writes in his memoir, *Sketch for a Self-Portrait* (1949), "it was but natural, although neither noble nor even wise, to harbour such an ambition, and to resent any question as to my right place in society" (50). *The Age of Innocence* (1920) examines the same issue from a female perspective.

The man Wharton knew had converted to Catholicism because the church, shorn of its theology, myth, and ritual, remained the mother and nurse of art.[23] Like her, he created a circle of close friends through which he defined himself. Berenson's sister Rachel once observed that "For diplomacy & intrigue the court of 'i Tatti' makes Henry of Navarre, Margot & Catherine de Medicis look like suckling babes."[24] The group at I Tatti differed from the inner circle in several ways. First, and more traditionally, it had a man of "genius" at its center. Second, Berenson negotiated with Harvard to make his villa what it is today, a "lay monastery for leisurely culture" (*S & T*, xiii), a museum. I Tatti stands as a monument (and a mausoleum) to its owner's knowledge of Italian art; it is the place he perhaps most thought the "House of Life," the permanent home of the soul.[25] To Wharton, Berenson was a courtly aesthete, a brilliant conversationalist, and the distinguished critic known for his expertise in attributing unsigned works of art. To him, she represented all of his past social aspirations associated with the patrician America of his friend Henry Adams. Although Wharton sometimes adopted a flowery voice when writing to him about art or scenic landscapes, together they shared a love of gossip—itself a form of subversive flirtation that rearranges all relationships, especially those of narrator and audience.

With these men—James, Sturgis, Berry, Lapsley, Lubbock, Smith, Norton, and Berenson—Wharton was beginning to fashion "a small human community, a society of friends," which not only extended, as R. W. B. Lewis writes, her "literary, intellectual, and social world,"[26] but also nurtured her own development as a woman and an artist. This Land of Letters existed on multiple levels: in the group's actual correspondence, in what the men themselves represented, in the art produced, and in the "characters" Wharton used to spell out her identity. Like many nineteenth- and early-twentieth-century women writers, she did not find the gulf between eros and art (what Elizabeth Stuart Phelps characterized as the thimble and the paintbrush) as unbridgeable as Phelps's *The Story of Avis* (1877), Kate Chopin's *The Awakening* (1899), Mary Austin's *A Woman of Genius* (1912), and Willa Cather's *The Song of the Lark* (1915) might lead one to assume. The equation of art and experience made less sense for a woman of her time and class than one between art and objectivity. Wharton may have envied George Sand's life, but she did not want to accept, as her remark to Lapsley about risks illustrates, the social and personal consequences of imitating it.

Wharton was denied access—especially in terms of sexual freedom—to the experiences Sand claimed as the birthright of "genius." This pattern of male artistic development, commonly characterized by the metaphor of the sacred fount, has as its counterpart the metaphor of the ivory tower. There an artist like Henry James or James Joyce's Stephen Dedalus observes and collects *les données*, the kernels for their fictions.[27] The legacies of class, wealth, and temperament made Wharton's enclosure in the ivory tower more insured and secured. Yet she could not escape another inheritance of gender that demanded she reinvent herself as woman and artist. In the process of defining herself, Wharton did not so much oscillate between matrilineal and patrilineal literary traditions—which she would have defined as the "sentimental" books her mother devoured and the leather-bound sets in her father's library—as gradually come to a greater understanding and appreciation, captured in *Hudson River Bracketed* (1929) and *The Gods Arrive* (1932), of their interdependence.[28] Unlike her earlier work, these late novels equate or "bracket" childbearing and writing; they argue that great books are not "motherless." After venturing, like Twain's Huckleberry Finn or Hemingway's Frederick Henry, into the wide world, where he is to acquire the broader view of art that Wharton assigned to men, whose "slice of life" novels win "Pulsifer" Prizes, Vance Weston realizes that he is incomplete without Halo Spear. He begins his career following the footsteps of Rip Van Winkle and ends it kneeling before the pregnant Halo. Placing herself with the majority of nineteenth-century American women writers, Wharton contends that home is where the heart and art reside.

For Wharton to be both woman and artist, she needed to find such a home, a metaphorical Land of Letters, where she could drink at the fount of experience at will (even if circumspectly), where she could immerse herself more fully and intensely in life without jeopardizing the roles, associated with class and gender, which buttressed her identity. Wharton may have believed that the artist was autonomous (an argument that Cynthia Griffin Wolff's biography supports),[29] but her relationship to the inner circle, a group that symbolically allowed her to appropriate and redefine the male traditions it literally embodied, belies that contention. In one sense she was, like male artists, the "paternal" ruler of a fictive world she created and then owned;[30] in another she was its product, its members as necessary to the production of herself as actors, audience, and playwright to the play. Foreshadowing Virginia Woolf's Mrs. Ramsay and Mrs. Dalloway (or her own Miss Bart), she could be either or both author and subject, composer and composition, painter and canvas. Men who were sexless or homosexual did not threaten either stance and may even have given Wharton a secret sense of heterosexual superiority.

In turn, the men of the inner circle, who viewed Wharton with affectionate skepticism, chauvinistically took their superiority for granted. Although Wharton figured as a subject in their correspondence and conversation, they did not need her presence as an occasion to meet or to participate in a kind of men's club where allegiances delicately varied. Having been a student of William James, Berenson felt a special tie to the brother, who was suspicious of the art critic's aesthetics. Because Lapsley and Lubbock were close friends, the others often mentioned them together: "I am lying like a birdcatcher behind the cage," Sturgis wrote Wharton in 1913, "baited with two lumps of sugar in the shape of Percy & Gaillard, holding my breath & hardly daring to move."[31] Lubbock turned to Lapsley, a sympathetic and partisan listener, when he had "black moods," experienced unrequited love or—more frequently—needed counsel about his conflicted relationship with Arthur Benson: "I said to ACB 'I won't show you what I have been writing—you would hate it.' 'No,' he said. 'I don't *hate* your work—but it seems to me like *death*. Fine and lofty perhaps, but the end of everything I enjoy & desire.'"[32] Editing Benson's diaries in 1926, Lubbock confided: "one turn of the screw is also a surprise to me—the reckless horrid way in which he apparently talked about me to people I hardly know—all noted down in the diary with a sort of *glee*—it's hard."[33]

Possessing a gift for disinterested friendship, Lapsley maintained relationships unmarred by jealousy and competition with all the members of the inner circle. James genuinely liked Berry, but he appears to have been in the minority. Wharton's worst traits—her snobbery and imperial manner—they generally blamed on Berry's influence, thereby avoiding any re-evaluation of her character or motives. James and Sturgis were most open and affectionate, commiserating over bad backs and nurturing one another in times of depression. *"Don't know this from me please,"* James wrote after passing on confidential information about Wharton's marriage.[34] Until James's death in 1916, they tried to meet monthly. Smith and Norton remained on the fringes of the group, connected to it by their ties to Lubbock and Wharton. James welcomed Lapsley, Lubbock, Berry, and Fullerton at Lamb House when they could get away and occasionally dined with Norton in London. He especially regretted seeing so little of Fullerton and addressed him in an erotically paternal voice: "If I could wish you to be anything in particular but what you are, I should wish you to have been young when *I* was. Then, don't you see, you would have known not only the mistress of *ces messieurs*,—you would almost, perhaps, have known *me*."[35]

Wharton's male friends were all representatives of the Land of Letters—of law, history, commerce, and art. She was their audience as much as they were hers. Their approval and affection validated the woman and the author; similarly hers, personally and professionally, validated them. "In our hurried world," Wharton writes, "too little value is attached to the part of

the connoisseur and the dilettante" (*ABG*, 150) Wharton's novels show
her admiration for these men's outdated or impossible standards, her appreciation of their refined sensibilities and love of beauty, her disdain for
their ineffectuality. With some blindness, Lapsley thought that Wharton,
like all women writers, was unable as a rule to get inside her male characters; she did not know "how their consciousnesses worked nor how they
behave when she is not there to observe them though she believes the
worst on principle" (GL, 44):

> Edith accepted the type exemplified by her brothers and their friends
> and contemporaries—men living on allowances or private means,
> who had often studied law and may even have had an office, but
> who had no practice, idle persons without responsibility or much
> conscience.
>
> (GL, 44)

Agreeing with Lapsley, Norton complained that Wharton, who admired
Theodore Roosevelt's virile self-sufficiency, "only grudgingly made concessions to the weaknesses of the other sex" (RN, 27). Percy Lubbock
thought Wharton's heroes modeled solely after Walter Berry, and he held
them partly responsible for, in his estimation, the ultimate failure of her
novels:

> Calm and strong, a man of the world and of the best world . . .
> master of himself and of his fate, a cool hand, a deliberate ob-
> server— . . . Will he never break down or flare up, never crash
> through his punctillo, never forget his manners . . . ? That is what
> this novelist in all good faith has taken for a man, and in all serious-
> ness has offered us as the flower of manhood.
>
> (*Portrait*, 228–229)

In the role of artist or critic Wharton extends her heroes a benevolent,
slightly condescending, sympathy. As connoisseurs, she treats her "over-
civilized" male characters—Selden in *The House of Mirth*, Amherst in *The
Fruit of the Tree* (1907), Manford in *Twilight Sleep* (1927)—more harshly,
showing how their acceptance of the status quo harms them only slightly
less than those who love them.[36] Protagonists like Ethan Frome, lawyer
Royall of *Summer*, or Martin Boyne of *The Children* (1928), who are mar-
ginalized by their own sexual or social inadequacies and consciously or
unconsciously prey on dependents or children, threaten society itself.
Newland Archer in *The Age of Innocence* is representative of those characters who find it impossible to change or leave a system that so benefits

them. Wharton's heroes, often as much victims as victimizers, stand as a critique of the "masculine" man and the culture that produced and protected him. ⌋

Wharton christened some of her male characters with her father's first name, George, others with his second, Frederic. They reflect her wish to explain, to realize, her father, whom she paints as a kindly distant figure hovering on the border of her understanding: "I remember his reading only Macaulay, Prescott, Washington Irving, and every book of travel he could find," she recalls in *A Backward Glance*.

> Arctic explorations especially absorbed him, and I have wondered since what stifled cravings had once germinated in him, and what manner of man he was really meant to be. That he was a lonely one, haunted by something always unexpressed and unattained, I am sure.
>
> (*ABG*, 39)

Meeting Wharton's needs for adoration and domination, her position at the center of the inner group recast and to some extent replicated what Freud called the "family romance."

⟦Wharton's fascination with the theme of incest has in part led recent critics to speculate that her father might have sexually abused her.[37] She chose, or perhaps had no reason, to leave us any concrete biographical information on the topic; interest is not proof. Would we wish to say that a writer like Ellen Glasgow, for example, who presided over the Society for the Prevention of Cruelty to Animals, wrote poems about dogs, and left a provision for her beloved Bonnie, had sexual fantasies about bestiality? Wharton's fictional use of a certain theme may have multiple sources. Who can know if Wharton survived incest or if she, following the tradition of many nineteenth-century novelists, incorporated the theme into the marriage plot?[38] Even something as conspicuously sexual as Wharton's unpublishable fragment about Beatrice Palamato is more of a cross between nineteenth-century sensation fiction and pornography than a confessional piece. "I've got an incest donnée up my sleeve that wd make them all [Faulkner's *The Sound and the Fury* and Céline's *Voyage du bout de la nuit*] look like nursery rhymes," she bragged to Berenson.[39]⟧

⟦Certainly Wharton's friends found nothing strange about her interest in incest.⟧ Sally Norton's memoir of Wharton suggests the link between forbidden knowledge and books that would partly explain Wharton's use of the metaphor.[40] Wharton made herself "mistress"—to use Norton's term—of the books forbidden to her in her father's library. Gaillard Lapsley offers a slightly different reason for her encouragement of talk that in itself might be classed as gossip or scandal: she wanted to know what people did and why they did it partly for purposes of direct literary documentation. In other words, Wharton was a complex personality whose use of a certain *donnée* probably had multiple sources and reasons. Berenson once complained that people "engaged in discovering the way a work of art or literature or music came to be" are now "sleuthing Henry James's sexual condition and Edith Wharton's possible illegitimacy as if those questions would solve the mystery of their careers as novelists."[41] Wharton chose a literary executor in Lapsley who agreed that the writer was entitled to decide what and how much the public may know.

Wharton surrounded herself with men like Lapsley, who were generally not sexually interested in her, because they left her core of self undisturbed. As confreres they were safe, the relationship defined on their part and hers. There was now no Lucretia Jones, no inhibiting or chastising mother; instead there were multiple, replicate images of her fantasized vision of her father. Like Ralph Marvell's dream of Undine in *The Custom of the Country* (1913), the unrealized, the unnamed, and the undefined, still belongs to us, while the actual forces us to confront our isolation.

The inner circle avoided topics they found distasteful or too personal, and this practice helped to preserve their sense of unity. In fact, they had no open disagreements until 1926 when Lubbock's impending marriage to Sybil Scott, the daughter of the Anglo-Irish earl of Desart and the widow of Bayard Cutting, threatened two of the group's central myths: its exclusivity and androgyny. Wharton considered Sybil an empty-headed chatterbox and a hypochondriac who had already annexed two of her friends: Sybil had had an affair with Berenson and then married his architect, Geoffrey Scott.[42] "*This kind of thing has got to stop*," she told John Hugh Smith.[43] Believing that Sybil had asked Geoffrey, who was involved with Vita Sackville-West, for a divorce in order to marry Lubbock, Wharton was seeing one of her own heroines come to life. Lady Sybil Cuffe-Cutting-Scott-Lubbock almost matched Undine Spragg-Moffat-Marvel-de Chelles-Moffatt in *The Custom of the Country*.

A journalist before her first marriage, a supporter of women's suffrage, and later the author of the memoirs *A Page from the Past* (1934) and *The Child in the Crystal* (1939), a book of fairy tales, a translation of four tales by Zélide, an anthology, and a travel book, Sybil was, of course, much more than the nonentity Wharton wished. Wharton—and Mary Berenson, for that matter—surpassed Sybil in wit and erudition, yet how were they to explain the appeal of this alluring and literary woman who fainted at the least provocation? Wharton told Mary Berenson "that she would have given all her brains and her art and the success they brought her to have been one of those women whom men find irresistible" (GL, 46). No matter how weak or flighty, Sybil seemed such a woman. Lubbock's de-

fection substantiated the author's thesis that men naturally prefer a perfectly complected, childish woman to what Paul Bourget, using Wharton
as a model, called "the intellectual tomboy."[44] Wharton disapproved of any
relationships that had the potential to remove her to the margins of her
friends' lives. For example, she objected to Robert Norton moving into
his second Riviera home, La Polynésie, which belonged to his devoted
friend Madame de Béhague. Instead of confronting or asking more of
Norton or Lubbock, she tended to redirect her anger at the perceived rival,
in much the same way that the men of the inner circle blamed her failings
on Walter Berry.

Sybil not only challenged Wharton's position, she also imposed herself
between the writer and her male mirror. The mirror was at best inadequate. Wharton's assumption that the inner circle felt the same as she
when reading the first novel of Alberto Moravia, viewing the Passo d'A-
prica, or mourning a friend mitigated her sense of "otherness" as it simultaneously kept her closest friends at arm's length. Most frightening of all,
Sybil presented Wharton with an image of the self she could have become,
a flirtatious society matron with intellectual pretentions and imaginary
illnesses.

After Lubbock's marriage, Wharton's opinion of his critical abilities dra-
matically declined. Informing Lapsley that she had had a letter from Lubbock "gloating over Sybil's having been very ill in Bombay ('*happily in
Government House*'!)," she wrote: "How he wd have jumped at that phrase
when he was doing 'Roman Pictures.'"[45] The situation bewildered and
saddened Lubbock, although his relationship with Wharton had shown
signs of stress before the intrusion of Sybil.[46] His defection was in some
respects a necessary step in claiming his independence—what Wharton
calls in *The Mother's Recompense* a right to buy one's own experience. If it
was also prompted by an unconscious need to establish himself as a writer
apart from her and the inner circle, it did not succeed. Lubbock's best and
last work after his marriage to Cutting in 1926 was *Portrait of Edith Wharton* (1947). When Lapsley asked him to supply the source of one of James's
phrases for *A Backward Glance*, he responded:

I thought I had ceased to feel pain in the matter, but your questions
bring up the old days—& I think what Howard would have felt &
said—& there is plenty of pain in it after all. It is very strange—I
shall never quite understand it. Of course it is irreparable now—
there is nothing to be done, I know that; for I can never bear to see
or hear from her unless she apologizes freely & frankly to Sybil for
the way she has treated her—& I know well she won't do that. Yet
to think that she can have borne to cut herself off—through these
years that have been filled for me with such sore anxieties & sorrows

[Sybil was an invalid, allergic to an unspecified protein]—to turn her back on it all—throw over the past without the slightest effort to save it—I shall never understand it. And the cruel thing is that it undermines & falsifies the past.[47]

Wharton, as Kenneth Clark once observed, divided the whole world into those who were inside her own charmed circle and those who were not. Lubbock's break with Wharton did not end his friendships with the other members of the inner circle, but it does raise the question—as he himself suggests—of a falsified past. A shared vision grants a sense of continuous identity; it also involves a form of negotiation that must to some degree "falsify" history and diminish the individual. In response, the individual has the means, like Lubbock, to empowerment through dissent or withdrawal. The inner circle's merging of masculine and feminine roles, while reflecting its members' basic refusal to commit, also provided a psychic space for self-creation without undermining their allegiance to traditions they benefited from and respected.[48] Unlike Wharton's clandestine affair with Fullerton (which to some extent also included James [see Chapter 3]), Lubbock's marriage openly challenged its androgynous orientation. The men's attraction to Sybil reinforced Wharton's sense of her own unattractiveness and made any Republic of the Spirit seem fictive or second-best. Sybil and what she represented—either in sexual or material concerns—implicitly undermined the group's self-definition: Was intimacy a form of disinterest? Were friends rivals?

Had Henry James been alive, he might have inspired Wharton with a more generous, certainly a more humorous, attitude toward Sybil. His death in 1916, about a decade before Lubbock's break with Wharton, had marked the end of the inner circle's first phase. The Land of Letters, mapped in his correspondence, was now in danger of becoming public. If that happened, each writer would no longer be the sole author of his or her identity; the reader would become—as Lubbock argues in *The Craft of Fiction*—a partner in the making of the book. Those members originally united in their affection and respect for James (Wharton, Sturgis, and Lubbock) increasingly sustained their relationships not on shared experience but on memory, transformed gradually into fact by the act of writing for a sympathetic reader. As individuals and as a group they wanted and perhaps needed to believe what Wharton wrote Lapsley: "We had a Henry that *no one* else knew, and it was *the* Henry we had!"[49]

In an attempt to keep the image of "*the* Henry" from being misrepresented and—perhaps more to the point—to keep their own privacy intact,[50] Wharton organized a campaign to control the publication of James's letters. To Edmund Gosse she wrote, "As you know, I have shared from the first your feeling that Percy Lubbock is the one person fitted for this very delicate task, & I wrote urgently to Howard Sturgis some time ago asking him to use all his influence with Mrs. James [the widow of William James] and to appeal to you for support." Wharton informed Gosse that she had conferred with Morton Fullerton, who also owned a large collection of letters from James:

> he and I are both unwilling to give our letters if the book is to be edited by the family, for the simple reason that we think it necessary that the work should be done by some one familiar with the atmosphere in which Henry and our small group communed together. The letters are full of allusions and cross-references that could not possibly be intelligible to any one who was not of the group; and when I say "the letters" I mean also those addressed to Howard Sturgis, Gaillard Lapsley, and Percy himself.[51]

The thank-you note that James wrote to Berry for a dressing case was one of the few letters that Wharton thought accessible to the uninitiated: "More prosaically, dearest Walter (if one of the most lyric acts recorded in history—and one of the most finely aesthetic, and one stamped with the most matchless grace, *has* a prosaic side,) I have been truly overwhelmed by the princely munificence and generosity of your *procédé*, and I have gasped under it while tossing on the bed of indisposition."[52] But Howard Sturgis's "Studies in Birdlife," full of the kind of cross-references (and nonsense) to which Wharton alludes, is similarly comprehensible. In it, he refers to James, John Hugh Smith, and himself, characterizing Wharton as "*L'oiseau de feu*," who "can carry off in its talons a 'fat Hen', or lamb from the lambhouse or even a small (H)ewe, & has been known to drag a heavy old goose of the *Quacker* species half over England, though these tough birds are notoriously hard to move."[53] These sample letters suggest that Wharton's concern about the intelligibility of James's letters was of less importance than the editor's discretion and perhaps the historical representation of the group itself.

Wharton wrote James's niece Peggy, recommending Lubbock's "extraordinary literary sense," "his experience in biographical work," and his "almost magical insight" into her uncle's point of view: "Not an allusion, not an association of ideas, seems to escape him; and his understanding of Mr. James's mind was so complete, that he appreciates the books on America as intensely, and with as complete an understanding of their local colour, as any American reader."[54] Wharton summarized the position of James's family and her strategy to Sturgis, who then was to pass her letter on to Lapsley:

They don't intend to do anything for five or six years (so they told Gosse), & if my proposal about Percy is not accepted, & they say they are going to do the book themselves, you might very well (supposing the alternative plan of 'Letters to a Group of Friends' is realized) say that your letters really belong to that group, & that, as they (the J.s) can do nothing for so long, you prefer to give your letters to Percy.[55]

Sturgis warned Wharton about "brusking" the Jameses. She replied that since they asked her advice it was "too good an opportunity to be missed."[56] She had not, however, anticipated the intensity of James's sister-in-law's opposition. Alice James had disliked Wharton ever since she had received a letter from her daughter stating that she had heard "things about Mrs. Wharton of which I had not dreamed. Her morals are scarcely such as to fit her to be the companion of the young and innocent."[57] For her part, Wharton thought Alice James unliterary and provincial. Each considered the other self-serving. During the fray, Lubbock was beside himself and complained to Lapsley: "Of course it is perfectly sickening that the Jameses elect to treat as a family matter what is not really much more of a family matter than the plays of Shakespeare. . . . *Imagine* that *literature* should positively be at the *mercy* of a pair of *women!*"[58] The family eventually consented to Lubbock as an editor, but not before warning him to avoid the influence of Mrs. Wharton.

More than the other members of the inner circle, Lubbock and Wharton needed to secure James for themselves, to place his narrative within their own. Referring to Wharton, Robert Norton writes that "it was almost axiomatic that he [James] was outside criticism" (RN, 48B). "I note in Percy such a different feeling for Henry from my own," Sturgis complained to Wharton in 1917. "He is so penetrated with his *greatness* . . . he seems to think of him so exclusively as the genius, the reputation, the possession of the ages; & I have such a weak human longing for the lost dear delightful angel man. . . ."[59]

Lubbock's caretaking or—depending on one's point of view—appropriation of James's memory is related to a belief he shared with James that art makes life, a premise that his own editing of the James letters supports. "Henry James might sometimes look back, as he certainly did, with a touch of ruefulness in reflecting on all the experience he had only enjoyed at second hand," Lubbock explains, "but he could never doubt that what he had he possessed much more truly than any of those from whom he had taken it."[60] The defense applies equally well to its author, who lived his own life in the context and shadow of a master so thoroughly that he sometimes sounded like him: "Your wonderful & beautiful welcome goes straight to my heart," Lubbock responded to Wharton's invitation to

Paris, "& I dwell on it & think of it & marvel at it—till I simply lose myself in the thought of this great blessing & possession which I am able to feel to be mine."[61]

Motivated by concerns similar to Lubbock's, Wharton's fight to control the letters recalls scenes from her childhood, when she hid stories and poems from the prying eyes of a mother capable of stealing or subsuming her identity. Perhaps she wanted to rescue James's remains (and by extension James himself) from the clutches of a family as supposedly unsympathetic and grasping as her own. Eleven years later, when Walter Berry died of a stroke in 1927, her behavior was curiously similar. This time the disputed items were books. Berry had left all his books to his cousin and heir, Harry Crosby, minus those that Wharton wished for her library. Soon Crosby began to fear that she would take them all. Wharton might have resentfully sensed that Crosby felt sorry for her, believing that Berry had not returned the force of her affection. Although Crosby generously excused the difficulties she caused him over funeral arrangements and the disposal of his uncle's ashes, which Berry had wanted "chucked out anywhere,"[62] she thought him "inexperienced and unmanageable." After sufficiently punishing him with the thought that she would claim the entire library, Wharton pronounced him a "cad" and took only seventy-three volumes and sets of books from the extensive collection. She had, however, gained possession of Berry's ashes, later buried in the Cimetière des Gonards at Versailles, where Wharton bought a double plot nearby. If we think of Berry's ashes (or life) like one of the books he willed, then Wharton might be said to have tried to insure a certain romanticized reading.

After the death of James, the inner circle experienced some readjustment. More than an attenuated social group, it now carried on as a literary workshop. Contradicting the popular image of Wharton's almost pathological separation of her professional and social selves, she increasingly shared her writing with the remaining members. Evenings at Hyères or I Tatti, which included a reading of work in progress, made the Land of Letters manifest. The happy few were her audience, duplicating the one that peeked into Mrs. Jones's bedroom as her daughter paraded to and fro, pretending to read from an upside-down book. The presence of listeners in the course of composition might in part explain the oral quality and the looser structure of Wharton's later work. With Robert Norton and "the collaboration of Gaillard Lapsley," she edited *Eternal Passion in English Poetry* (1939), a volume that reflects their personal preference for Robert Browning, Dante Gabriel Rossetti, and William Shakespeare. When Norton translated Claude Silve's novel, *Benediction* (1936), she provided an introduction. Wharton encouraged her listeners to be completely frank in their comments and suggestions and as a result of these discussions often rewrote a scene as many as four times. "In this way," Norton recalls, "I watched *The Glimpses of the Moon* [1922], *A Mother's Recompense* [1925], *The Old New York Stories* [1924], *The Children* [1928], *Hudson River Bracketed* [1929], and *The Gods Arrive* [1932], and many of the short stories and articles, take shape" (RN, 36–37). There grew up a little circle of intimates—Norton, Lapsley, Smith, the Berensons, Nicky Mariano, and Daisy Chanler—itself an extension of the inner group, with whom she "could talk book-shop from morning till night" (RN, 19). Believing that "in every society there is the room, and the need, for a cultivated leisure class but from the first the spirit of our institutions has caused us to waste this class instead of using it" (*ABG*, 95–96), Wharton employed her friends at Hyères. To her, reading and criticism were related arts that only born readers, "the Happy Few," as she wrote in "The Vice of Reading" (1903), could master.[63]

Wharton particularly valued Smith as a reader and had called *The Custom of the Country* their book, just as she later considered *The Gods Arrive* Walter Berry's book because he had always urged her to tell the story of an artist. Asking Lapsley's advice about the dedication to Berry, she wrote: "Under his initials I want to put the abrupt poignant opening phrase of Propertius's elegy on the death of the young woman he loved so much: '*Sunt aliquid manes* [spirits exist].' That seems to me the last depth of human yearning. But of course to Latinists it may be the worst of clichés—like 'that rare word gla-*mour*.' Do tell me, & in that case I'll refrain."[64] (She didn't need to.) Lapsley had also suggested that she preface "the book with a few lines that shd *not* be a magazine summary of the story, but—something very much better!" "If *you* can (& knowing your memory, I'm sure the 'if' is irrelevant)," she wrote, "do jot the idea down on a p[ost]. c[ard]. & shoot it off to me."[65] In turn, she offered Lapsley advice about making his academic writing more interesting. If he would change narrative chronology for dramatic effect and just add a touch of heart interest for the general public, indulged by cinemas and the detective novel, she teased, Lytton Strachey's best sales would pale in comparison.

Howard Sturgis may have been Wharton's most astute and dispassionate critic, Robert Norton her least. After reading *The House of Mirth*, for example, Sturgis faults the point of view. In a sense, he places her in the unwanted company of Mary Wilkins Freeman and Sarah Orne Jewett, those predecessors whom Wharton thought wore rose-colored glasses: it was unlikely anyone would know what Lily Bart "thought & felt on any particular occasion," he wrote,

> *but not impossible*, whereas what she thought & felt just before she dies alone, *she could not tell any one*, nor could she write it (being dead), & whenever I come across it in a book it falsifies the whole thing to me . . . I say . . . Mrs. Wharton *can't* know this; she's in-

venting; perhaps she has invented the whole thing; perhaps there never was a Lily Bart.[66]

Sturgis's criticism of *Summer* anticipates feminist interest in Wharton's revision of the seduced-and-abandoned plot: "What struck me was your courage in choosing one of the most time worn themes in the world, that had been done so over & over & over again that one would have thought there wasn't any a drop more to be squeezed out of it by any one, & then the amazing way in which you succeed in making it your own."[67] In contrast, Wharton found Norton, after reading the last chapters of what many critics consider her worst book, *The Gods Arrive*, "(literally) choking with emotion, & unable to ejaculate more than: '*Ah—parbleau!*'"[68]

From among these trusted readers, Wharton might have selected Lapsley as her literary executor because he had experience publishing and editing. At the time of his death in 1949, Lapsley was preparing a collection of Wharton's fugitive pieces designed to show her "training as an artist and her reflections about her art."[69] He intended to call the book "The Service of Letters," a phrase taken from her introduction to the play adaptation of *Ethan Frome* (1936). In it she had described herself as "a faithful servant of English letters." Lapsley's title would have delighted James, who commenting on the relationship between Wharton and her narrator in *Ethan Frome* had joked: imagine Edith (or her alter ego) a servant to anything! Lapsley had notes for an introduction that would state his interpretation of her general view of the art of fiction and its points of contact and dissent—notably that art is not the product of ideology—in relation to the younger generation of writers whom Wharton liked: Dreiser, Ferber, Lewis, and Fitzgerald.

Like Lubbock's editing of James's correspondence, this last project would reflect several voices. As Patricia Meyer Spacks writes of gossipers, the inner circle created a psychic space like that of Arden or Thessaly in which they wove their web of story, their drama of shared lives, and it allowed them to know themselves more intimately.[70] At the same time, one must wonder how much their collective story and the gossip that collectivized their memories (Spacks, 240) inhibited, while it protected, them from opening any closed doors in mind and heart. Somewhere in the blurred divisions between genres—whether fiction, history, biography, or autobiography, whether oral or written—lies the answer to how much the Land of Letters was a Republic of the Spirit and how much it was another kind of prison.

The inner circle never seems to have discussed these issues. Members tried to follow Berenson's maxim that "good friends should meet only when they are at their best to talk of things that interest them."[71] Nevertheless, the years found Lapsley and Berenson sometimes exasperated by

Wharton's "hatred and unreason," her "occasional outbreaks of anger or jealousy without any proportionate offence." After the illness that nearly killed her in 1929, "she did and said a good many things that one would gladly forget" (GL, 47). Despite these intermittent incidents of "demonic possession" or "moral dislocation" (GL, 47), the inner circle continued to meet and trade memories, to preserve in their letters and memoirs shards of the past for some future relic hunter. R. W. B. Lewis presents them at Hyères three years before Wharton's death in 1937: Norton now gray, Smith deaf and shouting down the length of the long dinner table for remarks to be repeated, Lapsley pompous and intolerant of anyone but "Angry-Saxons"—to use Berenson's phrase—and Wharton more restless than ever.[72] When she died, a cluster of old friends assembled around her grave to sing "O Paradise, O Paradise." This marked the last gathering of the inner circle. "Oh me, how thankful I am to remember that, whether as to people or as to places & occasions, I've *always* known the gods the moment I met them,"[73] Wharton wrote Berenson. And if she didn't meet them, she created them in letters.

CHAPTER TWO

The Inner Circle
and Bloomsbury

How one slides back into it all—back to Quacre—
you must try to come & see us—I want to talk about it—
I get the chance so seldom—indeed there aren't many
left to give it me.
(LETTER OF PERCY LUBBOCK TO GAILLARD LAPSLEY)

But tell me, who is Bloomsbury in your mind?
(LETTER OF VIRGINIA WOOLF TO GWEN RAVERAT)

REVIEWING PERCY LUBBOCK'S BOOK on Edith Wharton, Desmond MacCarthy envisioned himself in the world of Henry James's *The Ambassadors*, playing Lambert Strether to her Madame de Vionnet:

> I can imagine myself going to tea, talking, talking, and staying on to supper: a perfect *omelette baveuse*, cold grouse and a Moselle (the just perceptible violet bouquet of that wine harmonising with the slightly sour flavour of the bird) and then, a triangle of brie and a big yellow pear, both in perfect condition. Yes, I should have been content and most grateful.[1]

Wharton liked and would have welcomed MacCarthy. He was a link to James, who, during their fifteen years of friendship, had unsuccessfully warned him about the loneliness of writing: "If it runs after you and catches you, well and good. . . . for heaven's sake don't run after *it*."[2] She had not, however, approved of his association with Bloomsbury, a group she thought puerile and indiscriminate or "promiscuous." Neither the inner circle nor Bloomsbury, which saw its elders as anachronistic, would have supposed they had anything in common. Yet each responded to the modern's dilemma by creating its own version of a Republic of the Spirit. Like T. S. Eliot, the former sought meaning in the structure of the past and, like William Carlos Williams, the latter was excited with the possibilities for creating new artistic forms. Paired, they define one another as well as an age.

Bloomsbury raises the same kind of queries as the inner circle: If its members had no consensus of opinion or taste, was it in any ordinary meaning of the word a group? Or, was it, as E. M. Forster declared, "the only genuine *movement* in English civilization?"[3] "Who were the members of Bloomsbury?" Clive Bell asks. "For what did they stand?"[4] Critics tend to speak of an early and late Bloomsbury, separated by the First World War. In Leonard Woolf's reckoning, the thirteen members of "Old Bloomsbury" included himself and Virginia Woolf, Vanessa and Clive Bell, Molly and Desmond MacCarthy, Adrian Stephen, Lytton Strachey, J. M. Keynes, Duncan Grant, E. M. Forster, Saxon Sydney-Turner, and Roger Fry. Additions and deletions can and were argued by those who did or did not want to be associated with the group.

Despite Bell's claim that individuals held no distinguishing principles in common, there are some generalizations that are not too misleading. The early members were linked by the closest of familial ties and, unlike those of the inner circle, lived much as an extended family; nevertheless, intimacy was regulated, perhaps checked, by intellectual curiosity. Keynes gives an example of the things they used to discuss impartially: "If A was in love with B and believed that B reciprocated his feelings, whereas in fact B did not, but was in love with C, the state of affairs was certainly not so good as it would have been if A had been right, but was it worse or better than it would become if A discovered his mistake?"[5] The longevity of Bloomsbury, with its tangled skein of emotional and sexual attachments, probably owes something to its members' tendency to intellectualize questions of the heart. They triumphed, as Virginia Woolf wrote in 1925,

> in having worked out a view of life which was not by any means corrupt or sinister or merely intellectual; rather ascetic and austere indeed; which still holds, and keeps them dining together, and staying together, after 20 years; and no amount of quarrelling or success, or failure has altered this. Now I do think this rather creditable.[6]

All of Bloomsbury's original members except Saxon Sydney-Turner and Leonard Woolf belonged to upper-middle-class families that Noel Annan identifies with the new nineteenth-century intelligentsia. This is the same class that produced Percy Lubbock, John Hugh Smith, and Robert Norton. According to Annan, it emerged at the beginning of the century among a particular type of middle-class family whose children became scholars and teachers. Through intermarriage they eventually "spread over the length and breadth of English intellectual life, criticizing the assumptions of the ruling class above them and forming the opinions of the upper middle class to which they belonged."[7] Leonard Woolf wrote of them:

It was an intellectual aristocracy of the middle class, the nearest equivalent in other countries being the French eighteenth-century *noblesse de robe*. The male members of the British aristocracy of intellect went automatically to the best public schools, to Oxford and Cambridge, and then into all the most powerful and respectable professions. They intermarried to a considerable extent, and family influence and the high level of their individual intelligence carried a surprising number of them to the top of their professions.[8]

In *A Sketch of the Past*, Virginia Woolf records that every one of her male relatives was shot into the great patriarchal machine "at the age of ten and emerged at sixty a Head Master, an Admiral, a Cabinet Minister, or the Warden of a college."[9] At Cambridge, which Howard Sturgis, Robert Norton, John Hugh Smith, and Percy Lubbock also attended, the male members of Bloomsbury were inducted into the same clubs: the Apostles, the Midnight Society, and the X Society. Later in London they met on Thursday evenings and formed the Play-Reading Society, the Friday Club, and the Novel Club, among others. Prompted by Molly MacCarthy, the Memoir Club began about 1920 and continued until 1956 so that members could read their intimate recollections of the group to the group itself. When, as Nigel Nicolson writes, Bloomsbury began to weaken its hold on individual members during the late twenties, the Memoir Club functioned as an alumni association.[10]

With all the differences attributable to nationality, the American contingent of the inner circle originated from a process comparable to the one Annan describes. Over three centuries a group of bourgeois colonials and their republican descendants were transformed into a sort of social aristocracy, who appreciated "the concerted living up to long-established standards of honour and conduct, of education and manners."[11] Wharton explains that "even negatively, these traditions have acquired, with the passing of time, an unsuspected value" (*ABG*, 5). Such sentiment would seem anathema to Bloomsbury, which prided itself on "a barbarous incivility" and independence of manners.[12] Disliking empty social conventions and encouraging personal artistic expression, it tolerated a wider range of diverse ideas and behaviors than the inner circle.

Each group, composed of individuals whose interests roamed from economics to scholarship to art, had ties to France. The inner circle settled on the Right Bank; Bloomsbury visited Gertrude Stein on the Left. France appealed in particular to Wharton and Walter Berry as a civilizing force and to Clive Bell and Roger Fry as an index of the avant-garde. Bernard Berenson, who appreciated both views, had multiple connections to Bloomsbury. His wife had roomed with Stein when attending the Harvard Annex, and her daughters married a Strachey and a Stephen. He trusted Robert Trevelyan, poet, translator, and friend of the Woolfs, to read and correct drafts for stylistic excesses. Berenson and Fry served together on the board of *Burlington Magazine*. They were also competitors in the marketplace, especially after Fry began buying for the Metropolitan Museum in New York. Fry respected Berenson but disliked his need to display superior knowledge, while Berenson grew bitter about the other's independence, suspecting him of anti-Semitism. Berenson felt that Fry resented his authority in Bond Street, "and as good as declared war" against him if he did not "leave London to him." [13]

With an eye on his future reputation, Berenson did his best to court Bloomsbury. Members were not impressed. Clive Bell thought I Tatti "full of Old Masters, mysterious countesses and unspeakable Americans," and Vanessa—whose studies of spaces within spaces recall Wharton's gardens at Hyères—cursed the horrors of life there "in spite of the extreme comfort of the place, the Louis XV furniture, and exquisite breakfasts in bed." [14] Berenson later claimed that no one would believe his stories about the Bloomsbury set, which, by 1951, contained the "legendary figures" of Keynes and Fry: "I should be regarded as a venomous, self-absorbed, conceited egoist, who had a chip on his shoulder" (*S & T*, 208), he grumbled.

The 1910 Post-Impressionist exhibition of paintings, organized by Fry and including works by Picasso, Seurat, Cézanne, Van Gogh, Gauguin, and Matisse, brought Bloomsbury to the attention of the general public. In the decades following the 1910 exhibit, the public associated Bloomsbury with pacificism, feminism, the Hogarth Press, and the Omega workshops (1913–1920), founded by Fry to produce works of interior decoration, the subject of Wharton's first book, *The Decoration of Houses* (1897). If the inner circle occasionally regretted the public's neglect, Bloomsbury at times might have wished it. Edith Sitwell writes:

> In this world of superior intellect there were several models. There was, for instance, the amphibian model—with gaping mouth, glassy eyes staring at nothing in particular, and with a general air of slipperiness and, at the same time, scaliness.
> There was, too, the village idiot-model, drooling, and with a boastful exhibition of mental deficiency—also the deliberately awkward and blundering good-sportsman-and-cricketer-model. . . . All these beings lived in the shade of certain powerful and protective persons, eminent and accommodating divines. . . . [15]

Discussed as a movement and vilified by the Leavises as decadent aesthete parasites living on unearned income, Bloomsbury could not help but have a different kind of self-consciousness than the inner circle. The Memoir Club especially suggests that its members recognized and had a shared stake in defining their cultural and historical importance.

The friends of the inner circle were also protected in the way that Sitwell divined and resented, though the guarded, parochial society that they were born into generally preferred discussions of food, wine, horses, and travel to dialogues about art, music, or literature. This kind of protection was not enough for either group. In their personal lives, they needed continuity. For this reason perhaps, Bloomsbury was drawn to the work of G. E. Moore. Moore argued that "the greatest good we know" can be categorized into two classes: "aesthetic enjoyments, on the one hand, and the pleasure of human intercourse or of personal affection, on the other." [16] Moore's philosophy gave Bloomsbury what Henry James called "a standpoint in the universe." [17] From there they could question all else.

While members of the inner circle sympathized with Moore's emphasis on aesthetic enjoyment and personal friendship, they would have balked at his definition of "good" as something indefinable. Those who valued excellence in all things found his definition, or its lack, merely silly. Seeing Bloomsbury in the clouds and herself on Main Street, Wharton called an article by Moore "a precious piece of nebulosity." It made her "despair of England, from the literary point of view." "I had to press a sympathetic hand after reading [it]," she wrote Gaillard Lapsley. "Better, far better," she half-seriously continued, "Ala B. Campbell," whose misspelled solicitation for funds informs its readers that "the Dramus Producing and Releasing Corporation, officered and controlled by women have bought and are to produce 'THE SOUL OF THE VIOLIN,' the first great Dramatic Musical Photoplay." "I'm persuaded that the Releasing Co. she so eloquently represents believes Dramus to be the plural of Drama—" Wharton quipped, "proof in itself, surely, of definite cultural ideals!—" [18]

The inner circle had as its counterpart to Moore's teachings the classical thinking of Charles Eliot Norton, the Harvard fine arts professor. William and Henry James, Walter Berry, Morton Fullerton, Gaillard Lapsley, George Santayana, and Bernard Berenson all attended Harvard, joining, as Lapsley wrote, "a vast family, invisible, indeed, but nonetheless real, embracing at once the august past and the assured future, a moral idea rather than a legal fact." [19] As editor of the *North American Review* in 1864, Norton published James's first pieces. Thirty-eight years later, he recommended *The Valley of Decision* (1902) to William Dean Howells. Soon after their introduction in 1899, Wharton was driving the forty miles from her house in Lenox to Norton's in Ashfield, where she chatted with his daughters, Sara ("Sally") and Elizabeth ("Lily") and borrowed books related to the eighteenth-century Italian setting of her first novel.[20]

Professor Norton saw his mission as quickening, "so far as may be, in the youth of a land barren of visible memorials of former times, the sense of connection with the past and of gratitude for the efforts and labors of other races and former generations."[21] Wharton proved a lifelong devotee: traveling to Hyères from Avignon, she felt as if she were on holy ground, "for no corner of Mediterranean lands, with such blessings of climate, fertility and scenery, had played so continuous a role in European history."[22] Capable of imagining a handful of men in heavy armor plunging down on the Persian host at Marathon, she lived in a present so inspirited by the past that history seemed enacted in her immediate presence. Wharton would have agreed with Walter Berry that "[i]t was he," Charles Eliot Norton, "who opened my eyes to everything worthwhile."[23]

Reactionary and revolutionary, Charles Eliot Norton's vision of a present, whose meaning, richness, and very reality elusively (and allusively) reside in the past, summarizes the position of the inner circle. "It seems to me," Wharton wrote Lapsley in 1925, "that humanity is becoming one-dimensional. There is no substance, no depth, left."[24] After the war, she believed that "it was growing more evident" that the world she "had grown up in and been formed by had been destroyed in 1914" (*ABG*, 370–371). She particularly liked James's pronouncement in *The American Scene* (1907) that "it takes a great deal of history to make a little tradition, a great deal of tradition to make a little taste, and a great deal of taste to make a little art."[25] It takes, in other words, a certain measure of erudition, the kind that Wharton attributed to a dying breed of leisured connoisseurs and dilettantes.

The disdain that the happy few felt for the haphazard jumble of contemporary American society led to their immersion in foreign cultures. Their cultivated sightseeing in countries such as Germany, Italy, and Spain was motivated by a desire to experience their own humanity more fully, to reach across the barriers of time, culture, individual histories, and (to a much lesser extent) race, as when Wharton sympathized with the Moroccan women kept in the harem of a local dignitary. Following Goethe's lead, she believed that artists, sensitive to the whole range of human experiences, took upon themselves the problems of social milieu.[26] The novels of the twenties, for example, show her analyzing, if not assuming, these problems. *The Glimpses of the Moon* (1922), *The Mother's Recompense* (1925), *The Children* (1928), *Hudson River Bracketed* (1929), and even *Twilight Sleep* (1927), a surrealistic montage of a present lived only in the present tense, originate from a concern for the future of the family.

Bloomsbury may have felt less comfortable with the notion of universal feelings and standards, but both groups appreciated and seem to have been indirectly influenced by Frederic William Maitland, "the father of the pluralist tradition in English political thought."[27] Maitland was a friend of James, Lapsley's mentor at Cambridge, and the biographer of Leslie Stephen. He belonged to the Apostles, a discussion society which included Keynes, Strachey, Woolf, and Bertrand Russell, later the brother-in-law of Bernard Berenson's wife, Mary. His belief in the power of small groups and their ability to influence developing institutions provided a context for Lapsley's thinking about government as well as a justification for the historical significance of groups like Bloomsbury and the inner circle.

Maitland's commitment to civilization in its broadest sense helped to justify the expatriation of members of the inner circle and the conscientious objections of Bloomsbury. Roger Fry reflects his thinking when he writes that the mind has no national boundaries and can and should "guide the passions toward civilization."[28] To Fry, civilization and awareness meant the same thing. Forster expresses the logical extension of such thinking in *Two Cheers for Democracy* (1951): if asked to choose between his best friend and his country, he hopes that he would have the guts to choose his best friend. Although sympathetic to the spirit of Fry's definition, the inner circle would have rejected its consequences. Wharton's jingoistic war novel, *A Son at the Front* (1923), and James's letter about the bombing of Rheims Cathedral—"most unspeakable & immeasureable terror & infamy"—place the collective above the individual.[29]

From one perspective, the sightseeing of the inner circle was a noble attempt to capture—at least for an illusory moment—the collective or the universal. Berenson describes his friends' shared belief in an irreducible nugget of self unaffected by environment, unshaped by language itself: "The individual I meet in England, France, Germany or Italy," he writes, "is, in all but language and what language carries with it, pretty much the same human being. . . . even the Chinaman is much like the rest of us."[30]

From another perspective, the travels of the inner circle seem less benign. Because time increases the sense of alienation from the country of origin without fully erasing it from the country of residence, the exile is to some degree a Nietzschean figure whose self determines all physical and moral boundaries. The danger to the exile lies in believing that the self is paradigmatic of the universal; the opportunity lies in the latitude that the paradigm of exile grants.

More judges than mediators of culture, these "passionate sightseers" (as Berenson called himself) found their inherited and unexamined sense of standards and superiority reinforced. Howard Sturgis, for example, defined a whole country in terms of his class and experience. "I never was so impressed by the crass stupidity of the English as a nation," he wrote Wharton after he, Gaillard Lapsley, and Percy Lubbock attended a lecture that James delivered on Robert Browning.

This was an occasion of knowing the great dead, an assemblage by invitation of the "Literary Academy" of what might fairly have been expected to be an intelligent audience, not "smart" people, but scrubby aesthetes, whose dirtiness nothing but a claim to intellect could excuse. They all thrilled over Pinero, & went to sleep over Henry's most rich & delicate & exquisitely worded address.[31]

In the eyes of most of Bloomsbury and a younger generation of American writers, Sturgis, Wharton, and James were too hybrid, if not peculiarly high bred, although Virginia Woolf's comment on *The Wings of the Dove* (1902) reveals more about its author than James: "Very highly American, I conjecture, in the determination to be highly bred, & the slight obtuseness as to what high breeding is."[32] When one considers Wharton's disparaging remarks about women's suffrage, John Hugh Smith's anti-Semitism, or Robert Norton's cultivation of life—a little reading, a little painting, and conversation when available—as a fine art, the group seems bigoted and parasitic rather than old-fashioned.[33] The same might be said of Lytton Strachey's referring to Asians and Africans as "golliwogs" or Virginia Woolf using the term "darkies."[34]

Despite Woolf's observation about James, the members of the inner circle were not so much "guarders of the tower," inflexibly insistent upon absolute standards, as besieged themselves by a world that they perceived to have few standards left. Their social observations and memoirs conjuring past times involved them in a fierce and relentless dialogue with the present. Concerned with generating the most income from the sales of their books or, in James's case, the production of his plays, the writers tried to predict the popular taste they disparaged. The ahistoricity of James's later novels, Wharton's records of old New York, Sturgis's insights into the British upper classes, Lapsley's investigations of constitutional law, Norton's timeless, unpeopled landscapes, Smith's love of eighteenth- and nineteenth-century literature (from which he could quote at length), and Lubbock's taxonomy of fiction, not to mention his biographical writings, show the group's almost anxious response to or recording of an ever-changing reality.

With its social commitments and experiments in communal living, Bloomsbury tended to make the inner circle look Victorian. Yet to external observers, Bloomsbury appeared equally elitist. In 1947, R. L. Chambers wrote that the subject of Woolf's writing "was the little world of people like herself, a small class, a dying class, . . . a class with inherited privileges, private incomes, sheltered lives, protected sensibilities, sensitive tastes. Outside of this class she knows very little."[35] As a young poet in the thirties, Stephen Spender saw Bloomsbury—which reminded him of "those friends who at the time of the Plague in Florence withdrew into the countryside and told the stories of Boccaccio"—much as Bloomsbury eventually saw James: "the last kick of an enlightened aristocratic tradition."[36] Reading the essays of Lytton Strachey, Virginia Woolf, Clive Bell, Raymond Mortimer, and even Forster, he writes, "one sees how inevitably they interested themselves in the eighteenth-century salons and the English Whig aristocrats" (*WWW*, 128). The daily companionship of five or six people appealed to them as much as to Wharton. Spender could be describing one of the paradoxes at the center of the inner circle when he observes that Bloomsbury's "attitude towards an easy-going conventionality masquerading as traditionalism was critical: at the same time, they were deeply concerned with traditional values which they studied and restated with a vigour which made the old often have the force of the revolutionary" (*WWW*, 127). Where Bloomsbury most differed from the inner circle—more in practice than theory—was in insisting "on the necessity of expressing past values in the imagery and idiom of today" (*WWW*, 127).

Artistically and personally, Henry James bridged yesterday and today. Long a friend of Leslie Stephen, he was a fixture in the Stephen children's early years. Thoby Stephen's death from typhoid, following the deaths of mother, stepsister, and father, deeply disturbed him: "I haven't really borne to *think* of the bereavement of those brave and handsome young Stephen things (and Thoby's unnatural destruction itself)," James wrote, "and have taken refuge in throwing myself hard on the comparative cheer of Vanessa's engagement—quite as if it were an escape, a happy thought, I myself invented."[37] In reality, James intensely disliked Clive Bell, whom he described as a quite dreadful-looking, stoop-shouldered, long-haired third-rater. Perhaps he intuited a threat: after Vanessa, Clive, Virginia, and Adrian paid a visit to Lamb House in 1907, James prophetically punned: "And the hungry generations tread me down."[38]

At least two members of Bloomsbury, Desmond MacCarthy and Leonard Woolf, cite the influence of James during their Cambridge days. "We read *The Sacred Fount, The Wings of the Dove,* and *The Golden Bowl* as they came out," recalls Woolf.

> Lytton Strachey, Saxon, and I were fascinated by them—entranced and almost hypnotized. I don't know whether we thought that they were really great masterpieces. My enjoyment and admiration of them have always been, and still are, great, but with a reservation. There is an element of ridiculousness, even of "phoneyness" in them which makes it impossible to rank them with the greatest or even the great novels. But the strange, Jamesian, convoluted beauty and subtlety of them act upon those who yield to them like drink or drugs; for a time we became addicts, habitual drunkards—never, perhaps, quite serious, but playing at seeing the world of Trinity

and Cambridge as a Jamesian phantasmagoria, writing and talking
as if we had just walked out of *The Sacred Fount* into Trinity Great
Court.

(*Sowing*, 119–120)

After finishing *The Golden Bowl* in 1905, Woolf felt "astounded." "Did he
invent us or we him?" he asked Strachey. "He uses *all* our words in their
most technical sense & we cant have got them all from him."[39] The question delineates both the debt owed to James and the anxiety he inspired as
literary precursor, maybe the creator himself. How does one define the self
if nothing seems to belong to it? Despite MacCarthy's suspicion that James
"overvalued subtlety as an ingredient in character, and was perhaps too
'social' in his standards, employing, for instance, 'charm' too often as the
last test of character," no one could deny that he was "pre-eminently interested" in what interested Bloomsbury: "that is to say, in disentangling
emotions, in describing their appropriate objects and in showing in what
subtle ways friendships might be exquisite, base, exciting, dull or droll"
("HJ," 165). In 1909, James responded to an invitation from Geoffrey
Keynes, Charles Sayle, and Theodore Pembroke to visit Cambridge. "I feel
rather like an unnatural intellectual Pasha visiting his Circassian Hareem!"
he wrote Lapsley.[40] Once there he met MacCarthy and John Maynard
Keynes, both of whom initially bored him, and Rupert Brooke, who, for
probably unintellectual reasons, did not.

Bloomsbury courted James and ignored Wharton, whose antagonism
toward the group in the abstract—and Virginia Woolf especially—developed in the twenties as she felt her reputation threatened. Outraged,
she asked Lapsley if he had seen an article by Woolf in the *Saturday Review*, reporting Woolf's view "that no interesting American fiction is, or
should be, written in English, and that Henry, Hergesheimer & I are neg-
ligible because we have nothing new to give—not even a language!"[41]
Wharton retaliated in *The Gods Arrive* (1932). Her spokesman is Vance
Weston, an artist from the Midwest: "The fishers in the turbid stream-of-
consciousness had reduced their fictitious characters to a bundle of loosely
tied instincts and habits, borne blindly on the current of existence."[42]

After reading *Orlando* (1928), Wharton's disapproval became more per-
sonalized and more dated: the photographs in the advertisements for the
book made her "quite ill." Although not above posing in décolletage for
the frontispiece of *A Backward Glance*, she couldn't "believe that where
there is exhibitionism of that order there can be any real creative gift."[43]
The attack grows from two sources: Wharton's unwavering belief in the
necessary objectivity of the artist,[44] and her feeling of being overlooked by
younger authors. Long accused of losing touch with the native idiom, she

was not pleased after one English reviewer found *The Mother's Recompense* old-fashioned in comparison to *Mrs. Dalloway*.[45] Wharton's competition with Woolf reached its climax when Lady Aberconway commented upon Virginia's great curiosity. Wharton conceded that Woolf certainly had "a very imaginative mind, perhaps a very poetic mind—but was she fundamentally endowed with *true* curiosity?" That question among others proved to Lady Aberconway that Wharton's "curiosity about things and people exceeds even Virginia's."[46] Little did Wharton know that Woolf was similarly curious about her: "Theres the shell of a distinguished mind; I like the way she places colour in her sentences," Woolf wrote of Wharton to a common friend, "but I vaguely surmise that there's something you hated and loathed in her. Is there?"[47] The women's mutual consciousness oddly focuses on the quality of the other's mind. The questions may have been a disguised attempt at understanding the construction of the novels. Or was this vigilant dismissal a form of protection against unwanted influences itself a kind of homage? Struggling with the same problems of personal and artistic definition, each presented a mirror not to be gazed into too deeply.

Wharton's negative response to Woolf and Bloomsbury as an entity did not extend to its individual male members, who resembled those in her own circle—witty, informed, and (as Geoffrey Scott noted) "somewhat invertebrate" or not markedly "masculine." Desmond MacCarthy, essayist, drama critic, and literary editor of the *New Statesman*, Lytton Strachey, critic and biographer, and Arthur Waley, Orientalist, translator, and poet, suited her traditional tastes. "I had Arthur Waley here the other day," she wrote to Lapsley in 1928. "I had been told he was the incarnation of Bloomsbury, but found him rather the contrary—responsive, amiable, &, of course, supremely intelligent."[48] She praised MacCarthy, whom Logan Pearsall Smith (Mary Berenson's brother) had recommended for the task of editing James's letters: "oh, how well he writes! I remember some things in the extinct New Quarterly that thrilled me with quiet satisfaction."[49] Wharton saw Strachey, the irreverent biographer of Victorian England, without irony as the embodiment of "the old English culture." Hearing of his death in 1932, she told Berenson that "he was, with Aldous Huxley, the only light left in that particular quarter of the heavens."[50]

After *The House of Mirth* (1905), Woolf may have ignored most of Wharton's fiction, though she had qualifiedly kind words for Howard Sturgis's *Belchamber*: "A moving, in its way, completed story. But shallow. A superficial book. But also a finished one. Rounded off. . . . yet I like the design . . . a sensitive sincere mind—however, doing his embroidery and making his acute observation. Not a snob either."[51] Unlike Wharton, Sturgis could be read, enjoyed, and set aside. Woolf knew Sturgis through her aunt, Lady Ritchie, the daughter of William Makepeace Thackeray and herself an author. After Ritchie's death, each wrote essays that tried to excuse the loose structure of her novels: "her elusive charm baffles criticism," Sturgis explained. "Her books are written very largely in impression. The reader is sometimes left to infer the facts; the dates must take care of themselves; they do not always quite succeed in doing so. It is not dogmatically asserted that it is the best possible way of telling a story, but it was the best (because the only) possible way for her."[52] Sturgis's description seems particularly tailored to the niece, who consciously disrupted narrative to greater effect than her aunt.

The two groups were to become further connected through Percy Lubbock's wife, Sybil, who had divorced her second husband, Geoffrey Scott, following his affair with Vita Sackville-West, Virginia Woolf's friend and lover. Woolf's meeting with the new bridegroom in 1926 illustrates the generational difference in style between Bloomsbury and the inner circle: "We were egged on to discuss the passions. He mumbled like an old nurse that *he* never had such nasty things: whereupon, in the vilest taste, I contradicted him, never thinking of Lady Sybil, and he bubbled and sizzled on his seat with discomfort, and said, please Mrs Woolf leave *me* alone."[53]

"What can one say to Mr. Percy Lubbock?" Virginia Woolf asked Lady Ottoline Morrell. "By no means all one thinks."[54] She certainly could not say what she had thought of *Earlham* in 1922:

> I have read every word with great interest, trying to make out why in spite of every appearance to the contrary . . . it seems to me a thoroughly bad book—not a book at all in fact. I really cannot say why. . . . I suspect something hopelessly prosaic, timid, tepid, in his goal. The spirit of Earlham is undoubtedly the family butler. . . . that, to me, is the heart of the mischief—this conspiracy to misrepresent the human soul in the interests of respectability and, I suppose, of the defunct Henry James, until . . . nothing approaching bone or blood is left. And why should Percy, who is comparatively young, enter this conspiracy. . . . Oh the smugness of it. . . . really it is queer, how good it is and how bad, and why; and whether Percy himself is corrupt.[55]

Woolf seems to have harbored the same kind of moral suspicions about the inner circle that Wharton had about Bloomsbury. Ironically, her reservations about Lubbock foreshadow Chambers' about her. It leads one to ask, to what extent does Woolf's criticism reveal her own fears about misrepresenting the human soul, and how much does her antipathy toward Lubbock have to do with his being part of that "patriarchal machine," which spit out writers after admirals?

Woolf had not so confidently dismissed Lubbock's *The Craft of Fiction*

(1921), a book that owes its theoretical underpinnings to James's prefaces.[56] In the margin of the book, she commented, "This is all quite true, sound, & I daresay new."[57] To Forster, whose own *Aspects of the Novel* (1927) addressed Lubbock (as well as James), she wrote in 1927: "I dont agree with you that he's a critic of genius. An able and painstaking pedant I should call him; who doesnt know what art is; so, though his method of judging novels as works of art interests me, his judgments dont."[58] To be more than a female Henry James, Woolf had to reject Lubbock's judgments. She could not in good conscience, though, deny James's genius and criticized Forster for doing him less than justice: "Why is the pleasure that we get from the pattern in *The Golden Bowl* less valuable than the emotion which Trollope gives us when he describes a lady drinking tea in a parsonage?"[59] In a sense, Woolf was acknowledging James's influence and obliquely defending her own work, with its diminishing distinctions between life and art. Your definition of life is too arbitrary, she told Forster—who distinguished art from life but not author from narrator—and needs to be expanded.

Woolf's appreciation of James would have pleased even Lubbock. Whatever else he may have been, he was, Woolf tells us, "a great writer—a great artist. A Priest of the art of writing in his lifetime, he is now among the saints to whom every writer, in particular every novelist, must do homage."[60] David Garnett testifies that she kept a framed and autographed photograph of James on her writing table.[61] Although Wharton valued the man above the author, she too had to contend with his legacy. For both, then, those "huge tight-stuffed rather airless" books were "the bridge" one had to cross between the classic novel and "the novel of the twentieth century."[62]

To complicate matters about life and art, Woolf associated James with the father she loved and resented; and Wharton partly sought in him the father she never knew. Wharton's mingling or confusion of literary and biological fathers can be seen in the ghost story "Mr. Jones" (1930). The story's title conjures the ghost of George Frederic Jones, but its content has more to do with James and the ambivalence that Wharton felt toward literary traditions she defined as male and female. For centuries, Mr. Jones has prevented his female charges from speaking. First keeper of his master's deaf-and-dumb wife, now master of the female household servants, he tries to exert his control over the new owner of Bells, Lady Lynke. When Lady Lynke uncovers the history of Mr. Jones's initial prisoner, she gains control of her own house. She also gives her predecessor, known only by the inscription on her tomb—Also His Wife—her name (Miss Portallo), her very identity, back. On one hand, the story would have pleased Virginia Woolf. It warns women against supporting those who oppress them, evidenced by Mr. Jones strangling his second-in-command, the housekeeper Mrs. Clemm, whose name draws attention to the pinched or starved quality of her life. The story suggests that for an artist the past can open the door to new forms. Previously a sentimental travel writer, Lady Lynke now writes biography. On the other, Wharton treats Lady Lynke and her literary works lightly. The real fascination is with Mr. Jones, whether present or not.

The same kind of fascination can be seen in Woolf's many references to James. She remembers, for example, "the hesitation and qualification, the humming and hawing of Henry James' voice. So that no doubt I was supplied very early with a vision of greatness and great men. Greatness still seems to me booming, eccentric, set apart; something . . . now entirely extinct."[63] "Greatness," the word Woolf most frequently uses in her references to James, is something desired and disdained, something belonging to men of a certain age and temperament, something unattainable but dangerously capable of inhibiting or tainting one.

Like Wharton, whom Q. D. Leavis dubbed "Henry James's Heiress," Woolf could not prevent the inevitable comparisons. If Virginia were a race horse, David Garnett writes,

> I should expect to find Laurence Sterne and Henry James in her pedigree. The opening chapters of *Night and Day* have a distinct flavour of James. Later on, though the texture of her writing is quite unlike that of Henry James, there is the same kind of sensitive analysis characteristic of the novels of James's middle period.
>
> (*GF*, 177)

Both Wharton and Woolf felt it crucial to resist James's influence. As Woolf explains, "in life and in art the values of a woman are not the values of a man. Thus, when a woman comes to write a novel, . . . she is perpetually wishing to alter the established values."[64] Grounding the style of James's late fiction in a social milieu reminiscent of Wharton, Woolf (in some ways a hybrid of the two) altered the values these friends established. Her concern with psychological realism, the dominance of interior over external landscapes, and the examination of collaboratively constructed identity, especially in *The Waves* (1931), all recall James, cited as a forefather of everything from realism to impressionism.[65] Her emphasis on characters who survive beyond the turning of the last page matches Wharton's, and the historical, social, and cultural emphasis in works like *Mrs. Dalloway* (1925), *Orlando* (1928), or *Three Guineas* (1938) is analogous to that in *The House of Mirth* (1905), *The Custom of the Country* (1913), and *French Ways and Their Meaning* (1919).

Woolf and Wharton suffered from the dilemma of all successful women writers. First, rebel, then upholder of the status quo, each would have denied they had anything in common.[66] Although their aesthetic principles seem to assume different forms (Wharton's novels being more what Woolf might have considered "gig lamps symmetrically arranged" and her own "a luminous halo, a semi-transparent envelope surrounding us from the beginning of consciousness to the end"),[67] this distinction breaks down when one compares the spiraling structures of *Mrs. Dalloway* and *The House of Mirth*, the chronicle advances of *Orlando* and *The Custom of the Country*, or the circular designs of *Hudson River Bracketed*, *The Gods Arrive*, and *To the Lighthouse*. If, to some degree, Woolf's earlier books are novels of manners, then Wharton's later books delve into the fragmented consciousness of an age. Nevertheless, Woolf's insistence that "the 'book itself' is not the form which you see, but the emotion which you feel" would have struck Wharton as being like Moore's prose, another "piece of nebulosity"—Woolf's self-conscious manipulation of form undermining the assertion.[68]

Despite their differences, Wharton and Woolf shared some basic tenets that grew from their experiences with severe depression. Wharton felt besieged by the Furies and Woolf by "the great cat . . . playing with us once more."[69] Both felt an antagonism toward psychoanalysis, perhaps because it seemed to demand not only a reevaluation of the past but also a reconception of the self. Wharton's strict routine and love of order kept her world controllable. If writing allowed her to unloose the unconscious, it also gave her the means to contain it. Woolf was more cavalier: "Madness is terrific," she assured Ethel Smyth, "& not to be sniffed at; and in its lava I still find most of the things I write about."[70] Their dislike of James Joyce, which Forster shared, might have been tied to the ways in which he played fast and loose with consciousness.

Each woman believed—to quote from Woolf's essay "Mr. Bennett and Mrs. Brown"—that "all novels begin with an old lady in the corner opposite. . . . all novels, that is to say, deal with character, and that it is to express character—not to preach doctrines, sing songs, or celebrate the glories of the British Empire, that the form of the novel, so clumsy, verbose, and undramatic, so rich, elastic, and alive, has been evolved."[71] "Visibility in Fiction" (1929) shows Wharton in agreement: "the aliveness of the characters seems the novel's one assurance of prolonged survival."[72] Part of the release that Wharton, who rigorously supervised all aspects of her life, felt in writing was the moment when her characters took the reins from her hands and assumed control. Neither writer would have objected to James's contention that there is a "perfect dependence of the 'moral' sense of a work of art on the amount of felt life concerned in producing it,"[73] but their concern with verisimilitude led them to the same conclusion about *The Golden Bowl*: it was sheer style. Woolf called its characters not "live people" but "so many distinguished ghosts," and Wharton saw the actors suspended in the void.[74] For them, art must never be (as Woolf said of Lubbock's *Earlham*) "timid or tepid."

Agreeing that the effect of repression on women's writing often had disastrous results, the pair had little sympathy for those who could not "free themselves from the tyranny of sex."[75] That intolerance makes them seem elitist, though Woolf was a feminist in ways that Wharton—who had scant sympathy for extending the vote to all women—was not. An insistent believer in nothing less than total equality based on merit, Wharton refused to contribute scholarships designated solely for women with the observation that they would be better off staying home and having babies.

Wharton's politics seem to deny the history of the inner circle, for, in its own way, it challenged social and gender norms as much as Bloomsbury. The two groups had women at their center. Bloomsbury was able to incorporate several, though the rivalry between Virginia and Vanessa highlights how women artists often feel torn between equally compelling but seemingly exclusive needs; the desire for female community undermines the independence of one's vision. Both groups sought an androgynous ideal. Edith Wharton may not have appreciated the androgyny at the heart of *Orlando* or any other of Woolf's fictions, but its theory was crucial in her construction of self and in the formation of her relationships with her male confreres. "It is fatal for any one who writes to think of their sex," Woolf contends in *A Room of One's Own* (1929). "It is fatal to be a man or woman pure and simple; one must be woman-manly or man-womanly."[76] The definition approximates the inner circle's sense of the universal. Wharton herself attempted to be "woman-manly or man-womanly" when she called herself "a self-made man" and surrounded herself with the men Nicky Mariano called her "male wives."[77] These men frequently rebelled against and grumbled about her orders and counterorders, about going or not going for a picnic or a drive; nonetheless, they felt most comfortable with a certain type of woman whom, as Bernard Berenson writes, they saw as appealing, "not in the first place and perhaps not at all for reasons of sex, no matter how deodorized, alembicated and transubstantiated, but for the one deciding reason that . . . certain society women, are more receptive, more appreciative and consequently more stimulating" (*Sketch*, 12). Wharton found something similar with them, a space where she felt that irreducible spark of self freed from the confines of gender, from the trappings and demands of sex, where she felt accepted for herself.

As their attitudes toward gender, class, culture, and art illustrate, the inner circle and Bloomsbury believed in the principle of mastering, like Maria Gostrey in James's *The Ambassadors*, a hundred cases or categories.

Somewhere among all those categories or somewhere within their consolidation, the heart of things might lie. They came into existence for the same impelling reason and with the same goal: to create an oasis of civilization, humanity, and affection. Bloomsbury actively challenged the status quo, while the inner circle reacted to it, seeking to demonstrate the cultural ideals that Elizabeth Norton felt were lost in the late eighties: "about then also one began to realise that the society which seemed so aimless held voices unknown" (*Portrait*, 39). Each eventually straddled the two worlds separated by the First World War. Each belonged, as Forster observed of Wharton, to a tradition "that is ending."[78] No matter that members of both groups may have had a certain blindness about themselves and the future. With their passing—to quote T. S. Eliot's response to Virginia Woolf's death—"a whole pattern of culture" was broken.[79]

CHAPTER THREE

Edith Wharton and Henry James: Secret Sharers

I had never doubted that Henry James was great, though how great I could not guess till I came to know the man as well as I did his books.
(EDITH WHARTON, *A BACKWARD GLANCE*)

I love you all the while so much as ever, & there hasn't been a day when I haven't hung about you in thought & yearned over you in spirit, & expanded on your treasures of wonder & solicitude even as I have seen the hours & the days & the weeks go by.
(LETTER OF HENRY JAMES TO EDITH WHARTON)

IMAGINE HENRY JAMES AND EDITH WHARTON dancing their own minuet on the "dear old Aubusson carpet."[1] She flings him the handkerchief, literally casts it at his feet:[2] "The real marriage of true minds," she insists, "is for any two people to possess a sense of humour or irony pitched in exactly the same key, so that their joint glances at any subject cross like interarching search-lights."[3] "But, Edith dear," he amends, "the drama must speak charmingly."

Wharton saw herself and James communing like Milton's angels in her own Republic of the Spirit. For James, Wharton was the drama. "Oh how I want your news," he wrote her in 1909, "the real, the *intime*—how I want it, how I want it!"[4] She complied by providing him with a feast of *données*. "What is one's personality," she asks in *A Backward Glance* (1934), "detached from that of the friends with whom fate happens to have linked one?" (169). Wharton's question implies that "personality" is collaboratively constructed, and James's letters to her, written between 1900 and 1915, support this contention. She functioned as his alter ego, his secret sharer: "yours, dearest Edith, in constant participation,"[5] a participation which James aptly described as "supersensual & devotional."[6]

The relationship between James and Wharton was at once professional, parental, and so intrinsically personal that it extended in James's case to a perception of the "other" as himself. The roles each adopted dominate certain periods of their friendship but are by no means confined to them. The position of caretaker, for example, shifted according to need during Wharton's divorce and James's illnesses. Despite the differences in age, gender, and temperament, the two seemed to be parts of one person. Playing with this concept in the letters, James redefines gender. Without appearing unmanly or making Wharton unwomanly, he feminizes himself and masculinizes her. James creates a metaphoric home with Wharton, his own "Land of Letters" (to borrow her phrase), in which each can assume the social and sexual privileges attributable to the other sex, becoming, as discussed in Chapter 2, "woman-manly or man-womanly."

Initially James invited the younger novelist to send him her work and offered advice in favor of the American Subject: "Profit, be warned, by my awful example of exile and ignorance. You will say that *j'en parle à mon aise*—but I shall have paid for my ease, & I don't want you to pay (as much) for yours. . . . DO NEW YORK!"[7] His tone grew less mentorlike and more cordial after the 1905 publication of *The House of Mirth*, and by 1906 he was recommending his own literary agent, James Brand Pinker, to her.[8] Although he privately thought *The Fruit of the Tree* superior to *The House of Mirth*, James was unwilling to champion it and perhaps Wharton herself publicly in 1907. "I *want* to enthuse over you," he writes, "I yearn to, quite—."[9] The "quite" also exposes his hesitation about the journal in which his review of the book would appear, "a hole-&-corner publication," and the editor, who said that Wharton had "expressed a wish" for the piece. It was not until four years later that he unreservedly "enthused" over *Ethan Frome* (1911), "a beautiful art & tone & truth—a beautiful artful *kept-downness*, & yet effective cumulation."[10] James eventually granted Wharton the status of "book-maker" of the first rank with the 1913 acknowledgment that "for 'us,' & for our genius the act of attestation of the life of the mind & of the play of that genius is by itself a sovereign help, a condition indispensable." However, that acknowledgment seems offhandedly secondary, for it is embedded in the reassurance that work would soothe her spirit, "(even if *why* it should be so is a mystery) the most celestial balm flows from it."[11]

From the early stages of her career, Wharton seems to have needed James's professional (though she might have liked his public) approval far less than she needed his acceptance of her as a "confrere of the pen."[12] She was not above poking fun at his attacks of indigestion brought on "by eating orange fritters,"[13] parodying his style for Gaillard Lapsley, or despairing about his later novels, which she thought W. C. Brownell trenchantly critiqued:

What we see, what impresses us, is not the point of view, it is his own disinterested curiosity. . . . The novelist's personages are not sufficiently unified by his own *penchant*, preference, personality, to constitute a society of varied individuals viewed and portrayed from one particular point of view—as the characters of the great novelists do.[14]

James was equally judgmental of Wharton's fiction and more witty: "I do congratulate you, my dear," he informed her after reading "Les Metteurs en Scène," written in French and published in *Revue des Deux Mondes*, "on the way in which you've picked up every old worn-out literary phrase that's been lying about the streets of Paris for the last twenty years, and managed to pack them all into those few pages" (*ABG*, 183). After reading *The Custom of the Country* (1913), he "irrepressibly burst out": "But of course you know . . . that in doing your tale you had under your hand a magnificent subject, which ought to have been your main theme [life in the old French aristocracy], and that you used it as a mere incident and then passed it by?" (*ABG*, 182).

Wharton's account of their "literary rough-and-tumbles" in *A Backward Glance* illustrates the double game they played. Above all, she wants her readers to know that James accepted her as an equal; with her he could speak truthfully or "hit straight from the shoulder" (*ABG*, 184). Both writers would have denied their own competitiveness, but Wharton in particular makes sure that we are left with her version of the past, that we see her scoring the final hit: "What was your idea in suspending the four principal characters in 'The Golden Bowl' in the void?" she recalls asking its author in all innocence. "Why have you stripped them of all the *human fringes* we necessarily trail after us through life?" Her questions turn James's "startled attention on a peculiarity of which he had been completely unconscious," and he can only answer "in a disturbed voice: 'My dear—I didn't know that I had!'" (*ABG*, 191). One can almost hear Wharton repeating James's response to *The Fruit of the Tree*: I wanted to enthuse over you—"quite." While the anecdote seems prompted by unresolved competitiveness or the writer's need to assert her critical acumen, Wharton is also out-Jamesing James, the master of the left-handed compliment. When she echoes Emily Dickinson by calling him "Cher Maître," that form of address, if it was not ironic, reveals her need for a substitute father or a domineering lover as well as a literary mentor. "We who knew him well," she wrote Gaillard Lapsley after James's death in 1916, "know how great he would have been if he had never written a line."[15]

Wharton explained the special quality of James's friendship this way: "His one effort is to identify himself with the person addressed, to commune, in an almost mystic sense, with the friend whom his passionate imagination brings so near, whether the substance shared be the food of the gods or the humblest domestic fare."[16] James's vicarious participation in Wharton's life may have allowed him more fully to experience a woman's sensibility, but it also implicitly and morally began to demand an active involvement that made him uneasy. Not wanting to venture outside the "horizon of four brown walls,"[17] he preferred her to "hand over" her adventures "intact, at the very first opportunity."[18] That way, he could safely entertain or (depending on one's interpretation) exploit the "other's" point of view without dangerously relaxing his own boundaries of self.

In turn, Wharton profited materially and personally from James's example. She rejected his form of the psychological novel in favor of the chronicle, put an ocean between herself and family, and—encouraged by the inner circle's fluid definitions of masculine and feminine behavior—played with the parameters of gender.[19] For example, the woman who called herself a "self-made man" also kept a "Love Journal" during her affair with Morton Fullerton.[20] In it she recorded her own vulnerability, explored what she imagined other women felt—esoteric ecstasies and adolescent enthusiasms—and prepared herself for the inevitable: "My only dread," she wrote Fullerton, "is lest my love should blind me, & my heart whisper 'Tomorrow' when my reason says 'Today.' . . . To escape that possibility can't we make a pact that you shall give the signal, & one day simply call me 'mon ami' instead of 'mon amie'?"[21] Wharton embodied the rectitude of her lover's minister father and the "sensual effusiveness" of his overly solicitous mother.[22] With the bisexual Fullerton, she was able to explore not only her own eroticism but also that of James, Sturgis, Lubbock, Lapsley, and Norton. He supplied the one missing element in her relationships with these men, whose friendships prepared her to take a lover. Paradoxically, Wharton defined her unconventional liaison in the conventional terms of romance, allowing Fullerton to dominate her in a way no one else did. His bisexuality, perhaps implicitly placing a limit on the depth and scope of the relationship, might have made Wharton, who valued privacy and independence, feel safe. Although Wharton lived a fiction she disparaged, who is to say whether Fullerton was her creation or she his?

The same might be asked of Wharton's relationship with Henry James, whose letters employ metaphors that self-consciously underscore the sexual and collusive nature of their communication: "There have again & again, under the pressure of events, been words on my lips for which your ear has seemed the only proper receptacle—," he wrote Wharton five years after their correspondence began (1905), "and which for want of that receptacle, I fear, have mostly faltered & failed & lost themselves forever."[23]

The intimacy with Wharton intrigued James as much as it disturbed him, and the metaphors that he uses to describe himself, Wharton, and their relative positions show a gradual weakening of distinctions between author (James) and subject (Wharton). By 1907, the year that Wharton and Fullerton became lovers, James—who could have only guessed at their relationship—was characterizing himself in metaphors belonging to the domestic sphere. He would continue to use these or related images throughout their correspondence: "je rêve already over your presence," he writes in 1908, "& hold out my now empty cup—scoured quite clean of baser matter—for whole rich & thick flowing reports of everything."[24] James's own words seem to act like a self-administered aphrodisiac, enticing him on to greater verbal excesses. Here James highlights the erotic nature of their relationship by reversing the sexual imagery usually attributed to each gender. More frequently he used androgynous images that combined, rather than delineated, the sexes: "Your silver-sounding toot that invites me to the Car—the wondrous cushioned *general* Car of your so wondrously india-rubber-tyred & deep-cushioned fortune—echoes for me but too mockingly in the dim, if snug cave of my permanent *retraite*. I have before me an absolute year of inspired immobility—I am in short on the shelf." From there, envisioning "wild dramatic pleasure," he will watch her "on the Aubusson carpet," watching herself: "What sequels you will see to what beginnings, & into what deeper depths of what *abysses* you will find yourselves [she and Rosa de Fitz-James] interested to gaze!"[25]

In this letter, James presents himself as what he would actually become, a vicarious participant in Wharton's affair with Fullerton, her audience and accomplice.[26] Sending Fullerton to visit Wharton at The Mount, in Lenox, James literally cast him at her feet. James may have dispatched Fullerton as a substitute for himself, sensing that this literary Don Juan would ease the difficulties with Teddy. From then on, he hardly failed to end a letter to Wharton without coupling the names of her lover, whom he extravagantly admired, and her husband, from whose mouth, he wrote Sturgis, sprouted flowers of incoherency that bloomed in his "table-talk—or stable-talk—."[27]

James's benevolent attitude toward Wharton and Fullerton is particularly interesting in light of his behavior toward Violet Hunt: "I deeply regret and deplore the lamentable position in which I gather you have placed yourself in respect to divorce proceedings about to be taken by Mrs. Hueffer" (Ford's wife), he wrote her in 1909.

> . . . it affects me as painfully unedifying, and that compels me to regard all agreeable and unembarrassed communication between us as impossible. I can neither suffer you to come down to hear me utter these homely truths, nor pretend, at such a time, of free and natural discourse of other things.[28]

The public nature of the relationship between Hunt and Ford seems to have disturbed James far more than the fact of adultery. In contrast, Fullerton and Wharton were such souls of discretion that James could feel like a guardian angel, dining with them the night now immortalized in her poem "Terminus" (1909): "Wonderful was the long secret night you gave me, my Lover, / Palm to palm, breast to breast in the gloom. The faint red lamp / Flushing with magical shadows the common-place room of the inn."[29]

James's love of gossip—justified by the belief that "art is long & everything else is accidental & unimportant"—sometimes makes him appear almost ruthlessly detached from other people and their pain.[30] For him, gossip was an art, rather like Sturgis's intricate patterns of embroidery. Commiserating with Wharton about her husband's infidelities (itself an irony considering his knowledge about the Wharton-Fullerton liaison) and Teddy's embezzlement of her trust, James apologizes after making a slight joke: "Forgive my levity—it's only that my imagination & wonder play so fondly over the whole subject."[31] James advised her to depend on "the light & guidance" of her brother and Walter Berry and to "sit tight": "That keeps up our connection with life—I mean of the immediate & apparent life, behind which, all the while, the deeper & darker & the unapparent, in which things *really* happen to us, learns, under that hygiene, to stay in its place."[32] The conclusion is disturbing: James wants to roll the *donnée*, so to speak, around in his mouth, feel its surface, taste to the fullest its particulars, but he balks at the consequences of swallowing it whole.

All the frenetic, sexualized imagery that he, the islanded spectator, ascribes to Wharton, the soaring firebird, suggests both his fear of and fascination with the "other" who embodies oblivion in the form of pseudo consummation or domination. To Minnie Cadwalader Jones, James confided: "her powers of devastation are ineffable, her repudiation of repose absolutely tragic and she was never more brilliant and able and interesting" (Lewis, 323). Wharton's life and career forced James to evaluate his own. Her emphasis on plot and character challenged James's belief in the ascendancy of form—at least in the marketplace—while her spendthrift activity and hunger for new sights and new experience made his life of renunciation, sacrifice, and conservation seem a meager repast.[33] The magnitude of Wharton's equally compelling emotional and intellectual needs and the demand they placed on friendship can be inferred from the nicknames that James gave her, including "the angel of devastation," "wild woman," and "fatal woman." The first in particular captures the ambivalence that Wharton often inspired in men. Who in the James family could use the word "devastation" without thinking about "vastation," the word that Henry James Sr. used to describe the feeling that suddenly came over him, without warning or apparent cause, reducing him from "a state of firm, vigorous, joyful manhood, to one of almost helpless infancy?"[34] Because Wharton undermined a number of James's assumptions about art and the artist's relationship to life, she, "the fatal woman," had the potential of similarly reducing him. To borrow an image from Sylvia Plath's "Lady Lazarus," she might be capable of eating men like air. John Hugh Smith recalls that Wharton regretted that she had not known all that George Sand had known of life and love.

James's interest in Wharton grew from the anxiety she produced and the titillation she provided. His identification with her reached its climax at the height of her relationship with Fullerton, when he seemed to be drinking Wharton's life as thirstily as Dr. Jekyll drank his own elixir. That experience led him to a psychic border where meaning and identity threatened to collapse.[35] "Glad as I am that we 'care' for him, you & I," he admits to Wharton in 1909, "for verily I think I do as much as you, & that you do as much as I."[36]

James's letters to Fullerton foreshadowed the pattern of his to Wharton. In them, he goes through various transformations, the mentor becoming more fatherly, and the father becoming more loverlike, until he seems an alter ego. For example, in 1900, he tells Fullerton what he will tell Wharton in 1902: profit from my awful example:

> I *am* face to face with it, as one is face to face, at my age, with every successive lost opportunity (wait till you've reached it!) and with the steady movement of the ebb of the great tide—the great tide of which one will never see the turn.[37]

Six years later, James's offer of assistance has altruistically sexual overtones: "I am safe with you, and I am *whole* to you, and the thought of my being any good—of any fine use—to you—well, crowns the edifice."[38] And in 1906, he asks: "*Can* one man be as mortally, as tenderly attached to another as I am to you, and be at the same time a force, as it were, of some value, without its counting effectively at some right and preappointed moment for the brother over whom he yearns?"[39]

At the time that Fullerton and Wharton became lovers, James's tone toward each incorporated a kindly, slightly salacious paternalism—something that would not have offended Wharton, who herself liked to repeat stories that Robert Norton characterized as most unsuitable for the chaste New England ears of her earlier days. Not surprisingly, the erotic echoes in the letters grow stronger when triangulated. James is addressing Fullerton obliquely through Wharton, who in all likelihood will show or repeat parts of the letters: "Kindly assure him [Morton] of my absolutely consistent affection & fidelity & ask him to have a very small further—a scrap of divine—patience with me. I plead—I plead; also I bleed [from the lash of his own reproof] (with—attenuated—shame)."[40] What amounts to an apology for not responding to Fullerton's article "The Art of Henry James" links James metaphorically, physically, and emotionally with Wharton as surely as his reference in the same letter to himself as "a poor old croaking barnyard fowl" aligns him with Fullerton, a younger and more splendid version of the old rooster. The situation, like the house of fiction described in the preface to *The Portrait of a Lady*, had any number of possible windows. At will, James, an indirect participant and observer, could be both lover and beloved or, in his subsequent accounts to Sturgis, both author and narrator.

In short, James was involved in a kind of ménage à trois: "tell him [Morton] with my love that I am as much in his skin as he is himself; & that my idea of a proper affection for my friends is to *be* to that degree in their skins (with my faculty of dédoublement not exhausted by the above feat I am really at present as much in yours), without being in their way."[41] James's image of being in another's skin is unsettling because it literally is a form of possession. Although Wharton had feared this very thing from her mother, Lucretia Jones, she seems to have welcomed James's participation and interpreted it as a sanction. His hunger for the news she doled out met her needs for adoration and domination, perhaps rewriting the childhood story that contained an absent or—as some critics imagine—an abusive father.[42]

The form of James's participation in his friends' affairs changed in 1909. Rousing James from the deep seat of his sofa,[43] Wharton asked him to help her rid Fullerton of the demands of his former mistress, that "accursed woman."[44] The combination of drama and delicacy proved impossible to resist: fronting for Wharton, James agreed to send Macmillan the price of the incriminating letters they then would advance to Fullerton for a book on Paris. The two hoped that the plan would serve practical and ideal ends, converting Fullerton's "stricken & comparatively sterilized life into a life worthy of his admirable intelligence & capacity."[45] Apprised of the extent of Fullerton's personal and economic woes, James imagined a more honest and intimate relationship with him:

> The clearing of the air lifts, it seems to me, such a load, removes
> such a falsity (of defeated relation) between us, that I think *that* by
> itself is a portent and omen of better days and of a more workable
> situation.[46]

The plan underscores the novelists' naivety and their patronizing attitude toward their protégé. James pities Fullerton "with the sense that the normal & possible expanding & living man was lost in it [the strain of the situation], lost to himself & lost to *us*."[47] Speaking of Fullerton as if he were Sleeping Beauty, James fully expects "the release of his mind, his spirit, & his beautiful intelligence from a long bondage."[48] To Wharton and James, Fullerton is a text in need of revision: "Tell Morton," he writes her, "how I go on appreciating àpropos of such beautiful processes— *him*."[49] James was doubly naive, for Wharton, worried about his deepening depression and anxieties about money, made him the beneficiary of her largesse (in much the same way she did Fullerton) just three years later in 1912: Scribner's agreed to divert her royalties to James, who would get $4,000 on beginning and $4,000 on completing *The Ivory Tower*.

Wharton and James eventually lost patience with Fullerton's procrastination over the project for Macmillan. Fullerton's acceptance of Wharton's money may have violated the code of the gentleman, but the extenuating circumstances of the artist justified it. James's exasperation grew as it became clearer that Fullerton was neither. "It isn't quite for me to goad him about his book," he wrote Wharton, "but if I could only get nearer to him (which everything else seems to prevent), I would urge him not to wait for any ideal *readiness* to begin it, but to let a beginning *make* that readiness, which shall defy him then to *distinguish* from the ideal."[50] Speaking plainly to Fullerton, James advised: "My own belief is that if you really *break* with her [the blackmailer]—utterly and absolutely—you will find yourself *free*—and leave her merely beating the air with the grotesque *gestes* and absolutely 'getting' nowhere. . . . take your stand on your humour, your manhood, your courage, your decency, your intelligence and on the robust affection of your old, old, and faithful, faithful friend Henry James."[51]

As James's disillusionment with Fullerton grew, he felt increasingly impotent. "What an ineffable blessing you must be," he writes Wharton, "you in your embrowned saloon—to the harassed Morton, to whom I send my impotent homage—& of whom I feel that without you I shouldn't just now have courage to think at all."[52] Finally James was forced to concede: "You tell me that Morton the book-maker *defaillit*. There it deplorably is—that he isn't,—won't be, probably *can't* be—a bookmaker. And his intelligence has such perversities! What is to be done about it?"[53] Wharton had no answer, and Fullerton's failure to complete the Paris book contributed (to borrow one of her favorite metaphors) to the unbandaging of her eyes.

The psychic effect of the James-Fullerton-Wharton triangle is suggested by stories James and Wharton wrote during that time. In James's "The Jolly Corner" (1908), Spenser Brydon returns to the home of his youth for the purpose of surprising his alter ego, the man he would have become if he had not chosen exile. Night after night he roams from room to room in search of his other, projected self. But when that self is revealed, it has the face of a stranger, and Brydon (like Sara Clayburn in Wharton's "All Souls'") swoons. Although the alter ego is definitely described as male (albeit an effeminate male), he comes from a "corner" that is obviously feminine: "more in the likeness of some great glass bowl, all precious concave crystal," which holds "this mystical other world, and the indescribably fine murmur of its rim was the sigh there, the scarce audible pathetic wail to his standard ear, of all the old baffled foresworn possibilities."[54] Unlike "All Souls'," "The Jolly Corner" has a contrived happy ending. Brydon awakes from his faint (a kind of "feint") and promptly plights himself to Alice Staverton. A form of rescue and reassurance, marriage keeps Brydon from confronting the supposedly monstrous or feminized part of himself. The story ends with the destruction of the alter ego, the secret sharer. In this, it perhaps reflects the homosexual panic that Eve Sedgwick reads in "The Beast in the Jungle."[55]

Wharton did not write anything as self-exploratory as the "The Jolly Corner," but "The Pretext" (1908) and "The Letters" (1910) provide a veiled commentary on her friendship with Fullerton. In the former, the wife of a staid professor, Mrs. Ransom, falls in love with a young visitor from England, Guy Dawnish. The perfectly chaste affair takes place in silence, for "he had understood that only on those terms could their transcendant communion continue—that he must lose her to keep her."[56] After he returns home, Mrs. Ransom reads that his longstanding engagement has been broken and assumes that she is the reason. A simple question destroys her illusion: "*Who is the woman,*" Dawnish's aunt demands of her, "*since you are not?*" ("Pretext," 653). "A pretext," she realizes, "she had been a pretext" either to shield some one else or to escape from a wearisome situation ("Pretext," 654). How much, Wharton might have asked herself, was Fullerton's former lover a pretext for extracting money? How much does Mrs. Ransom embody her author's fears of growing old before tasting the joys of youth, of appearing ridiculous, of ransoming her future to a man who constantly demanded signs of affection and then withdrew?

In 1908, Mrs. Ransom's Roman spring cannot counterbalance all the lonely years left to live. In 1910, Wharton was more philosophical. "The Letters" tells of Lizzie West's romance with her married employer, Vincent Deering, their three-year separation after his wife's death, and their subsequent reunion and marriage, made possible by her inheritance of an unexpected fortune: "the fact of her letters—her unanswered letters—having on his own assurance, 'meant so much' to him, had been the basis on which this beautiful fabric was reared."[57] The act of writing those letters made Deering her own creation, just as Wharton's letters to Fullerton and the love journal she kept made him hers. Even Lizzie's stumbling upon the knowledge that her letters were unopened does not alter the fact of the present she has created. Dismissing the idea that "everything he had ever done and been was a lie" ("Letters," 203), she concludes: "The years had not been exactly what she had dreamed; but if they had taken certain illusions they had left richer realities in their stead" ("Letters," 206). The same might be said of Wharton, whose art now spoke authoritatively about sexual passion, love, longing, accommodation, and rebellion.[58]

After James's participation in the Fullerton affair, his ways of addressing Wharton become less "supersensual" and more "devotional." The experiment of relaxing those boundaries between self and "other" having proved too dangerous perhaps, James increasingly characterizes himself in reassuringly retrogressive and erotically infantile terms. Wharton may be soaring "off over the mountain tops," he wrote in 1913, but he doesn't grudge her a hoot of her pace. "I only just lie down flat to take it—I mean the passage over me of the whole—where I can best blubber into the carpet. In that posture I shall lie until you come & pick me up again."[59] James seems simultaneously defeated, masochistic, and "devastated." The following year, their positions were reversed, and James adopted the desexualized paternal voice that he most often assumed from then on: "That you feel weary & worn comes home to me as the dove to its nest; I *know* how you feel even as if I had drawn up the 'specifications' for it in every detail."[60]

When the First World War threatened all the inner circle held dear, "taste, reverence, continuity, and intellectual honesty,"[61] they supported the Allies zealously. The war not only politicized the group, it also gave them an arena in which they could marshall and exercise their social consciences beyond personal charities; patriotism transformed patronage and further blurred distinctions between traditionally masculine and feminine behaviors.

Fullerton had seen warnings of the conflagration as early as 1906. His *Problems of Power* (1913), which had a foreword written by Theodore Roosevelt, minutely analyzed the origins of a possible war in Europe and went into a second printing in 1914. Infused with the spirit of Walt Whitman, who tended Civil War casualties, Lapsley spent weeks in Boulogne sitting by the bedsides of old pupils. (In the next war, he worried about consuming food that could go to others and eventually returned to the United States.) Lubbock worked for the British Red Cross in France, Egypt, and London. James made his Watchbell Street studio available to Belgium refugees, chaired the American Volunteer Motor-Ambulance Corps, and helped Wharton collect pieces for *The Book of the Homeless* (1916). Sold for the benefit of the American Hostels for Refugees and of the Children of Flanders Rescue Committee, the book included works—to name some— from Sarah Bernhardt, Rupert Brooke, Jean Cocteau, Thomas Hardy, Igor Stravinsky, Claude Monet, Auguste Rodin, and John Singer Sargent. Norton joined the British Admiralty; Smith was commissioned first in the Yorkshire Regiment and then in the Coldstream Guards and awarded the Military Cross and the Croix de Guerre; and Sturgis took lodgings in London and read, censored, and readdressed the correspondence of German prisoners.

Having been born in Paris, Berry strongly identified with France. He had great influence among the city's rich Americans, acting as their banker and lobbying against the noninvolvement of the United States. With characteristic exaggeration, Marcel Proust wrote, "Theorem, France could not win the war without America. Walter Berry made up America's mind. *Ergo*, Walter Berry is the conqueror in the greatest of all wars."[62] Berry helped to find Berenson an appointment in the Intelligence Section as a first class interpreter assigned to duty with the American Mission in Paris. The two met regularly, Berry introducing Berenson to Proust in 1918 and providing him with the subject for a 1924 essay, which argued that an illuminated antiphonary seen in Berry's apartment was the work of the fourteenth-century artist Lippo Vanno. Berenson later served as an observer at the Peace Conference at Versailles.

The inner circle agreed with pacifist members of Bloomsbury that war was a barbarous affair, but they also believed, as Berenson wrote, that "it is necessary for so long as we remain the barbarians that we are, violently impatient, unable to use our reason." From war, we learn "to look facts in the face and use them for repairing our old or for designing a new House of Life."[63] Maynard Keynes might have felt some sympathy for the logic of this thinking, though its complacency would have appalled most of Bloomsbury.

Unlike James, Wharton continued to write. *Summer* (1917), set in the Lenox landscape, and *French Ways and Their Meaning* (1919) illustrate her related responses to the war: the former marks an imaginative return to a home threatened by dark forces which emanate from the nearby mountain; and the latter, ostensibly interpreting French culture for American servicemen, criticizes American culture and attitudes.[64] Published in 1915, *Fighting France: From Dunkerque to Belfort* is a kind of propagandistic travel book that describes the mood of the country and the intelligent courage of its population (which Leonard Woolf also admired),[65] the armies of refugees, and Wharton's visits to the front.

During this time, James's letters to Wharton, who spent the war period in Paris, show a marked shift in tone. They begin by paying tribute to Wharton's frenetic activity and end with the almost submissive confession that from her he was learning "what it really is to live."[66] "It's an immense inspiration to myself that you speak of 'doing something,'" James writes her in 1914; "it's so what I myself am trying."[67] Wharton's "something" amounted to nothing less than creating a second front. Far more than someone like Vera Brittain, who did her own form of battle as a nurse, Wharton felt the need to assume whatever control over the course of events she could. Rejecting the ancillary roles traditionally assigned to women, Wharton marshaled her tremendous powers of organization, establishing and superintending—with the help of Elisina Tyler—the American Hostels for Refugees, an organization that encompassed a free clinic and dispensary, a workroom that supplied a clothing depot, a grocery distribution point, a child-care center with classes, and an employment agency. Wharton waged her war against domestic havoc, providing assistance to 9,330 refugees. Near the end of 1915, as R. W. B. Lewis observes, her organization had served 235,000 meals, found 3,400 jobs, distributed 48,000 garments, and provided 7,700 people with medical care.[68] Legitimized by its concern with the family, the Napoleonic effort bridged traditionally feminine and masculine worlds, home and battlefield. James applauded: "I can't sufficiently rejoice in you & be proud of you."[69] In recognition of her work, Wharton received the Legion of Honor and was named Chevalier of the Order of Leopold.

Because Wharton's letters from the front allowed James a way of participating in the most intense and what he perceived to be the most noble drama of his life, they also humbled him: "all my powers of being anything else," he acknowledged, "have gone to living upon your two magnificent letters, the one from Verdun, and the one after your second visit there, which gave me matter of experience and appropriation to which I have done the fullest honour."[70] James writes in the language that wives and mothers might have used to husbands and sons, but he speaks as one comrade to another. It is her art, the letters, that make her most precious to him and, as his tone indicates, most inaccessible: "I myself feel almost as abject in my ignorance of that land [Brittany] as I have lately felt in my disgraceful, my humiliating state of unfitness; but I had always rather your sensorium, instead of mine, were exposed to any of the forces of nature, or art, or life—so just as much, virtually, do I sooner or later gain by it, with the comfort added that you don't lose."[71] No matter how loved, the elevated, sexless heroine of James's drama is somehow beyond the earlier and more human form of their correspondence. In this last letter, Wharton's "Cher Maître" seems to be passing on the mantle.

In *A Backward Glance*, Wharton admits that the story of her years with James, their gaiety, jokes, and laughter, "must be taken on faith" (256). Yet she knows, and draws our attention to, the metamorphosis that begins once it assumes written form. Her narrative becomes a history that holds its characters suspended in the story itself. Wharton makes the same point fictionally in her allegory of life with James, "The Hermit and the Wild Woman," in which two isolated but complete souls tend their own gardens until they are joined in death and art—what Wharton called the Kingdom of Heaven. Art alone, she believed, has the power to give us a sense of lightness and liberation, to melt the hard walls of individuality and merge us in the poet's deeper interfusion, without our losing the least sharp edge of self. The friendship between Wharton and James strove for this ideal, to make art love and love art.

Edith Wharton writes in her memoir that any account of her own growth must include an account of Henry James's stimulating and enlightening influence. Similarly, any account of the inner circle must evaluate the effect of the relationship between James and Wharton on the group itself. What drew James to Wharton and the inner circle? How did the group accommodate two such commanding presences?

When Wharton moved to Europe in 1907, Henry James was preparing the New York edition of his selected fiction. Begun in 1905 and completed four years later, the monumental project represented his lifetime's work. James hoped that the edition would secure his future, but neither its critical reception nor its financial rewards met his expectations, the first royalty statement in the fall of 1908 especially knocking him "rather flat"—"a greater disappointment than I have been prepared for."[72] Roger Fry observed that "when people like Henry James they have ceased to be true Americans. . . . The people here loathe and detest him, and simply don't know what it's all about because they haven't got that sense of things at all. Life to them is simple and blankly sentimental."[73] James's disappointment grew so severe that his friends thought him suicidal, drawn into an abyss where his vision had no value or replacement. It was during this time of artistic and personal crisis that James's involvement in the inner circle reached its height. Consisting of Britons and transplanted Americans, as well as an intellectual American princess, the group presented him with a cast of characters literally following in the footsteps of his fictional pilgrims. They supported William James's postulate that truth *happens* to an idea: "Its verity *is* in fact an event, a process: the process namely of its verifying itself, its veri-*fication*. Its validity is the process of valid-*ation*."[74]

If the world largely ignored James's vision of the international theme, the inner circle affirmed it,[75] replicating what he called in the preface to "Lady Barbarina" "the sublime consensus of the educated": "*There*, if one will—in the dauntless fusions to come—is the personal drama of the future."[76] For them, as for all James's characters, Europe was the new frontier, its voices and choices, sensuousness and sensuality, temptations to idleness, and inspirations to work a colossal challenge. Experiencing the same condition of exile that James had articulated in the first three novels of the edition—*Roderick Hudson*, *The American*, and *The Portrait of a Lady*—the happy few had to resolve questions of individual, national, and collective identity. How were they to integrate themselves into an old and complex civilization—a process mirrored in the construction of the group—without losing a sense of self grounded in the past? In other words, how were they to become citizens of the world or what James called "cosmopolites."

"There comes a time," he wrote in 1872,

> when one set of customs, wherever it may be found, grows to seem to you about as provincial as another; and then I suppose it may be said of you that you have become a cosmopolite. You have formed the habit of looking for points of difference and of resemblance, for present and absent advantages, for the virtues that go with certain defects, and the defects that go with certain virtues.[77]

The inner circle not only illustrated and justified James's vision, they *were* the vision, partially blank pages waiting further inscription. The group's loose structure and reliance upon correspondence exactly suited James's nature, which craved participation from a controlled, safe distance.

Although connected to other groups such as Romney Marsh (which included H. G. Wells, Ford Madox Ford, Joseph Conrad, and Stephen Crane),[78] James was the heart and perhaps the conscience of the inner circle. The members acknowledged his greatness and congratulated one another on knowing a Henry hidden from the rest of the world. Because his benign and seemingly omniscient presence held them to a high standard (which deteriorated after his death, culminating in Wharton's quarrel with Lubbock over the marriage to Sybil Cutting), James in part shaped the tale of the inner circle. Not surprisingly, the story incorporates the major themes of his novels, which in the broadest sense might be seen as the quest for self-definition and the clash of cultures. The vision, definition, and genius of his artist figures coalesce only in exile. One may be, as Madame de Mauves observes and the inner circle demonstrated, very American and "arrange it with one's conscience to live in Europe."[79] Like James's protagonists, the happy few fashioned identities, independent and ultimately alone. While they sustained a collaborative fiction of accord, they knew—as "the virtuous attachment" between Mme. de Vionnet and Chad Newsome in *The Ambassadors* highlights—that it cannot to some extent escape being a lie. From *Roderick Hudson* (1875) to *The Golden Bowl* (1904), James's characters choose a life tangential to community in order to preserve the vision upon which their identities rest. The pathos of his work comes from this solution, the abstract tie to humanity rather than the concrete connection to community that the inner circle strove to achieve but never fully realized.

James believed that "for a stranger to cease to be a stranger he must stand ready . . . to pay with his person."[80] Having himself "paid" by settling in England, he now observed the inner circle doing the same: Gail-lard Lapsley torn between his family in the United States and his life in Great Britain, Howard Sturgis holding court for Eton and Cambridge alumni at Qu'Acre every Sunday, Walter Berry parading with rich Ameri-cans in the lobby of the Paris Ritz, and Wharton penetrating the inner sanctum of the Faubourg. Sturgis and Lapsley in particular might have reminded James of the Touchetts—"they have their own habits, their own language, their own food—some odd religion even . . . of their own"—in *The Portrait of a Lady* (1881), a novel that flirts with theories of the rela-tionship between national and individual identities.[81] At best one be-comes, like Madame Merle, unplaceable. "If we're not good Americans we're certainly poor Europeans," she tells Isabel, pessimistically explaining the dynamic of exile: "we've no natural place here. We're mere parasites, crawling over the surface" (*PL*, 171). In contrast, the inner circle hoped, like Isabel, to wed "great knowledge with great liberty" (*PL*, 361), believ-ing, as Lafcadio Hearn did, that "anyone who wishes to be purely *himself*, must be isolated in all countries."[82]

Like Roderick Hudson, caught between the disparate worlds of Chris-tina Light and Mary Garland, these friends had to break with the past in order to enjoy a future in the Old World. Because James ironically posits the past—immediate and personal—in America and the present, "visible, palpable, measureable,"[83] in Europe, his characters who stay in or return to America appear to be retreating from life. Instead the inner circle chose to remain in Europe and, as James wrote in *The Ambassadors* (1903), Eu-rope changes one's sense of proportions, "and the proportions were at all times . . . the very conditions of perception, the terms of thought."[84]

Exile provided them with a future replete with new forms but not with-out the problems inherent in grafting the New World to the Old that James had outlined in *The American* (1877). As Christopher Newman learns, the self has a better chance of thriving in a social climate favorable to it. Despite its endless opportunity, Europe, both finishing school and stage, teaches an old and necessary lesson: the parameters and limitations of self. Journeying into the wilderness of the Old World, Newman unwit-tingly discovers that "everything's terrible . . . in the heart of man," includ-ing his own, capable of blackmail.[85] Literally paying with his person, he surrenders a congruent and harmonious vision of the world. There is no going back; nor would it be desirable to sacrifice individuality and return to type, "the American." The cost of knowledge is exile, for only "in the presence of new measures, other standards, a different scale of relations" (*Amb.*, 77), can one experience, like Lambert Strether, what James would later call "the personal drama of the future," "the sublime consensus of the educated." Wharton called this consensus "the inner circle," and membership encompassed the loss of a past and an increasingly alien self whose ghost reappears in memoirs, such as Percy Lubbock's *Earlham*, James's *Notes of a Son and Brother*, or Wharton's *A Backward Glance*.

The inner circle believed, as James wrote to Fullerton, that one sets out from the port of "the essential loneliness of life": "and it seems to be the port also, in sooth to which my course again finally directs itself!"[86] According to Virginia Woolf, this view led James to become more and more

> confirmed in his conviction that an artist can neither live with the public, write for it, nor seek his material in the midst of it. A select group, representative of civilization, had at the same time protested its devotion, but how far can one write for a select group?[87]

Certainly from about 1904 to 1915, the inner circle formed part of that group. And Wharton, far more than James, wrote with this private audience in mind. Those friends who gathered around her fireplace at Hyères and listened to the morning's composition and revisions mitigated a loneliness that James described as being deeper than "genius," "deeper than pride," "deeper, above all, than the deep countermining of art."[88] James paints a panoramic but static world, deaf to the changed voices of his protagonists, who, without an audience, are, in reality, silenced.[89]

James's feeling of an absolute solitude helps to explain why the cosmopolitan communities in his novels seem manifestations of diminished dreams. In the preface to *The Spoils of Poynton* (1896), he writes that "the free spirit, always much tormented, and by no means always triumphant, is heroic, ironic, pathetic or whatever, and . . . 'successful' only having remained free."[90] Marriages dissolve or remain unconsummated because they could in part repair a condition that James thinks irrevocably linked to the production of art and thereby the continuation of culture. Without a true marriage between the New and Old Worlds, both worlds stay sterile, America—to borrow a phrase from Wharton's *French Ways and Their Meaning*—remaining in the kindergarten stage of development and Europe settling into a dissipated old age. In the end, each remains cut off from tradition, either at the root or the flower. Except for *The Europeans* (1878), a comedy of manners, James consistently resists a real marriage between Europe and the United States. Isabel Archer's exists between two expatriates, who can no more belong to each other than they can to their adopted Italy; Milly Theale's spiritual marriage to Merton Densher in *The Wings of the Dove* (1902) is consummated in death; and Lambert Strether returns to Mrs. Newsome, an American invalid.

Despite the romantic exploration of "otherness" leading to a fuller understanding of one's own isolated individuality, itself the tragic vision and history of the happy few, the unsatisfactory conclusions of James's novels contain an implied criticism of the perversity and idiosyncracy of exile—a conclusion that the success of the inner circle, its assimilation and continuity, perhaps reassuringly undercut. In James's fiction, Europe and America ultimately function as rhetorical and symbolic devices used to explore the otherness at the heart of self and art. James intensifies the experience by having his protagonists see with the eyes of someone of the other gender—Strether, for example, adopting Mme. de Vionnet's point of view. Each new category that Strether masters shades and expands his vocabulary, transforming both thought and personality. Wharton's presence in the inner circle presented the men, as well as herself, with the same opportunity for introspection.

In 1907, Edith Wharton might have stepped out of the pages of a number of James's novels. Recalling Isabel Archer, whom she resembled intellectually and temperamentally,[91] Wharton played Maria Gostrey to John Hugh Smith's Lambert Strether and Mme. de Vionnet to Morton Fullerton's Chad Newsome—part gentleman, part Pagan. The remove to France presented her with the same problem that faced Isabel Archer. How does one reconcile being a woman, an artist, and a citizen of the world in a society that makes the Emersonian ideal of unfettered selfhood impossible for women? How does a woman live a male plot, what Isabel defines as "the union of great knowledge with great liberty" (PL, 361): "the girl presently made up her mind that to be rich was a virtue because it was to be able to *do* and that could be sweet. It was the graceful contrary of the stupid side of weakness—especially the feminine variety" (PL, 182).

Wharton could not escape social and familial obligations, the confines of history, but she did choose one corner in "the great round world" (PL, 216) to cultivate. If we accept, as James implies, that great knowledge and great liberty can exist solely in an imagined kingdom of self, then Wharton succeeded, much as Isabel, by learning to cherish the single occupancy of her innermost room. Because it preserves a sense of continuous self, silence confers power. It creates, as Newland Archer in *The Age of Innocence* (1920) knows, an inner sanctuary as impregnable as the church walls enclosing Claire de Cintré. Wharton would never have denied herself knowledge, despite knowing that knowledge was—and perhaps cannot be anything other than—a form of molestation, capable of making—as James writes in *The Turn of the Screw* (1898)—the friendly hour lose "for the unspeakable moment all its voice": "I continued unmolested," the governess explains—"if unmolested one could call a young woman whose sensibility had, in the most extraordinary fashion, not declined but deepened."[92] Having traded liberty for knowledge, Isabel, the most imaginative of women, is also the saddest. Notwithstanding her protests, she has, after all, needed the aid of her clever and corrupt husband to teach her how to live. Isabel's decision leads us to ask, as Yeats does of Leda: "Did she put on his knowledge with his power / Before the indifferent beak could let her drop?" ("Leda and the Swan").

James not only read bits and parts of his own heroines in Wharton, he also saw a fresh sheet, for his letters to Walter Berry, Howard Sturgis, and Gaillard Lapsley show him creating the character of Edith Wharton and then directing the play: she was a monumental wake and he its survivor clinging thankfully to shore. Wharton joined in the fun, inviting Smith to dine with Woollett in the rue de Varenne and telling Lapsley: "Isn't it lucky I didn't go to [Qu'Acre]? Henry & Howard would both have as-cribed their attacks [of illness] to my devastating presence!"[93] She never suspected that sometimes Lapsley too found her irritating. Describing her in society, he writes:

> behind it all there was the rather anxious hostess cumbered with many cares and trying to look after everything—who, if she saw you smoke after tea when everyone had refused, would rebuke you by pointedly asking you to pass the cigarettes. All this was extremely exhausting, and it became the more so, if you recall the tempera-mental restlessness which raged under restraint.
>
> (*Portrait*, 58)

The role Wharton played—firebird, lioness, whirlwind—confined and trivialized her power even as it granted her license and latitude. It made her strengths, ambition, energy, and authority less threatening to her timid male confreres. James's fascination with and fictionalization of Wharton made her a presence, if not a cautionary fact, in his relationships with the other members of the inner circle. His portrayal of her intruded on those friendships even as it helped to cement them. In this context, Wharton's relationship to James replicates that of Mrs. Anerton to the poet Vincent Rendle in the story "The Muse's Tragedy" (1899). The world sees her as the Silvia of *Sonnets to Silvia*, and she knows herself to have been a rhetorical convenience of "a cosmic philosophy, not a love poem; addressed to Woman, not to a woman!"[94] The men's tolerant bemusement and erudite gallantry at best neutralized Wharton's devastating presence. To some degree, James's characterization, like Strether's of Mme. de Vion-net, interfered with pinpointing the actual reality and consequences of her being. When art is innocence and innocence "all an art" (*Amb.*, 230), as in James's relationship with Wharton, new definitions, maybe a new lan-guage replete with new metaphors, are needed.

By assuming the rights of both sexes, Wharton defied categorization, and her position threatened women as well as men. (James's sister-in-law and his niece, Peggy, for example, thought her immoral.) Her attraction to "feminized," asexual, or homosexual men allowed her to achieve what she most desired and could most trust, the Platonic ideal of a marriage of minds, unmarred by fluctuations of passion. Wharton may not have needed, like Isabel, a clever man to teach her how to live, but she did need clever men to make her feel accepted regardless of pretty looks or ways. This "ideal of friendship" (*PL*, 163) is made possible in *The Portrait of a Lady* by Ralph Touchett's illness, which assigns him (as it eventually did Sturgis) to a female plot of passivity. A conclusion reminiscent of the ending to *Jane Eyre*, it suggests that some form of debilitation must exist to make men and women equal partners. Doubly diseased with tuberculosis and "femininity," Ralph is as maimed as Rochester. Readers who reject this interpretation must envision a different kind of partnership.

Wharton accepted the role James assigned because it had its benefits. "She felt perhaps safer with men," writes Lubbock, "safer from the claims and demands of a personal relation: from some of which she shrank so instinctively that intimacy, what most people would call intimacy, was to her of the last difficulty" (*Portrait*, 54). "To understand Edith," Paul Bourget writes,

one must recognize that she is *une sensitive*—so much so that the presence and proximity of people, were they even the most familiar of friends, seemed to check or chill her response, and to the end they might scarcely know, unless sometimes her letters showed them, that she needed and returned their response.

(*Portrait*, 54–55)

Explaining her passion for gardens, Wharton told Elisina Tyler, "I like to love, but not to [be] loved back."[95] If Wharton had difficulty in establishing real intimacy, the role she played may also have served as a vehicle for friendships, giving them form. "After all," she wrote Lapsley in 1923, "when I'm gone, who's going to joke the old jokes with you?"[96]

No less than James, Wharton imagined herself a character. Seeing "everything in terms of a potential story, her mind was all the time busy spinning its plots."[97] Robert Norton testifies that "the habit of transposing everything into terms of her art extended to herself":

She saw herself, I am convinced, in "situations" even while she was dealing with them. An experience that in the living of it had been a series of *contretemps* she would reset as she would have wished it and was thereafter convinced that it had happened so.

(RN, 49)

This literary distancing from self and experience was a practice that the fact of exile intensified and the inner circle, with its countless allusions and repartee, fostered. In a sense, the missives and daily narratives of self involved its members in a continual writing and rewriting of their lives together, which was potentially as "fictional" as Wharton's rewriting of the contretemps Norton remembers. Each member of the inner circle, like James's exiles, was an artist to the degree that she or he created an individual history in the context of a tradition emended by the process itself. This holds especially true for those who left memoirs or reminiscences, now a part of literary history.

In Wharton's telling, the history of the inner circle resembles *The Golden Bowl*: "we're selfish together—we move as a selfish mass," Amerigo tells Maggie. "You see we want always the same thing . . . and that holds us, that binds us, together. We want each other only wanting it, each time *for* each other. That's what I call the happy spell; but it's also a little—possibly—the immorality" (*GB*, 2: 91–92). The immorality, in the group as well as the novel, lies in tinkering with or authoring another's life. The fiction of togetherness that Maggie fights to prolong matches Wharton's vision of the inner circle always in accord. Maggie's text achieves congruence by sacrificing Charlotte, her dilemma and her fate recalling Percy Lubbock. Because she knows that the Ververs see her as a possession, bought to give them a life, Charlotte asserts her humanity and individuality by having an affair.

Maggie must sustain her fiction at the cost of integrity. She has both everything and nothing to fear in the history her husband shares with Charlotte, for only by understanding that history can she and he have a true marriage. With her guiding hand, she and Amerigo begin to write "some new history that should, so far as possible, contradict, and even if need be flatly dishonour the old" (*GB*, 2: 16), bereft of irony and ignorant of the fall. Their marriage comes closest to achieving, even as it questions the desirablity of, what James calls in his definition of the cosmopolite spirit "a dauntless fusion."

The new history demands a coauthor, but Maggie forces Amerigo to conform to her plot. "When, next to God, her husband is not the tribunal to which her heart and intellect appeals," wrote another young wife, "the golden bowl of affection is broken."[98] And because "*les grands seigneurs*, persons of her husband's class and type, always know how to reestablish a violated order" (*GB*, 2: 220), Amerigo's submission may be as suspect as the embrace that Maggie bestows to hide the triumph in her eyes. If the self must always remain a guest in another's inmost room, then complete collaboration seems undesirable as well as impossible.[99] For artists like Maggie (or James or Wharton), the fullest participation in someone else's life might well precipitate the averting of one's eyes. How can art or truth, themselves forms of self-embroidering, escape from being false?

Participation in another's life can be only fleeting, bits of embroidery stitched together to give the illusion of a whole canvas. Howard Sturgis's *Belchamber*, Percy Lubbock's *The Region Cloud*, James's novels from *Roderick Hudson* to *The Golden Bowl*, and Wharton's from *The Valley of Decision* to *The Buccaneers* all speak eloquently of the inability to make more than an imaginative connection between the self and other. Yet all contain protagonists who, despite fear, despite approbation, strive for nothing save that. No matter how worthy the struggle, one wants to protest. Renunciation may allow us to retain ourselves and keep our idealization of the other, but it also permits us to remain untried, to bury our fear. What if there is, in truth, nothing out there, Isabel Archer or Lily Bart asks, except the fiction of a fiction? Whether peopled with a benign Cher Maître or the whirling dervish of a woman, the story belies the truth as it gives it an imposed form.

After spending a summer afternoon with James at Bodiam Castle in Sussex, England, Wharton wrote:

> in such solitude the moment held us. . . .
> Clear we saw,
> Through the clear nether stillness of the place
> The gliding images of words and looks
> Swept from us down the gusty tides of time,
> And here unfolding to completer life;
> And like dull pebbles from a sunless shore
> Plunged into crystal waters, suddenly
> We took the hues of beauty, and became.
> Each to the other, all that each had sought.[100]

The beauty and the success of the inner circle lie in Wharton's last line, an echo of Emerson "Each and All." But no matter how dauntless, the fusion can only remain incomplete. The tension in James's novels and his relationship to the inner circle grow from the desire to repair history and restitch the drifted continents, to convert one's port of call from the essential loneliness of life. The country that exists between self and others, public and private, past and present, communal and individual, inevitably makes this attempt impossible, makes us all exiles, united, as the happy few, in the pathos of our shared and yearning humanity.

CHAPTER FOUR

Howard Sturgis, Percy Lubbock, and Bernard Berenson

How many people have read Belchamber *today?*
E. M. FORSTER, *ASPECTS OF THE NOVEL*

*I have read your novel, but believe me, Howard, it shall
make no difference between us.*
THOMAS WARDE-COOKE

The author's voice is disguised in the voice of his spokesman.
PERCY LUBBOCK, *THE CRAFT OF FICTION*

PERCY LUBBOCK FOUND A SECOND HOME at Qu'Acre, where he could drink endless cups of tea with local dignitaries, stroll in Windsor Park with Howard Sturgis's infirmary of old dogs, or sit companionably and knit, while his host, "composed as a dowager and audacious as a streetboy," designed a new piece of handiwork.[1] On the surface, these friends seem to have lived uneventful lives. Sturgis had settled at Qu'Acre in 1888 after the death of his much-loved mother. Four years later, the household expanded to include a distant cousin, William Haynes Smith (nicknamed "The Babe"), whom Sturgis treated as child and wife. Despite a proclivity for high-risk investments on Smith's part, the two lived comfortably together until Sturgis's death. Smith later married a cousin.

Lubbock's life seems hardly more dramatic. Before his librarianship of the Samuel Pepys collection at Magdalene College, Cambridge, he wrote occasional literary articles for the *London Times*. His most productive years followed the death of Henry James. In the 1920s, he edited James's letters and the diary of Arthur Christopher Benson, wrote two novels, three memoirs, and *The Craft of Fiction* (1921), the book of criticism for which he is best remembered. At forty-seven, in 1926, he married Lady Sybil Cutting. The couple spent the Second World War in Switzerland, where Sybil died in 1943. According to Bernard Berenson, Lubbock passed his remaining years in Lerici, Italy, all but totally blind, a displaced, slightly bitter old man whom time had left behind, "his only company the clouds, the waves, the sea's sunshine and sorrow, and books. . . ."[2]

Unlike Sturgis and Lubbock, Berenson led a life of astonishing successes, which took him from a ghetto in Lithuania to the halls of Harvard, the drawing room of Isabel Gardner, and the "court" of I Tatti. Comparing I Tatti to Voltaire's Ferney, one visitor observed: "There was the same cosmopolitanism, the same coming and going of celebrated persons, the same atmosphere of esprit and 'enlightenment' and the same centering of attention on the Master of the House." If sometimes Berenson "displayed," as George Santayana thought, "the air of the Renaissance,"[3] he did it with opulence and authority. "Two golden Giottos, a tiny Perugino, deep green and red, and part of Sassetta's great altarpiece dedicated to St. Francis, other fragments of which are in the Metropolitan Museum in New York, London's National Gallery and the Louvre," graced his sitting room.[4] His study *The North Italian Painters of the Renaissance* (1907) brought order and method to a largely undefined field. After seven decades of writing numerous books and articles, he ended his career with *Homeless Paintings of the Renaissance* (1969). "Not many have gone through life," he wrote in *Sketch for a Self-Portrait* (1949), "with so few restrictions to their freedom of action, freedom of contact and, need one add, freedom of thought."[5]

While Berenson left diaries and memoirs that detail his inner life, we know little about those of Sturgis and Lubbock. How much were their own identities influenced by their friendships with Edith Wharton and Henry James? Among the happy few, they were defined like the Tin Man and the Scarecrow at the end of *The Wizard of Oz*, Lubbock valued for brains, Sturgis for heart. "If ever an intellectual young person felt . . . a child," Lubbock tells us, "it was with Howard—who wasn't intellectual, who could often be fractious and naughty, but whose insight was a needle, piercing to the bone" (*MC*, 62). "You & Percy have always had the meanest opinion of that large woolly part of me," Sturgis wrote to Wharton. "It's my warm stupid heart you value, even when most amused at my 'ideas' & 'opinions', & at the queer grotesqueness of my claiming to have any other. I never can grasp which it is."[6]

These narrow characterizations—like Wharton's as the wild or fatal woman—shaped and limited their self-portraits. Sturgis mistrusted his own form of artistic intelligence, which he saw as intuitive rather than analytical, and Lubbock deprecated the writing in which he excelled, literary biography and autobiography. Although twenty-five years separated these men, they faced the same dilemma: how could they claim the title of "book-maker" in the company of two renowned and prolific (and in Wharton's case profit-making) writers? Berenson, who defined himself as a friend of Wharton and not a member of the inner circle, had no similar problem; his reputation was firmly and independently established.

The inner circle's hierarchy of affection and talent only increased Sturgis's and Lubbock's personal and professional anxieties. As a character in Lubbock's *Earlham* (1922) observes, the lives of our elders may be a show for our benefit, but "there seems to be a need of self-protection."[7] Lubbock at one time found Wharton's criticism the only standard by which his work deserved to be judged,[8] and Sturgis poignantly joked that "the little Rye-bird [James] is very prolific, & lays a quantity of beautiful grassgreen eggs, much prized by epicures for their exquisite & delicate flavour. . . . the Quacker Goose only lays three eggs in its life, & these are addled."[9] E. M. Forster summarizes the popular version (substantiated by Wharton in her memoir) of Sturgis's career: "he wrote to please his friends, and deterred by his failure to do so he gave up the practice of literature and devoted himself instead to embroidery, of which he had always been fond."[10]

If Wharton had to become a self-made man in order to write, Sturgis and Lubbock underwent a similar transformation. Their homoeroticism or sexual difference exiled them to the territory feminist critics assign to women writers: a kind of no man's land.[11] This might in part explain why the pattern of their artistic development seems "female" in the sense that they began writing nearer to forty than twenty or mastered a genre other than the novel first. It is always something of a masquerade when a woman writes as a man,[12] Sarah Orne Jewett warned. It is no less a masquerade when a man with homosexual sympathies writes as a heterosexual. Unlike Forster, who had the courage to write what he came to think unpublishable (or even worthy of publication) in *Maurice* (1971), or Virginia Woolf, who explored and spoofed the connections among androgyny, homosexuality, and creativity in *Orlando* (1928), Sturgis and Lubbock tell their tales (as Emily Dickinson says of the truth) "slant." The opposite, Berenson was fascinated with the myth of Narcissus and wanted to give the impression in his diaries of telling his directly, recording thoughts as they occurred and without revision. Sturgis and Lubbock most resemble Willa Cather, and their novels *Belchamber* (1904) and *The Region Cloud* (1925) share with hers an ambivalent and sometimes confusing tone. As in *My Antonia* (1918) or *A Lost Lady* (1923), their heroes are literally divided between two texts: the overt story of events lived in time and the covert story of illicit desire.

The story surrounding the publication of *Belchamber* contains perhaps its own *donnée* of illicit desire. It can be imagined with what trepidation Sturgis—who "wallowed" in *The Golden Bowl*, reading every sentence twice, rolling it round his tongue, and saying it aloud—accepted his friend's offer to read the book's proofs.[13] After reading a third of *Belcham-*

ber, James had two major reservations: first, he questioned Sturgis's representation of the English upper classes; second, he wished that the hero had more of "a constituted and intense imaginative life of his own."[14] For a novel that so minutely explores the consciousness of its feminized protagonist, this second criticism seems curious. James may have found his reading less reconstructive—to use his own word—than deconstructive, the novel forcing him to confront Sturgis's, if not his own, ambivalent sexuality. Sturgis (most likely feeling betrayed or embarrassed) responded to James's suggestions with the news that he intended to withdraw the novel from publication. "If you *think* of anything so insane you will break my heart and bring my grey hairs, the few left me, in sorrow and shame to the grave," James answered.[15] "I *would* write a book if I could," Sturgis later told Wharton. "I really would, in spite of all the trouble it is, & the fact that people hate it when it's done, but I'm obstinately barren."[16]

Making no connection between his friend's depression and the unsuccessful response (his own included) to *Belchamber*, James exasperatedly wrote Wharton in 1907 that Sturgis

> is literally in pieces, as far as "character" goes, and I don't see his future at all. It's the strangest disintegration of a total of which so many of the pieces are good—and produced by no cause, by no shocks, reverses, convulsions, vices, accidents; produced only by charming virtues, remarkable health and the exercise of a *cossue* hospitality. It's all irritatingly gratuitous and trivially tragic.[17]

Sturgis did not write another novel; he did continue to write reviews and several short stories, the best of which, "The China Pot," readers must seek in an unpublished dissertation.

Described as "a thinly disguised account of Sturgis's response to James's criticism of *Belchamber*,"[18] "The China Pot" reflects its author's conflicting feelings toward both James and himself. Like Sturgis, the protagonist, Jimmy, idolizes and imitates a Jamesian character named Throckmorton, whose evaluation of his friend's novel replicates in tone and meaning James's judgment of *Belchamber*: "It's at once too early and too late to criticize; I wish I could have seen it sooner, before it took final shape; and yet on the other hand there are things which at first sight don't recommend themselves to me" (Borklund, 267). His ego as delicate as a china pot, Jimmy commits suicide. The death breaks Throckmorton, who knows but won't admit his own involvement in the tragedy. Throckmorton may understand more than his compatriots about "the conception of literary work and the spirit in which it should be attempted" (Borklund, 267), but his knowledge of the human heart, of life, and, by extension, literature itself has proven inadequate.

Although Sturgis clearly directs our sympathies toward Jimmy, his own are divided. Jimmy's devotion forces Throckmorton to live perpetually with a parody of himself, to sit eternally before a distorted mirror ("CP," 334). Worse, Jimmy's death makes it necessary for him to betray the nature and source of his art by concealing the truth in "a cloud of words" ("CP," 339). Sturgis seems fully aware of the harm that uncritical affection can cause the giver and the recipient. Defining the line that all the inner circle walked with James, "The China Pot" indicts the artist who cannot take criticism as much as the one who dispenses it. The story illustrates the dynamics of a group in which each member is potential subject, author, and critic. When those roles overlap, can the individual sort out his or her motives? "A cloud of words" protects or exposes the speaker as well as the listener.

If we accept Percy Lubbock's argument that an author's method must tell us something about the quality of his imagination, then Sturgis's thrived—to its own detriment—on Henry James. The same might be said of all the men of the inner circle, who seemed to feed on anecdotes about Wharton's life but really lived on James's words. Did they find it easier, as does Jimmy, to talk in a voice other than their own?

Despite its focus on James, Sturgis's imagination more closely resembled Edith Wharton's—or hers, his. Eleven years before the publication of *The House of Mirth* (1905), he staked out the territory that would become her métier. His ironic second novel, *All That Was Possible: Being the Record of a Summer in the Life of Mrs. Sybil Crofts, Comedian* (1894), dispels myths about women's sensibilities and sexuality while criticizing the double standard for women's behavior: "A man may do almost anything, and still be thought a very good fellow (and be so too)," Sybil argues. "I can't see why the same tolerance should not be extended to women. I suppose men laid down the laws originally on this subject, and so made them conveniently for themselves."[19] Coming from the corrupt world of the stage, Sybil learns to define herself, as will Ellen Olenska in *The Age of Innocence* (1920), by the standards her lover has discarded: "It was not any new belief in the sacredness of marriage as such," she tells a friend, "but a sudden sense that for such love as I felt for Robert Henshaw only the highest form of union, whatever it was, would be endurable" (*ATWP*, 308). Above all, Sybil and Ellen are artists, and their authors seem to concur that their well-being depends upon renunciation: integrity demands the repression of sexuality and creativity. Women cannot separate, as men can, their public and private lives. The publicity or "promiscuity" of their situation either robs them of a rich, interior self or banishes them to the margins of polite society. Sturgis's sympathy encompasses what Wharton, with a nod to Ida Tarbell, would later call "the business of being a woman."[20]

In Sturgis's next novel, *Belchamber*, Wharton found a model for another heroine, Undine Spragg of *The Custom of the Country* (1913). Her initial review of *Belchamber* called Cissy, the hero's wife, the most brilliant study in the book: she is an "extreme expression of a selfish nature's unwillingness to pay for what it has got."[21] But, like Undine, Cissy is not entirely unsympathetic. Before marriage, she is frank and open, admitting that young girls know far more than their elders suppose. (Sixteen years later May Archer will echo her.) When Cissy's mother sells her—as Mrs. Bart planned to sell Lily—to the highest bidder, the power of her position perverts her. All the training that makes Cissy a desirable woman also makes her deceitful and calculating.

Sturgis's analysis primarily differs from Wharton's in its more obvious emphasis on how inflexible gender roles hurt both sexes. His title character, a lord nicknamed Sainty, seems a prototype for what Wharton— referring to Lawrence Selden in *The House of Mirth* (1905)—called her "negative hero."[22] Her interest in the method, design, and "lifelikeness" of *Belchamber* were all related to the way that Sturgis presented this character:

> Mr. Sturgis has evidently said to himself: "I am tired of the so-called manly hero, the brawny and beautiful being who has pervaded English fiction for the last fifty years, always brilliant, victorious, and irresistible. I will show that, in real life, this showy person often produces his effects at the cost of a great deal of suffering and shame inflicted on the adoring group about him; and by way of contrast I will present as my protagonist a man at odds with life, at odds with his situation, a man crushed under his rank and wealth . . . I will show how this man, ridiculed, misunderstood and exploited by those about him, gives his life to repairing the evil wrought by the brawny and beautiful being who, according to the conventions of fiction, ought to be the hero of my book."
>
> (*Bookman*, 308)

Sainty is a grown-up version of Sturgis's first hero, Tim Ebbesley (of *Tim* [1891]), who dies of a broken heart when his idol—a good-natured young man in the tradition of Thomas Hughes's Tom Brown—forsakes him. His death suggests that men of artistic temperament must either kill the feminine in themselves or face the adult consequences of homoerotic desire.

Belchamber's failures grow from Sturgis's own ambivalence toward his hero. Sainty's feminine sensibilities constitute the novel's moral center, but they are also the object of his author's scorn. Acknowledging his wife's illegitimate child in order not to appear ridiculous, he colludes in his own emasculation. Any hope for the future dies with Cissy's son, for Sainty's abdication of his marital rights insures the future plundering of Belchamber and the symbolic demise of civilization itself. Following the strategy of many nineteenth-century women writers, Sturgis creates a protagonist who embodies his own characteristics or desires and then punishes or destroys him. Self-flagellation, which masquerades as revenge, allows the writer to exist both within and outside the norms and mores of contemporary society.

Why Sturgis failed to see the connection between his work and Wharton's may have something to do with a number of reasons that range from issues of gender to dismissal of his own (and, by an intuited extension, her) gifts. Believing that men could do anything better than women once they set their minds to it, he may not have welcomed comparisons. The men of the inner circle praised, coddled, and loved Wharton, but they ultimately believed in and prided themselves on the supremacy of their own sex. Wharton's ambivalence about women scholars shows how even she could not always disentangle herself from her context. Those who rebelled against rigid patterns of behavior also established their own, complacently accepting the sense of continuity they granted and ignoring the ossification they insured. The group in part reflected a kind of cultural misogyny they often consciously disdained and unconsciously practiced. The very "masculine" story Sturgis tells—of conflicted sexuality, homosexual desire, and homosocial allegiance—is one that would interest D. H. Lawrence in *Sons and Lovers* (1913) and Ford Madox Ford in *Parade's End* (1928).

Wharton's failure to see the connection, the influence of Sturgis's thinking and work on her own, was in part self-serving. She wanted posterity to couple her name with successful men like Walter Berry and renowned writers like James, Paul Bourget, George Eliot, and Emily Brontë, whose depiction of the Yorkshire moors inspired the landscape of *Ethan Frome*. At best, Wharton had mixed feelings about Sturgis's output. Although she advocated the American publication of *Belchamber* and couples it in *A Backward Glance* with David Graham Phillips's *Susan Lenox*, a book she thought another "neglected masterpiece," she refers to *Tim* and *All That Was Possible* in the same sentence as "charming, if slightly over-sentimental tales."[23] *Tim* is sentimental, even bathetic. Still her dismissal of the latter surprises, until one remembers her internalization of the standards by which her work was found wanting.

Particularly sensitive to charges of influence, Wharton saw her reputation, like those of all American writers, lying on her originality. Seen as a lesser James, she was not about to promote herself as a greater Sturgis. Wharton's denial of her indebtedness to those who came before also undermines her view of civilization. "If only people who can't create wd realize that those who *can* (in the great sense) owe their 'procédé' to their own vision of life, & not to any one else's," she wrote Gaillard Lapsley.[24] Wharton's irritation is understandable but misguided, for her reading of Sturgis's books enriched her own. Here is perhaps the greatest fiction at the heart of the inner circle, one that Percy Lubbock would have said was governed by point of view—"that is the question of the relation in which the narrator stands to the story."[25]

With some irony and perhaps more nostalgia, Henry James once called Percy Lubbock "the only *man of letters* in England."[26] Edith Wharton saw his career and his blending—or at least blurring—of genres more pragmatically. "I wish that he'd write books that go into categories," she told Lapsley after the publication of *Earlham*, "the public always takes to them more readily."[27] Lubbock himself knew, as he writes in *Roman Pictures*, that "[p]eople are never happy till they have decided that you are this or that, some recognizable type,"[28] yet the tone of his books, whether biography or fiction or a combination of both, repeatedly raises the question of his relation to the subject: is Lubbock the dispassionate scholar he presents himself to be, or is he, the first-person narrator, the main character?

In all of Lubbock's work, the critical eye masks the "I" of the narrator. This seemingly voluntary self-effacement lends his voice a note of omniscience. By suppressing his authority, Lubbock stresses it. He cleverly argues, for example, that James's biography could only be composed in his letters because most of the novelist's "incessant adventure" was internal: "so much of it as he left unexpressed is lost . . . like a novel that he might have written, but of which there can now be no question, since its only possible writer is gone."[29] Nevertheless, Lubbock's editing is itself a "*re*construction," which illustrates what he later argues in *The Craft of Fiction* (1922): if books are written by those who interpret them, no less are lives.

There seems a direct connection between Lubbock as a child peering into every corner of Earlham, the family estate, and making it his own and the adult biographer who begins describing and ends appropriating. His first book, *Elizabeth Barrett Browning in Her Letters* (1906), became the model for every succeeding memoir. Its form is one that he continued to perfect, the presentation of primary material woven together with strands of narrative that supply necessary biographical facts and personal commentary. Tentative, delicate, and privileged, its tone became his trademark: "Indeed, criticism of her [Barrett Browning's] work tended generally to concentrate itself upon her style, which was a misfortune in a way. It obscured the real point, which was that her thought needed clarifying first. She was not careless; indeed, she was, if anything, too full of theories about rhymes and metres."[30]

To some extent, Lubbock's voice reminds one of Lytton Strachey

(1880–1932) or Gore Vidal (1925–): employing inverse snobbery, it irreverently reveals the weaknesses and vanities of the very personality it is supposedly promoting. Despite his sympathy for Barrett Browning's imprisonment in her father's house and his appreciation of the courage it required for her to correspond with other writers, Lubbock criticizes her seriousness as a writer. How could she speak of her poetry "as simply as she might have spoken of her needlework, if she had had any"?

> It is an attitude which women seem to find easier to preserve towards their work than do men, partly, no doubt, because to a woman art is a more detachable thing than to a man; it is not often to her the sharp concentrated flame into which all the material of life must be cast, that it is to the male artist.
>
> (*EBB*, 30)

Viewed in the context of his near idolization of James, Lubbock's condescension toward women writers made him master, not sycophant. Nowhere is this more evident than in his *Portrait of Edith Wharton* (1947): "But with the kingdoms of the earth lying open to view, sparkling under the sky, she couldn't have the patience to rake the grasses at her feet. In the course of time there might be a chance for all, even for those who are left behind. Let her go; some day one may overtake her."[31] Lubbock does, in this way, "overtake" Wharton; his unflattering memoir affords him the last word.

Lubbock secured his position as a man and a judge of letters by disparaging the achievements of women authors, whose problems of self-definition matched his own. Mary Cholmondeley and Rhoda Broughton, for example, had different but equally intimidating models in Wharton and James, and worked, as did he, in nontraditional or emerging forms.[32] Although Lubbock sought these women as confidantes and mentors, he treats them as harshly as Sturgis treats Sainty in *Belchamber*. Lubbock's need to separate himself from female rivals recalls Wharton's efforts to distinguish her work from the "lavender pages" (*ABG*, 294) of local colorists. If Wharton, who seemed to share his sense of divided loyalties, felt her sexual (feminine) and her authorial (masculine) identities to be competing, Lubbock felt torn in a comparable way. Whether a product of his time or personality, his misogynistic treatment of women artists appears self-defeating and demeaning.

Lubbock's studies usually pair women writers, to their detriment, with male counterparts. They assert a masculine right / write / rite, a masculine literary tradition. Cholmondeley's sister, for example, confessed her disappointment to Wharton: "'friends of Mary's' thought it odd that Henry

[James], Rhoda [Broughton] & Howard [Sturgis] should have been given the centre front."[33] Lubbock presents Rhoda Broughton as "a smart maiden lady to be seen in many a country-house-party of the shires" (*MC*, 36). She is "not for the world a novelist" (*MC*, 36). In Lubbock's memoir of Wharton and her "little literary talent, pretty as it was" (*Portrait*, 243–244), James again takes "centre front": "As for Henry, though he blessed her worldly adventures he couldn't stay to share them. For her the triumphs to which she was returning, which she would quickly be extending; they were very well for her and rightly hers. A greater lot was his—to be alone with his genius" (*Portrait*, 7). When writing of Samuel Pepys and George Calderon, the playwright, his tone may be quizzical or critical but never condescending: "I am not going to say that George's academic discipline was anything but wholesome," Lubbock warns. "Yet it may be that in studying the ways of theatrical drama he tended to think more of details and moments than of the wholeness and continuity of a subject fully wrought into form."[34]

Lubbock's attitude toward his subjects was both defense and predication. Supported by the labors of butler, gardener, stableboy, nanny, coachman, and cook and ruled by an "angel in the house," Earlham provided him with a liberal education that ignored any except the most comic and kindly of Dickensian characters. Every winding path, tendril of ivy, and broken gate on the property invoked the memory of the indefatigable Aunt Richenda who drew them a century before. It was part of the "order of things"—both feudal and Victorian—that Lubbock's grandmother bring sympathy and bounty to the poor and bedridden while the latter give gratitude: "She believed in the distinction, took it as real and lasting; no words were needed, but without words she made it unmistakable that everybody had his due station and degree" (*Earlham*, 205). Resembling Wharton's old New York, Earlham "safely and sharply divided" (*Earlham*, 149) its inhabitants from the rest of the world. It "lay apart, sufficient to itself, following its own ways and talking its own language—or no, not revealed indeed, but hinted at, implied and assumed, in the friendly incursions of the neighborhood," "an appendage of Earlham" itself (*Earlham*, 139, 204). Seeing the globe in similar terms, the household naively and imperially funded missionaries, who ventured forth to enlighten the heathens.

Lubbock's memoir (like Wharton's *The Age of Innocence*) questions what it in part venerates. Valuing the experience embodied in the manor's walls and timbers, Lubbock presents himself as belonging to a class that Wharton's heroine Nan St. George of *The Buccaneers* (1938) admires: people who live in houses so old that they carry them in their bones. Ironically, the memoir reveals him pandering to the class snobbery he faulted in Wharton. His own homelife was more prosaic: "Now let me start on this fair white page," he wrote Gaillard Lapsley, "& see if I can't talk composedly & contentedly to you (of course I can) while my father dozes in one armchair (6:30 p.m.) & Roy in another reads what appears to be a catalogue of mowing-machines & Alan (the youngest) in another studies very solemnly an 18th century folio on the antiquities of Westminster Abbey."[35]

Earlham demonstrates that "memory will give one everything, will even give one, at the right hour, the chance to forget the unnatural security in which it guards the past" (*Earlham*, 180). Excluding his own parents from the text and placing himself as a direct descendant, if not heir, to the tradition his grandmother, Laura Pease Gurney, represents, he becomes what he perceived her to be, "the vessel of the old tradition" (*Earlham*, 217). When Lubbock disparages women writers, he forgets that he learned narrative technique at his grandmother's knee: listening to her husband's sermons, Laura Gurney translated them into her own language, thereby making his (His) words her own. "I want people who will give me time," Lubbock once told Lapsley, "won't make up their minds about me too quickly—won't let me see them 'placing' me—don't you agree?"[36] In other words, he wants the power and the protection of anonymity, the power James attributed to the artist-observer.

Like *Earlham*, Lubbock's best-known book, *The Craft of Fiction* (1922), guards the past; it also anticipates the future. Read by generations of university students, it is both derivative and innovative: derivative in the sense that Lubbock defines, interprets, and extends the theories of James's prefaces; innovative in the ways that he foreshadows reader response theory and emphasizes the psychological approach his contemporary I. A. Richards popularized. Lubbock did not demur from pronouncing on literary questions that James—believing that "discussion to be really luminous, would have to rest on some perfect definition of terms as is not of this muddled world"—avoided.[37] As a result, his text is more of a handbook, which introduces a technical vocabulary and exhibits a modernist preoccupation with form, memory, and individual consciousness.

Because the book is written in straightforward prose, it allows readers to bypass the intricate, retrospective meanderings of James's creative imagination. For artists such as Virginia Woolf and Ellen Glasgow, who owned well-marked copies, it provided a way of examining James's theories of fiction without hearing the imposing, and often intimidating, voice of the man himself. Woolf finally decided that Lubbock's ideas about writing did not apply to her "tunnelling process": "the fact that I've been so long finding it proves, I think, how false Percy Lubbock's doctrine is—that you can do this sort of thing consciously."[38]

Two passages that address the relationship between writer and reader illustrate the transformation of James's thinking into Lubbock's. "As the historian of the matter sees and speaks," says James:

> so my intelligence of it, as a reader, meets him halfway, passive, receptive, appreciative, often even grateful; unconscious, quite blissfully of any bar to intercourse, any disparity of sense between us. Into his very footprints the responsive, the imaginative steps of the docile reader that I consentingly become for him all comfortably sink.

(*AN*, 335–336)

Extending the idea, as well as the power of the reader, Lubbock writes:

> The reader of a novel—by which I mean the critical reader—is himself a novelist; he is the maker of a book which may or may not please his taste when it is finished, but of a book for which he must take his own share of the responsibility. . . . The reader must therefore become, for his part, a novelist, never permitting himself to suppose that the creation of the book is solely the affair of the author.

(*CF*, 77)

Lubbock comes to this conclusion because he was a critic first and foremost; whereas James used criticism to explore, articulate, and defend his own technique and vision. James, who believed that the writer invents, then governs, characters and readers, narcissistically imagines himself as a female reader ("passive" and "grateful") penetrated by the "blissful" experience of reading. Lubbock envisions the process as a meeting of confreres, not a seduction; a book's merit depends in part on the quality of its reader's imagination.

Lubbock most agrees with James when he locates the transformation of art into life in the dramatized consciousness of the individual character. In his hierarchy, "everything in the novel, not only the scenic episodes but all the rest, is to be in some sense dramatized" (*CF*, 123): "Drama, then, gives the final stroke, it is the final stroke which it is adapted to deliver; and picture is to be considered as subordinate, preliminary and preparatory" (*CF*, 269). Its antithesis is the "panoramic" or "pictorial" method, which becomes—as in Thackeray—"the representation of the author's experiences, and the author becomes a personal entity, about whom we may begin to ask questions" (*CF*, 114). After faulting *War and Peace* for its lack of unity and praising *Madame Bovary* because "the story stands obediently before its author" (*CF*, 60), Lubbock credits James with developing a new technique that fully dramatizes "the picture of the mind" (*CF*, 156): "I do not know that anywhere except in the later novels of Henry James, a pictorial subject is thus handed over in its entirety to the method of drama, so that the intervention of a seeing eye and a recording hand, between the reader and the subject is practically avoided altogether" (*CF*, 185). According to Lubbock, James is—as James himself once wrote of Morton Fullerton and Wharton—in the reader's skin without being in the way.

The Craft of Fiction does not mention Wharton or Sturgis. By Lubbock's literary standards, Sturgis remained amateurish and Wharton insular: "she had so controlled her craft that it had little history to relate, indeed perhaps too little" (*Portrait*, 70). "Didn't she realise that the true makers of art and shapers of thought were to be found elsewhere," he asks, "that those who could read and understand her aright were awaiting her where she had failed to observe them, perhaps on the very doorstep from which she had launched her flight?" (*Portrait*, 70). The criticism could apply equally to James, and it shows Lubbock defining and claiming a tradition, which largely excluded his own uncategorizable books. Little did he understand Wharton's brand of the panoramic vision, exemplified by her chronicle novels, or her attempts to enlarge—what Howells calls—the "bounds of civilization."[39] *The Craft of Fiction* allowed him, like Jimmy in "The China Pot," not just to mimic his friend's voice and intonation, but to project himself into his mind, "to think his thoughts" ("CP," 304).

The Region Cloud encompasses the principles set forth in *The Craft of Fiction*. Referring to the novel's homoeroticism and Lubbock's relationship with Sybil Cutting, Wharton wrote Lapsley that "Percy's book is indeed a strange product in the light of his private affairs."[40] The tale traces a young man's disillusionment with a man of genius. When the two meet, Channon, a renowned painter, asks Austin: "Mighn't there be something in the thought of attentive eyes, clear and critical eyes, following one's accomplishment in the world? not, you see, with any notion of helping or of being helped, but in mere calm appraisement of the thing one does, the sort one is."[41] James could have asked the same of Lubbock, who, in turn, possibly wondered if he abdicated, like May Bartram in "The Beast in the Jungle," "sole possession of himself" (*RC*, 289).

With the "desperation of a great-hearted lover," Austin vows, "I *will* be used" (*RC*, 301). Channon accepts the sacrifice. "You'll do nothing," he tells Austin:

> "You would never have come here at all, you would never have given your mind away to me as you did in the beginning, if you had needed yourself for any purpose of your own. I always saw that. I, when I was young, was of another fashion. I could no more have

offered up my genius to another man than I could have worn another man's head. But you were different, and I did you no wrong."

(RC, 397)

The speech could be a direct comment on Lubbock himself, who similarly
characterized his own relationship with James: "Intercourse with him was
not quite easy. . . . But it was enough to surrender simply to the current
of his thought. . . . No words seem satisfactory in describing the dominance he exerted by no overriding or ignoring of the presence of others,
rather with the quickest, most apprehending susceptibility to it."[42] The
description recalls James's analysis of the relationship between reader and
writer; it makes one speculate whether Lubbock ever felt Austin's need to
reclaim the self he surrendered.

In many ways, *The Region Cloud* seems a response to James's "The Lesson of the Master" (1888) and Wharton's "The Potboiler" (1908). To Paul
Overt, the hero in James's story, the "full, rich, masculine, human, general"
life of the distinguished writer Henry St. George seems ideal.[43] But
St. George demurs, citing his domestic and social complications: "They've
given me subjects without number, if that's what you mean; but they've
taken away at the same time the power to use them" ("LM," 266). That
confession persuades Overt, himself an artist, to leave the woman he loves.
When he returns from Europe with manuscript in hand, he finds her be-
trothed to St. George who explains: "I wanted to save you, rare and precious as you are" ("LM," 282). "The Potboiler" repeats the point. With
the hope of earning enough to marry, Wharton's artist does studies of
society women draped in pearls. Refusing the sacrifice, his sweetheart becomes engaged to another because "though his pictures are bad, he does
not prostitute his art."[44] In Lubbock's novel, Austin learns "the lesson of
the master"; he learns to be ruthless, driven, and self-justified in the name
of art. Whether Channon used Austin or Austin Channon is arguable. A
cynic would say the same of James and Lubbock. Echoing a character in
Roman Pictures, Lubbock might explain: "I have played many parts, acting up to the theory and expectation of my different companions; it
saves trouble, it spares one the effort [and the consequences] of [overt]
assertion" (19).

If James and Wharton supplied the *donnée* for Sturgis and Lubbock,
they did not take away the power to use it. Lubbock's experiments with
form, genre, and memory and Sturgis's insistence on the interrelatedness
of identity and gender in texts that might be characterized as homoerotic
show that they too have lessons to teach. Like Wharton, they give us another "vision of life," another answer to "the question of the relation in
which the narrator stands to the story"—whether that of the inner circle

or the twentieth century. They make us rethink what separates the masters from the practitioners.

Bernard Berenson made a career of separating the masters from ordinary practitioners. As early as 1896, he wrote: "My ambition now is to have done with all but the few great masterpieces of art, and in art as in life to meticulously keep away from the sordid, the second-rate, and pettily personal."[45] By the time that Berenson and Wharton considered themselves friends (1909), he had not succeeded in shunning the sordid: Isabel Gardiner's husband had suspected him of inflating the prices of her purchases, and he had begun his dubious association with the Duveen brothers, who, in hopes of cornering the market on Renaissance art, preferred that unsigned works be attributed to better-known (and higher-priced) painters.[46]

Berenson's method of making attributions depended on the sixth sense of the connoisseur developed through arduous study, rather than on material considerations. With his painter's eye, the smallest details acted as a signature. Roger Fry, both an admirer and a rival of Berenson, approached the artist's imagination from a slightly different angle: "one needn't care a rap about the artist that created it, but surely the idea that the thing was created for the special purpose of arousing the emotion does add something."[47] Berenson's clients had to believe implicitly in his "God-given" gift and in his integrity (*AP*, 186).

The rumors that surrounded Berenson probably intrigued Wharton, whose interest in art was more than amateurish. In 1894, for instance, she correctly identified a series of terra cotta groups mistakenly attributed to the seventeenth-century artist Giovanni Bonnelli as being the work of the fifteenth-century artist Giovanni della Robbia (Lewis, 72–73). The question of influence, which so affected Sturgis and Lubbock, did not seem to concern either Wharton or Berenson, even though her early travel book *Italian Backgrounds* (1905) seems shaped by his theories. "It is only in the background," she asserts, "that the artist finds himself free to express his personality."[48] Wharton might be commenting on Sturgis and Lubbock's relationship to the inner circle.

Berenson loomed in the foreground of Wharton's life, but until the twenties he remained in the background—an intense spot of color—for most of the other members of the group. While Berenson advocated a scientific or "quantitative" approach for defining the motives and general ideas of an artist,[49] his reliance on an informed intuition troubled Henry James, whose objections may have had more to do with the man and his sensuous exuberance than his aesthetics. James too assumed a certain trust among artist, audience, and critic, but the latter's function, as exemplified by Berenson, might have struck him as parasitic.

James's reservations did not trouble Wharton, and Berenson's friendship with her was "one of the most satisfactory" of all his "human relations": "No devoted sister could have been more concerned for my comfort, more eager for my happiness. As an elder sister she never hesitated to reprove and advise, and for that I loved her" (*Sketch*, 25). Four years before Wharton's death in 1937, Berenson summed up their relationship:

> I got such a comfy feeling just being in the same room with her. We have known so many people together, travelled together, gossiped together, discussed together, that now it seems quite enough just being together. She is such a Tory & I the last almost of would-be aristocrats.[50]

In spite of Berenson's snobberies, Wharton adopted a tone with him that occasionally echoed hers with James, le Cher Maître: "And the palaces of Trapani!—how do they happen to be so much finer than any at Palermo? And why was Selinus built on a stretch of coast without harbour? And what song did the sirens sing—&c, &c? Oh, how many things I want to ask you."[51] Their correspondence rings with a Pater-like ardour of the sort that Charles Eliot Norton found distasteful: "the stillness, the greenness, the exuberance of my flowers," Wharton enthused about The Mount, "the perfume of the hemlock woods, & above all the moonlight nights on my big terrace, overlooking the lake."[52] With Berenson, Wharton recovered and revised the teacher-pupil relationship she had enjoyed with Professor Norton, whose death (1908) almost coincided with the beginning of her more playful friendship with Berenson. No matter how hard life seemed, they found human nature (the title of a volume of short stories Wharton dedicated to Berenson in 1933) fascinating and felt it "well worth the trouble of getting born."[53]

Prior to meeting Berenson, Wharton had outlined her aesthetic principles in *The Decoration of Houses* (1897), a book written in collaboration with Ogden Codman, an interior designer. *The Decoration of Houses* articulates a classical belief in tradition and an organic approach to form, content, and function. "Originality lies not in discarding the necessary laws of thought," she argues as T. S. Eliot would in "Tradition and the Individual Talent" (1917), "but in using them to express new intellectual conceptions."[54] Success in any art, which must be "based on common sense and regulated by the laws of harmony and proportion" (*DH*, 198), depends on "a due regard for the limitations of the sense to which it appeals" (*DH*, 67). More generally, the book advocates the cultivation of artistic taste because it will indirectly broaden "the whole view of life" (*DH*, 183). Wharton's subsequent interest in novels of manners would not have surprised Berenson, who, in 1892, wrote that architecture and manners are "perhaps more closely connected than any two other expressions of the human personality, manners being in the van, because closer to the person. . . . through Consular, and Empire manners you finally get to us, finding the same forms in the manners that you find in the architecture."[55] Wharton often uses the two, manners and architecture, to shed "light on our moral experience."[56] In *The House of Mirth*, for example, Lily Bart's economic and social descent—from Mrs. Penniston's parlor to Gus Trenor's study to Mrs. Hatch's hotel suite to the boardinghouse's common room— marks her spiritual rise.

Although Wharton never abandoned the precepts of what Fry called a "conscientious art,"[57] she did begin to appreciate a wider range of responses. In 1905, she complimented Sara Norton for writing obituary verse (a practice that Mark Twain had satirized in *The Adventures of Huckleberry Finn* [1885]): "I am very glad you sent me the lines on Ethel, dear Sally, not only because of my own interest in reading them, but because I know how deeply they will touch Henriette's heart. . . . They are charmingly done, & I am now wondering why you have kept this gift so long a secret from me."[58] Three years later, she asks in *A Motor-Flight through France* (1908):

> Is there not room for another, a lesser order of appreciation, for the kind of confused atavistic enjoyment that is made up of historical association, of a sense of mass and harmony, of the relation of the building to the sky above it, to the lights and shadows it creates about it—deeper than all, of a blind sense in the blood of its old racial power, the things it meant to far-off minds of which ours are the oft-dissolved and reconstituted fragments?[59]

Berenson asked himself the same question when he wondered if distinctions between the beauty of "fine art" and the "picturesque" were not a form of "culture-snobbery" (Samuels, 345). Percy Lubbock did not address this question in *The Craft of Fiction*; rather, he outlined standards for judging the merits of literature often applied today—scope, depth, verisimilitude, and a dramatized central intelligence. Despite minor misgivings, Wharton and Berenson, like all the inner circle, supremely valued "Anglo-Saxon humanity." In societies where art flourished, they were largely willing to overlook the miseries caused by a rigid class system, whether intellectual or economic, for "then a few of the highest class can devote themselves solely to culture without harm, and perhaps to the great advantage of the community" (*BBT*, 38).

In the teens and twenties, Wharton's aesthetics became more elastic, focusing, like Berenson's, on the unique vision of the artist. In "The Criticism of Fiction" (1914), for example, she argues that "all intelligent criticism of any art presupposes an intelligent criticism of life in general." Fore-most, it is concerned with the point of view of the creator. She ends the essay by applying Berenson's definition of a connoisseur to her own of a critic:

> it is the critic's office, and his peculiar honor, to dwell most on the nature of their highest gift, on that divining and life-evoking faculty which, whatever method it resorts to for expression, is the very foundation of the novelist's art, and the result, not of this or that rule or theory, but of the intense and patient pondering on the depths of life itself.[60]

Berenson's voice similarly echoes Wharton's in *The Study and Criticism of Italian Art* (1916): "what is true of life is true of art: its ultimate aim is ecstasy." Wharton blessed him for articulating "so thrillingly" what coincided with her own "aesthetic."[61] Eight years later in *The Writing of Fiction* (1925), a book that presents a more "romantic" aesthetic than *The Decoration of Houses*, she acknowledged Berenson's emphasis on psychology and technique: "a creative mind combines with the power of penetrating into other minds that of standing far enough aloof from them to see beyond, and relate them to the whole stuff out of which they but partially emerge" (*WF*, 15). Inspiration must be nursed much like the connoisseur's intuition, yet one must also recognize and accept the strengths and limitations of the individual imagination; style is itself a form of discipline (*WF*, 24).

Unlike Wharton, Berenson had an irrepressible faith in what he liked to call humanity and she called the rabble. The two, nevertheless, shared a sense of something they considered an almost mystical connection to the universe. Berenson named this feeling "IT":

> IT is every experience that is ultimate, valued for its own sake . . . IT is aesthetical and, to the large extent that the two can be kept separated, not ethical. . . . IT is the most and immediate way.

> (*Sketch*, 150)

As Wharton aged, her own version of "IT" (though she did not use the word) moved from a historical to a more spiritual aesthetic. In 1908, she wanted "to keep intact as many links as possible between yesterday and to-morrow, to lose, in the ardour of new experiment, the least that may be of that long heritage of human experience" (*MF*, 11). Writing, which took place "in some secret region on the sheer edge of consciousness" illuminated by "the full light" of critical attention (*ABG*, 205), provided a "link" between the past and IT: "To the artist his world is as solidly real as the world of experience, or even more so but in a way entirely different; it is a world to and from which he passes without any sense of effort, but always *with an uninterrupted awareness* of the passing" (*WF*, 120). Wharton's late interest and increasing emphasis on the immaterial led her friends to speculate about her possible conversion to Catholicism. "My heart goes out to her confessor," one friend joked.[62]

Although Wharton's relationship with Berenson seems to have been less conflicted than hers with Lubbock or James's with Sturgis, one of her short stories from *Tales of Ghosts and Men* (1910), "The Daunt Diana," suggests an ambivalence toward the type of connoisseur Berenson (and to a lesser degree the men of the inner circle) represented. Berenson brought a new definition to "dilettantism": "the real selfish passion for training oneself to have enjoyment of one exquisite and beautiful thing, leading on to the enjoyment of one even more beautiful" (*BBT*, 43). Earlier in "The Dilettante" (1904), Wharton had criticized this endeavor as leading to "the descent of man"—the title of the volume in which the story appears. "The Dilettante" recalls James's "The Beast in the Jungle" (1903), for the protagonist learns that the cultivation of sensibility has excluded the possibility of love. Sixteen years later Wharton had not altered her view of this kind of connoisseurship. In *The Age of Innocence* (1920), Newland Archer is "at heart a dilettante, and thinking over a pleasure to come often gave him a subtler satisfaction than its realisation."[63]

"The Daunt Diana" exposes the dangers of attribution mongering and incorporates Berenson's theories of tactile values and space composition. The statue of Diana, coveted by the protagonist, Humphrey Neave, originally belongs to Daunt, a man insensible to beauty. Neave is a natural connoisseur but poor. His long inquisitive fingers "seem to acquire the very texture" of the thing they touch—whether bronze or lace, enamel or glass—"until its essence has been secreted."[64] Neave's gift can also be read as a perversion, a sanctioned rape. Years of study, "a long process of discrimination and rejection" ("DD," 53), have honed his ability as much as Berenson's. "This intimate realization of an object comes to us only when we unconsciously translate our retinal impressions of it into ideated sensations of touch, pressure and grasp," Berenson explains in *The Central Italian Painters of the Renaissance* (1897).[65] Inheriting an unexpected fortune, Neave buys Daunt's entire collection only to find that he can take no pleasure in what he has not hunted, scraped, and bargained for himself:

> there'd been no wooing, no winning. Each of my little odd
> bits—the rubbish I chucked out to make room for Daunt's glo-
> ries—had its own personal history, the drama of my relation to it, of

the discovery, the struggle, the capture, the first divine moment of possession. . . . they had become a part of my imagination.

("DD," 57)

Neave sells the collection at a great loss because people assume he found it second-rate. Then he spends the next years buying it back. In the center of his tiny room smelling of neighbors' cooking and packed pell-mell with treasures, the Daunt Diana reigns again. "I always cared—always worshipped—always wanted her," Neave confesses. "But she wasn't mine then, and I knew it, and she knew it . . . and now at last we understand each other" ("DD," 59–60). His obsession or "possession" has little to do with mutual understanding, for Diana remains sphinxlike and self-possessed.

The Daunt Diana might serve as a metaphor for Wharton's position with the happy few, who tried collectively to possess this often daunting woman. The inner circle recognized that from the cradle to the grave one is playing to an audience, as did Sturgis and Lubbock for James, Wharton for the group, and Berenson for the world. Berenson's peripheral relationship to the inner circle reminds us of its flexible and intangible nature. James may have been the original guiding spirit for the group, but the shape and realization of its imaginative reality was Wharton's. If, as Berenson argues, "the story of these audiences succeeding one another" forms "an important part of a biography or an autobiography" (*BBT*, 193), then the story of the inner circle presents a kind of concert. The author's voice may be disguised, as Lubbock reminds us, in the voice of a spokesman, but it is also revealed by a choice of spokesmen.

CHAPTER FIVE

Love and Exile: Edith Wharton's Fictional Selves

No matter what your talent as an author, where are you to catch yourself en flagrant délit of being yourself, yours individually, privately, yet representative and consistent?
BERNARD BERENSON, *SKETCH FOR A SELF-PORTRAIT*

Every additional faculty for exteriorizing states of feeling, giving them a face and a language, is a moral as well as an artistic asset, and Goethe was never wiser than when he wrote: "A god gave me a voice to speak my pain."
EDITH WHARTON, *FIGHTING FRANCE*

IMMEDIATELY AFTER THE ARMISTICE ending the First World War, Edith Wharton began transforming a long-deserted estate outside Paris into a gathering place for the happy few. Today Pavillon Colombe sits relatively undisturbed, surrounded by acres of immaculate grounds. Both the house, with its corridor of rooms that appear to march in step, and the gardens, ringed by hedgerows to form an outdoor's equivalent, reflect Wharton's need for order. "It would have required a microscope to find a speck of dust in any room," Robert Norton testifies.[1] Despite their formalism, the spaces are cozy, the grandeur contained to a human scale. If a woman's nature is like a great house full of rooms (as Wharton wrote in "The Fullness of Life"), then her own embraced the competing decors elegantly balanced at Pavillon Colombe. Here Wharton "exteriorized" an interior domain, that innermost room, where the soul sits alone and holds court. As a canvas, this study of controlled intimacy, which recalls the architectonic structure of novels like *The House of Mirth* (1905) or *The Custom of the Country* (1913), needs no signature.[2] Pavillon Colombe captures the essence of Wharton's relationship to the inner circle.

Wharton's lived fiction informs her published ones. Her heroines seek to duplicate the delineation of public and private space found at Pavillon Colombe. Resembling their author, they too are driven by often incompatible forces: "the dissecting intellect" and the "accepting soul." At best, they can become one of the rare few, "whose daily life reveals the inner harmony 'through chinks that grief has made.'"[3] From *The Valley of Decision* (1902) to *The Buccaneers* (1938), these women learn that while the unsustainable dream of the accepting soul feeds desire, the dissecting intellect undermines it. Those who stake all on the dream—Lily Bart in *The House of Mirth*, Justine Brent in *The Fruit of the Tree* (1907), or Mattie Silver in *Ethan Frome* (1911)—wind up imprisoned, maimed, or dead. Those who escape such punishment—Sophy Viner in *The Reef* (1912) or Kate Clephane in *The Mother's Recompense* (1925)—do what Wharton herself did: they choose exile, a problematic space that can accommodate intellect and soul. Instead of realizing themselves in or through another, they discover, like Vance Weston in *The Gods Arrive* (1932), that what they most want is "to be alone."[4] The innermost room is now a "hidden cave" where the artist hoards "secretest treasures."[5]

The ambiguous fates of Wharton's exiled heroines have long been debated. Is Wharton, as Louis Auchincloss writes, harsh on Sophy Viner?[6] Does she condemn Kate Clephane to a needlessly lonely future? Why are those women who claim the self's supremacy emblematically ostracized?

The answer partly lies in Wharton's ambivalence about intimacy. Neither marriage nor love gave her the happiness she found living tangentially with others. Wharton needed strict routine to make her world more manageable. "If ever by any unthinkable *contretemps*, some cogwheel in the elaborate machinery of the day were blocked," Norton explains, "the resulting confusion would be held a disaster of the first magnitude! But it was the machinery and its oiling which enabled her to get through so much" (RN, 34–35). Guests at Hyères sometimes found this kind of regimen disconcerting; yet the men of the inner circle tended to share Wharton's own need. Gaillard Lapsley's niece remembers that during his visits the household revolved around his schedule: mornings were devoted to correspondence, after lunch he read the newspapers and went for a walk, there was tea at 4:30 sharp, and a drink before dinner at 7:00.[7]

To an extent, the structure of the inner circle inhibited intimacy. Norton describes the group as bonded by "rational intercourse" and "the rarest of luxuries, a common field of values and interests, in which a general measure of familiarity could safely be assumed. No need to explain or elaborate" (RN, 20). Lapsley recalls Wharton moved beyond control on just two occasions—the death of his brother and the death of Walter Berry. He believed that friendly companionship with men was what the author understood best, though it was not what she professed to value highest. Nicky Mariano was perhaps the closest in characterizing the importance of the inner circle to the author when she called its men "Edith Wharton's wives."[8] These men offered Wharton what they could, maybe more. They provided the emotional support and encouragement that Halo Spear gives

Vance Weston. Despite the relationship with Morton Fullerton demanding a surrender of self and a suspension of critical thinking, it promised, as she herself wrote, the knowledge of what other women feel. No one gave her the consummate love she alleged to want, but probably did not. As a group, the inner circle succeeded in creating an alternative that served them well: a "companionate" marriage. In *The Story of Avis* (1877), Elizabeth Stuart Phelps asks, How many generations will it take to create a woman artist, if it takes three to form a gentleman? Wharton might have asked how many it will take to make a woman artist's ideal friend and lover.

While many people tend to view stable marriages as an index of health and happiness and are suspicious of those, like Henry James or Gaillard Lapsley, who appear to lead celibate lives, solitude can give us a greater awareness of our deepest feelings.[9] Linked to self-realization, it may be a vital condition for people as creative as the happy few.[10] For Wharton, exile was a desired state precisely because it placed her outside the unsatisfactory story of romantic rescue told and retold in the novels of her contemporaries. Wharton knew the independence that Ellen Olenska claims in *The Age of Innocence* (1920) threatened society as well as the family; the continuation of civilization—to paraphrase Freud—depends upon discontent, the thwarting of passion and the subjugation of will.

How could Wharton write a novel of manners and marriage that incorporates an artistic siren like the Countess Olenska? She does so by telling two stories. The first demands the banishment of those heroines most like herself who do not fit into the marriage plot. The second gives them a life which must be imagined. This unarticulated ending is "beyond the ugliness, the pettiness, the attrition and corrosion of the soul."[11] It is the homeland her couples seek, and its existence undercuts the philosophical framework of her fiction. Repudiating Newland Archer's notion of his dull but honorable past, Ellen Olenska proves that one does not have to accept "a succession of pitiful compromises with fate, of concessions to old traditions, old beliefs, old charities and frailties."[12] Ellen's defection, which ostensibly preserves society, foreshadows its gradual dissolution.

Wharton's first story resembles those of eighteenth- and nineteenth-century heroines torn, as Nancy Miller and Rachel DuPlessis write, between love and quest. If the love plot ends in the heroine's integration (marriage), the quest ends with her disintegration (death).[13] Wharton's second story asks the reader to complete its ending, to envision Sophy Viner, for example, with a different future than that of her sister, Mrs. MacTarvie-Birch. Although Wharton combines and comments on the plots that earlier women writers found mutually excluding,[14] she largely determines the "single tale" her readers will invent: denial and self-control bring rewards; they allow the heroine to form her own community, to win her "way in the world." [15]

In Wharton's fiction, the dissecting intellect guarantees an "unhappy" ending. The language her heroines seek to master masters them. This is her tale of the failed artist. No word can release the self and define the self anew. Resting on inequality, the vocabulary and tropes of romance leave little room for adult sexuality and intellectuality. The women, who want to escape the inhibiting story lines of domestic fiction that have also given them pleasure, power, and connection to others, play a kind of Russian roulette with their identities; the latent power of language can people or destroy this most tenuous—and ultimately most fictive—of worlds. As Wharton's heroines acquire knowledge and maturity, they write themselves out of the only scripts they have known. *Summer* (1917) exemplifies the paradox. Seduced by words that make love "as bright and open as the summer air," [16] Charity Royall is denied access to her upper-class lover's world when he stays her budding vocabulary with inattention or swallows it in kisses: "But once more, as she spoke, she became aware that he was no longer listening. He came close and caught her to him as if he were snatching her from some imminent peril" (115). Wharton diverges from a pattern commonly found in twentieth-century American women's fiction, for the embryonic emergence of Charity's voice imperils her more than the system her lover or guardian represents. Its acquisition places her outside protection: "I want you should marry Annabel Balch," she tells him. "I feel I'd rather you acted right" (151). Harney's sweet talk leads to her final imprisonment in lawyer Royall's house, but it has also opened a new world in which she communicates with her baby in a kind of prelanguage of impulses not shaped into thought.[17] Caught between two worlds, one known, the other longingly fancied, Wharton's heroines usually settle, like their nineteenth-century sisters, for a third founded on compromise. Those who refuse to give up the right to an inner life lead the richest lives in exile.

Three of Wharton's better known novels of female artistry, *The House of Mirth*, *The Reef*, and *The Age of Innocence*, serve to illustrate her analysis of the topics central to her lived and fictional lives: language, space, and exile.

Published the year before the first partial gathering of the inner circle at Qu'Acre in 1906, *The House of Mirth* combines two plots shown to be incompatible: the romance and the *Künstlerroman*, the former thriving on the lack of definition the latter demands. The novel, which relentlessly strips Lily of every hope of romantic rescue,[18] asks a series of questions that are all to be answered negatively. Are there "right" words? Is there a land "free from everything—from money, from poverty, from ease and anxiety, from all the material accidents" (*HM*, 108)? Reflecting perhaps

Wharton's own anxieties of authorship, Lily Bart's tragic end highlights the deforming as well as the transforming power of a language she cannot govern or replace.[19] When Lily "writes" her personality, she also becomes involved in a process of unwriting. Because the present narrative often depends on a revision of a past self, it demands a relaxation of the boundaries that define identity.

A reader of sentimental fiction and Edward Fitzgerald's translation of *Omar Khayyam*, Lily wants to believe in Lawrence Selden's accepting soul and the word, never spoken, which will free her to assert her own eager individuality. The struggle to articulate her feelings forces her to confront the disfigured image that stares from her glass, the self capable of sexual exploitation and blackmail. As with Isabel Archer, everything that belongs to her becomes a limit, a barrier. In this she differs from those around her, who subscribe to Madame Merle's belief that "one's house, one's furniture, one's garments, the books one reads, the company one keeps—these things are all expressive" of one's self.[20]

Lily's exile and subsequent death result from her insistence on dividing language from its context. Dismissing her history of competition and enmity with Bertha Dorset, she supports the myth of Bertha's platonic relationship with Ned Silverton. Her opposite, Selden reads words only in context. "I shall look hideous in dowdy clothes: but I can trim my own hats" (*HM*, 117), Lily tells him on their walk at Bellomont. Seeing the woman and what is said of her as one, Selden, who later confuses Lily with Mrs. Lloyd, the *tableau vivant* character she portrays,[21] loses the meaning of her words in the hum of Percy Gryce's returning motor. He does not perceive that she lacks the "patience, pliancy and dissimulation" (*HM*, 60) necessary for the self-deception that will permit her to deceive and marry Gryce or any of her other suitors, including Selden.[22]

The things practiced but not named in the Trenor-Dorset set—adultery and sanctioned prostitution—form the substance of Gerty Farish's work, the bond of Nettie Struther's marriage, and the subject of Wharton's fiction.[23] Lily needs love to survive, yet the places where she finds it—in Gerty's arms and Nettie's kitchen—do not conform to the plot of a redemptive marriage, ironically capable of resurrecting her at Bellomont. Gerty and Nettie have established communities that grant them linguistic freedom outside the fiction of romantic and economic deliverance Lily still holds dear. The plasticity and receptivity that make Lily a good model make her a poor inventor. She hopes to recover old ways of seeing that will not disrupt the decorum of her carefully constructed text. Words that are even worse than George Trenor's touch—"mistress" and "blackmail"—ensnare her as securely as Harney's kisses silence Charity.

Although the discovery of her own integrity and voice are simultaneous, Lily finds only a measure of freedom from her prison of inarticulateness.

Telling Rosedale her version of the business dealings with Gus Trenor, "[s]he made the statement clearly, deliberately, with pauses between the sentences, so that each should have time to sink deeply into her hearer's mind" (*HM*, 472). Lily cannot reconcile the temptation to use Bertha's letters with the vision of her beauty serving a greater good. The original exile that made her a social pariah is increasingly self-imposed, as her tale becomes a kind of secularized spiritual autobiography. Like Edna Pontellier of *The Awakening* (1899), she has swum into a beyond that preserves a sense of self by destroying it.[24] Succumbing to the struggle to understand and to be understood, Lily leaves Selden her ideal self, martyred on the pyre of Bertha's letters.

Presenting the shadow side of the Land of Letters, *The House of Mirth* shows what happens when collaboration becomes appropriation. The novel ends with Lily, who has consistently resisted marriage and its attendant violation, with a room of her own and the wolf (literally in the form of Selden rushing to her rescue) at her door. Gerty and Selden are now free to construct her story from the fragments she left behind, the check to Trenor, the empty vial.[25] Illusion will again prevent disillusionment. While the plots of romance and female artistry exist side by side, embodied in Lily's dream of Nettie's baby girl asleep on her breast, the former is culturally privileged; in the shape of the baby, Marie Antoinette, and the seduced-and-abandoned theme she symbolizes, it literally weighs Lily down.

The house of mirth becomes a house of mourning because its foundation rests on the belief that another can awaken the slumbering soul. *The Custom of the Country* (1913) makes the point more bluntly. Wharton worked on the book during her affair with Morton Fullerton, whose demands for written signs of passionate avowal and affectionate abjection probably made her ironically aware of the differences between language and meaning. "Sometimes I feel that I *can't* go on like this," she wrote him in 1908, "from moments of such nearness, when the last shadow of separateness melts, back into a complete *néant* of silence, not hearing, not knowing—being left to feel that I have been like a 'course' served & cleared away!"[26]

Novel reading (*When the Kissing Had to Stop* and *Passion in the Palace*) has formed Undine Spragg's speech and thought as much as Lily's "with the vocabulary of outraged virtue, and with pathetic allusions to woman's frailty,"[27] but traditional story lines have no power to deflect her from her desires. She subscribes to them only in retrospect and when they suit her purposes:[28] "she gradually began to look on herself and Ralph as the victims of dark machinations . . . and implied that 'everything might have been different' if 'people' had not 'come between' them" (*CC*, 210). Undine has no "poky" qualms about keeping Van Degen's pearls, what sensational fiction would call "the price of her shame," if their price can launch a new phase of her European career.

Undine's power and terror lie in her ability to twist old plots and to imagine new ones. "You come among us speaking our language and not knowing what we mean," Raymond de Chelles contemptuously tells her,

> "wanting the same things we want, and not knowing why we want them, aping our weaknesses . . . and we're fools enough to imagine that because you copy our ways and pick up our slang you understand anything about the things that make life decent and honourable for us!"
>
> (CC, 307)

Undine is more frightening than any imagined "other" because she is so familiar. The isolation or solitude at the center of the novel, based exclusively on a false self, borders on the pathological. The range and depth of Undine's eloquence—limited to "I want"—serves as Wharton's warning. Undine might wrest the pen from Ralph Marvell's poetical hand,[29] but she turns the stuff of sonnets into tabloid copy. Her predicament underscores the plight of the woman writer who has no satisfactory alternative to the tradition she has rejected.

In *The Reef* (1912), Sophy Viner and Anna Leath are caught in a similarly undefined space. Recalling *The Golden Bowl* (1904), the novel centers on four people either related or soon to be related by marriage. Anna's efforts to learn the truth of her lover's relationship to Sophy explode the book's central myths: nothing distinguishes her from the younger woman except class; her stepson's engagement to Sophy is anything but an old-fashioned case; and learning the right words does not shorten the distance between lovers circling one another like those on the Grecian urn. Words can only strive to coincide with action: "she would have been happier if there had been less discrepancy between her words to Sophy Viner [pledging to renounce George Darrow] and the act which had followed them [making love to him]."[30]

The second book opens with Anna literally suspended between past and present, community and self, civilization and nature: "In the court, halfway between house and drive, a lady stood" (*Reef*, 81). Like Maggie Verver, she must learn to fill out "her appointed, her expected, her imposed character"[31]; she must create a place for herself in the void. Her actual home is Givré, an estate set in the cultivated wilderness of the French countryside. Within its walls, Anna has lived a dutiful life, secretly nourished by the stuff of great poetry and memorable action. Givré and all it represents in terms of personal, social, and cultural histories has the power to predetermine one's perspective, displacing, for example, the reality of Anna's fiancé with the memory of her late husband, Fraser Leath.

The geographical and cultural isolation of Givré, the seat of American expatriates, reflects Anna's own. She is, in a sense, caught like many female artists between the competing and complementary traditions housed there. Those traditions, embodied in Fraser Leath and George Darrow, threaten her autonomy. If life with Fraser resembled a walk through a carefully collected museum, life with Darrow promises less: "she was like a picture so hung," he thinks, "that it can be seen only at a certain angle: an angle known to no one but its possessor. The thought flattered his sense of possessorship" (*Reef*, 129). The awkward juxtaposition of "possessor" and "possessorship" underscores the future institutionalized transformation of woman into object, artist into artifact. Anna longs to share her innermost room; she wants to learn the words that will save her from waning "into old age repeating the same gestures, echoing the same words she had always heard" (*Reef*, 29). But because she is not willing to accede to the formulas men have by heart, there is no place where she can "speak her pain." Anna knows that if she and Darrow should begin "to talk intimately they would feel that they knew each other less well" (*Reef*, 108).

Finding a voice and "exteriorizing" it are not necessarily subsequent steps in Wharton's novels. If Mattie Silver had died, Mrs. Ned Hale tells the narrator of *Ethan Frome* (1911), "Ethan might ha' lived," sustained by the vision of his lost love or a dream briefly realized.[32] Silenced by wife and lover, he no longer has the power to tell the story we hear through an intermediary narrator. His future will pass—much like his tale—in servitude to the whims of others. Heroines such as Charlotte Lovell in "The Old Maid" (1924) achieve power by what they do not say as much as what they say. They assume, to some extent, the stance of the disenfranchised, who know the "other" better than the "other" can know her or himself. While the silencing of Ethan marks a loss of power, a shift from potential author to captive audience, Anna's silence leaves her free to imagine; it fosters and perpetuates, in this way, art. She learns that the "visioned region" (*Reef*, 85) of self cannot, and perhaps should not, be fully shared. This principle maintained the inner circle and its fiction of togetherness for nearly four decades; it determined what materials Wharton marked for her biographer. Following her author, Anna chooses self over community, and, depending on one's interpretation of the novel's ending, civilization, no matter how imperfect, over untamed nature. Forced to explore the source of Sophy's "otherness," Anna finds it in herself,[33] and this process of discovery and articulation helps her to carve a space in the traditions which would normally exclude or engulf her.

Sophy's flight to India insures that silence reigns at Givré; the telling of her story might have given the estate another mistress. Her story exists outside the narrow world of Givré, outside the "first world"; it presents an alternative to that of Anna working within the confines of tradition. Foreshadowing Kate Clephane in *The Mother's Recompense* (1925), Sophy means to keep the experience she has bought, and her acceptance, rather than denial, of the past asserts her individual worth, her right to a world—not just a room—of her own. Like Kate, who returns to the home she fled eighteen years before, Sophy chooses exile over any dumb "conspiracy of rehabilitation and obliteration."[34] It lets her keep memories and identity intact;[35] it preserves an imaginative connection to those left behind.

With the exception of her exiled heroines, Wharton's characters are trapped in mutilated fictions she knew to be destructive and still half-yearned to live: "I don't think she ever quite accustomed herself to the social freedom she had taken at the instance of her taste and reason," observed Lapsley, "and she sometimes suggested to me an emancipated feminist conscientiously practicing free love."[36] Brought up like Aggie in James's *The Awkward Age* (1899)—with what they are *not* to learn, her heroines envision a future replete with new forms of speech and behavior. Because they want a wife to interpret them to the world, the men resemble more sophisticated versions of Christopher Newman.

The terms of romance favor Wharton's heroes but trap them as well.[37] In *The Custom of the Country*, for instance, Ralph Marvell mistakes the Dynamo, representative of a closed, entropic system, for the Virgin, the force that Henry Adams pronounced the greatest and most mysterious of all energies. His desire to save Undine Spragg from Van Degen and Degenism—"the 'call' for which his life had obscurely waited" (*CC*, 49)—teaches him the difference between Mallory's universe and Dreiser's. Responding like a James character in *The Wings of the Dove*, he turns his face to the wall: "the ghost of his illusion . . . he had somehow vivified, coloured, substantiated by the force of his own great need—as a man might breathe a semblance of life into a dear drowned body that he cannot give up for dead" (*CC*, 128).

If Wharton's heroes destroy themselves, like Marvell, or permanently retreat to their libraries, like Newland Archer, her exiled heroines have the chance of securing a space reminiscent of her own:

> As a stranger and newcomer, not only outside of all groups and coteries, but hardly aware of their existence, I enjoyed a freedom not possible in those days to the native-born, who were still enclosed in the old social pigeon-holes, which they had begun to laugh at, but to which they still flew back.
>
> (*ABG*, 258)

Of all Wharton's heroines, Ellen Olenska of *The Age of Innocence* (1920) comes closest to finding a place that accommodates both intellect and soul. Three decades after their parting, Archer speculates:

> she had spent the long interval among people he did not know, in a society he but faintly guessed at, in conditions he would never wholly understand. . . . she had doubtless had other and more tangible companionship.

> (*Age*, 359)

Ellen flourishes in a community which resembles the inner circle, one the artist considers inspirational. "Good talk," Wharton writes, "seems . . . to pass into my mind with a gradual nutritive force sometimes felt only long afterward; it permeates me as a power, an influence, it encloses my universe in a dome of many-coloured glass from which I can detach but few fragments while it builds itself up about me" (*ABG*, 171). "Good talk" showcases, shelters, and renews the self; it provides, in Wharton's mind, all the glories of communion with no attendant violation. "People talk more for themselves," she told Bernard Berenson, "and write more for their correspondents."[38] The Republic of the Spirit, to borrow the metaphor from *The House of Mirth*, is inevitably an existential realm, a kingdom of one. The perfect soulmate may be at most a conglomerate of friends, like the happy few, lovingly but loosely connected, who can give partial voice to each other—Wharton, for example, helping Henry James to continue work on *The Ivory Tower* or Gaillard Lapsley mediating between her and Percy Lubbock.

Ellen is an artist who constructs her identity in much the same way that she metamorphosizes Medora Manson's sitting room—taking the best materials at hand and making them uniquely hers. Having left a realm of "European witchery" (*Age*, 7)—a cross between the court of the Borgias and the stuff of Cinderella's dreams—she enters a world of dull, dignified domesticity governed by "The Family." "Is there nowhere in an American house where one may be by one's self?" she asks Archer. "You're so shy, and yet you're so public. I always feel as if I were in the convent again—or on the stage, before a dreadfully polite audience that never applauds" (*Age*, 132). In old New York, Ellen, who is neither maid nor widow, has no position, no privacy, no place. The Mingotts, the Van der Luydens, and the Lefferts will shelter her if she agrees not to divorce her profligate husband. The solution substitutes one jailer for another. "More's the pity," her grandmother Mingott confides in Archer, "her life is finished" (*Age*, 152).

Mrs. Mingott would have been more accurate observing that Archer's life was over, for the novel (following the format of *The Custom of the Country*) neatly reverses traditional male and female plots: after removing the bandages from Archer's eyes, Ellen adventures into the world beyond, and he remains behind, trapped by familial obligations and social conventions. Archer's domestication succeeds to the degree that even after the death of his wife, May Welland, he is powerless to envision a new life. Although he prides himself on his facility for command, he seeks domination. All the women in the novel—including Ellen, who holds him to his vows—conspire to cage him. Shown off during his engagement "like a wild animal cunningly trapped" (*Age*, 67), he realizes that the years will transform "Newland Archer" into the "Wellands' son-in-law."

Archer rebels in the manner of *The Golden Bowl*'s Prince Amerigo: he makes love to Ellen, a woman who represents all that is not domestic. The dream of escape and rescue feeds his desire no less than it does that of Wharton's heroines. Recalling Sophy, Ellen does not conform to type; she is both the woman "one loved and respected" and the woman one "enjoyed—and pitied" (*Age*, 96). Archer's Ellen Olenska resembles Lambert Strether's Mme. de Vionnet: she is "some fine firm concentrated heroine of an old story, something he had heard, read, something that, had he a hand for drama, he might himself have written."[39]

These men author the women they love much as the men of the inner circle authored Wharton. For them, the allure of a woman lies in the imagined mystery or the art of her speech. Strether best knows Mme. de Vionnet as the possessor of "a language quite to herself . . . a charming slightly strange English" (*Amb.*, 310). Beaufort, who understands "every turn" of Ellen's dialect and "speaks it fluently" (*Age*, 137), is the one man with whom she can be a confrere; Archer never fully comprehends her. He lives "in an atmosphere of faint implications and pale delicacies" (*Age*, 16) where passion and pain, such as Regina Beaufort experiences, have no voice. Wondering "when 'nice' women will begin to speak for themselves" (*Age*, 80), he is not prepared for Ellen's answer. Words such as "adultery" and "mistress," which have a recognizable place in her vocabulary, have no bearing on his individual case. Once they do, his ways of ordering experience crumble, for "'nice' women, however wronged, would never claim the kind of freedom he meant" (*Age*, 43). Archer feels that Ellen represents "reality," then insists on its opposite: a country where one is free from such words. Japan, whose language neither he nor Ellen speaks and which he—like the majority of nineteenth-century travelers—associates with erotic adventures, represents such a land to him. He wants to replicate the world he shares with May, a world where problems are ignored or passively resolved. The original ending to the novel, in which the lovers flee and then separate, makes clear that in six months Ellen's silences will become as intelligible as May's. Better than Ellen, Archer loves the image he invents of himself as a moral Beaufort.

Without invention the Countess Olenska never could have fallen in love with the priggish, slightly fatuous young man we meet at the opera. Initially she imagines him as a bridge between her past and present: "You had felt the world outside tugging at one with all its golden hands—and yet you hated the things it asks of one; you hated happiness bought by disloyalty and cruelty and indifference" (*Age*, 171). Archer's readiness to make Ellen his mistress, his misunderstanding of her relationship with M. Rivière, his eagerness to purchase happiness at May's expense, all contradict Ellen's original assessment. Increasingly she finds that she does not speak his language, that more than any other of "these kind people" he asks her to pretend, to embrace the "real loneliness" (*Age*, 77) of being, like Cassandra, not heard. Too intelligent not to be honest with themselves, Wharton's heroines find that self-communion inhibits desire.

Ellen rejects Archer's proposal to elope and lessens the division, upon which his love rests, between her public and private selves. Following Isabel Archer, he learns the terrible consequences of his theory: "Women ought to be free—free as we are" (*Age*, 41). His final imprisonment insures Ellen's freedom, prevents her from ever becoming another version of Lydia Tillotson, whose marriage to her lover in "Souls Belated" (1899) will make her "nice" and negated (selfless). The alternate ending to the story is read in Lily Bart's or Ralph Marvell's lifeless body. Archer is as "incorrigibly romantic" as Medora Manson, and this makes up "for many things" (*Age*, 164), including his marriage, which in retrospect becomes more than "a dull association of material and social interests held together by ignorance on the one side and hypocrisy on the other" (*Age*, 44).

The reader cannot help suspecting that Archer's redemptive thinking is, in fact, "a humbugging disguise of the inexorable conventions that tied things together and bound people down to the same pattern" (*Age*, 43). He never realizes the full implications of being a spectator rather than a participant in life. Like John Marcher, he confronts his own beast in the jungle, but the realization that he is destined to be the one man "to whom nothing was ever to happen" (*Age*, 227) holds no horror. Watching the sun set outside Ellen's apartment, he thinks, "It's more real to me than if I went up" (*Age*, 362). Wharton saw, and his immobility proves, that old plots had some uses. The episode with Ellen keeps Archer a faithful husband, just as Darrow's interlude with Sophy prods him and Anna toward a true marriage. Nevertheless, it seems cold comfort to believe, as Lambert Strether does, that "it doesn't so much matter what you do in particular, so long as you have your life" (*Amb.*, 132).

The Age of Innocence has no place for an Ellen Olenska or, for that mat-

ter, an Edith Wharton. It cannot survive the spoken, never mind the written, word: "Don't destroy my last illusion," Mr. Welland pleads (*Age*, 272).
Wharton's exiled heroines, to quote Julia Kristeva, cut "through language,
in the direction of the unspeakable."[40] Their paths may be solitary, yet
they lead to a surer sense of self; they lead to the sacred fount of experience
and art. The vocabulary of unusual situations often belongs to fiction and
the stage, but May's last words survive, transformed from platitude by her
son's insistence on defining "the thing most wanted": "She said she knew
we were safe with you, and always would be, because once, when she
asked you to, you'd given up the thing you most wanted" (*Age*, 356). They
suggest that May spent the years of her exile, both within the marriage
and literally from the novel's plot itself, in writing her own fictions.

Ellen and Archer represent the two sides of renunciation. For her it
means greater freedom, while for him it means "only a closer self-impris-
onment."[41] Old New York excluded artists, musicians, and "those who
wrote" (*Age*, 100). If the ideal is, as Archer argues and Wharton's expatriation seems to support, a fusion between these two groups, then it is
not difficult to imagine Ellen creating "a stage [in both its meanings] of
manners where they would naturally merge" (*Age*, 103). The inner circle
certainly combined these two groups; for Wharton, it was the stage Archer intuits, one shaped by a long history and tradition, one that gave its
actors scope. "It's worth everything, isn't it," M. Rivière asks Archer, "to
keep one's intellectual liberty, not to enslave one's powers of appreciation,
one's critical independence?" (*Age*, 200). Archer does neither and misses -
"the flower of life" (*Age*, 200). "The prisoner of a hackneyed vocabulary"
(*Age*, 309), his final message to Ellen is an excuse: "Say I'm old-fashioned"
(*Age*, 361).

Ellen retains her intellectual liberty without selling her soul. How those
terms are defined and synthesized lies outside the scope of the novel and
outside the parameters of the marriage plot. As readers, however, we recognize that the tale of the Newland Archers is as obsolete and obscure to
us as it is to their son, Dallas, and his fiancée, Fanny Beaufort. Ellen keeps
the right to her own story and its publication. She presents a blank page
only to the society she has abandoned. In Paris, her withdrawal is a kind
of dialect, which speaks eloquently of a withholding, itself a retention and
an assertion of self. Ellen's story is the story of the inner circle. Challenging
the values of old New York, it demands that we write an ending to relegate
Archer's nostalgic and sentimental vision to its rightful place, the past.

The Reef and *The Age of Innocence* suggest that the stories of Wharton's
exiled heroines can only be secret. Told, they would begin, much like
Vance Weston's first novel *Instead*, with "the mysterious substitution of
one value for another in a soul which had somehow found peace" (*HRB*,
322). The story of the secret soul must remain undecipherable, if one imag-

ines it housing, as Weston does, a mysterious stranger, "closer than one's bones and yet with a face and speech forever unknown to one" (*HRB*, 45). The formation and practices of a soul at peace is, with the exception of her memoir, a story Wharton never wrote. There she hints at the rich, inspired life she leads in her "secret garden" when she becomes "merely a recording instrument," her hand never hesitating because her mind has not to choose, "only to set down what these stupid or intelligent, lethargic or passionate, people say to each other in a language, and with argument, that appear to be all their own" (*ABG*, 202). Maybe the fictional representation of this process would not have had enough tension; maybe it required a new plot, one that does not unite Vance and Halo Spear at the end of *The Gods Arrive*;[42] maybe she thought it too close to the "me-novels" she disdained, each version reducing, rather than expanding, "the irreducible core of selfness" (*HRB*, 272) she valued.

The "central mystery" remained for Wharton "as impossible to fix in words as that other mystery of what happens in the brain at the precise moment when one falls over the edge of consciousness into sleep" (*ABG*, 198). If creativity is dependent upon solitude, then Wharton had a story no one might want to read, a story whose ending is antisocial and whose nontelling gave her a sense of power that matches Charlotte Lovell's:

> What happens there is as real and as tangible as my encounters with my friends and neighbors, often more so, though on an entirely different plane. It produces in me a great emotional excitement, quite unrelated to the joy or sorrow caused by real happenings, but as intense, and with as great an appearance of reality. . . .
>
> (*ABG*, 205)

As a writer, Wharton considered herself a "realist," and she rejected the ending that belonged to sentimental fiction for two reasons. First, it did not accurately represent what she believed to be this welter of a world: "all the cranks and the theorists cannot master the old floundering monster, or force it for long into any of their neat plans of readjustment" (*ABG*, 379). Second, and more important, the happy marriage rests on a merging, as opposed to a delineation, of identities. The closest relationships in her novels take place between women, like Anna and Sophy or May and Ellen, who forge bonds as a preliminary step to finding themselves.

In relationships between men and women, renunciation becomes the most satisfactory answer, a form of protection that allows one to make adjustments by simply not participating. The solution brings to mind the image of Henry James snugly surrounded by his four brown walls. It reflects Wharton's belief that creativity flourishes in the quietude of one's inmost room, the place where the artist summons characters to life. Solitude may be, as James, Wharton, and the other members of the inner circle thought, a necessary condition for "genius," but does it then follow that all relationships must remain unrealized? Believing that "intellectual companionship between lovers was unattainable" (*GA*, 390), Wharton found with the happy few a satisfactory alternative to what she termed "the miserable poverty of any love that lies outside of marriage, of any love that is not a living together, a sharing of all" (*Portrait*, 103).

In Wharton's life, no man came to the rescue; in the universe of her fiction, no man seems capable of it. The larger and most irrevocable sympathies of her heroes generally belong to the society in which they live. Loving convention and the status quo more than any woman, they perpetuate a patriarchal system that bonds men ultimately and most securely to other men. They support Anthony Storr's argument that "human beings are directed by Nature toward the impersonal [whether writing history, running a bank, or painting landscapes] as well as toward the personal" (Storr, xiii). At the same time, Wharton seems to imply in *The House of Mirth* that this yearning for the impersonal or the "universal," this Republic of the Spirit, is another kind of fraternity: "Why do you call your republic a republic?" Lily asks Selden. "It is a close corporation, and you create arbitrary objections to keep people out" (*HM*, 113). Although this republic particularly excludes Lily who, like all single women in her world, is forced to sell herself to the highest bidder, it also does not belong to Selden: "It is *not* my republic," he stresses. It is, though, his to enter more freely.[43] Lily's question and Selden's answer underscore the fallacious notion of a "universal," even for those whom we think define it.

As the only woman in a group of men, Wharton could not escape the fact that she was an anomaly. The "otherness" that was a source of pride was also a source of fear, another form of linguistic and spiritual exile. Wharton never mentions any connections between the lives portrayed in her fiction and those she encountered among her friends, but her best-known ghost story, "The Eyes" (1910), seems to present a corrupted version of the inner circle. Wharton asks: What happens when you confront a stranger in yourself? What if you have never known your closest friends?

A story within a story, "The Eyes" is both parable and mirror. The protagonist, Andrew Culwin, tells a group of intimates about the two times he saw a pair of disembodied eyes. The first visitation occurs after he insincerely proposes marriage. At night he wakes, haunted by eyes whose "orbits were sunk," whose lids were "like blinds of which the cords are broken."[44] They continue to haunt him until he abandons his fiancée and the novel he is writing and flees to Europe. The second visitation follows a similar betrayal in which he lies to a young protégé about the merit of the younger man's work. This time the eyes are worse: "Worse by just so much as I'd learned of life in the interval; by all the damnable implications my wider experience read into them" ("Eyes," 126). They vanish only after he admits what he thinks: the stuff's no good. As Culwin finishes his story, he glances in the mirror and sees—as does his latest protégé—the eyes he has described glowing from his own congested face.

The eyes come from Culwin's betrayal of others and his betrayal of himself. Their appearance is directly linked to Culwin's abandonment of art in the first instance and the falsification of it in the second and third. Wharton argues that artistic and personal integrity cannot be separated. Despite her assertion that "the 'moral issue' question must not be allowed to enter into the estimating of a ghost story," "The Eyes" contains a moral.[45] Culwin's personal and artistic failures occur because he refuses to confront his own doubleness. The company of those happy few who mirror his thoughts and feelings has allowed him to avoid this other, horrifying self.

From Culwin's point of view, the story also suggests what it means to be "other," what it must feel like to be watched by reproachful, accusing, judgmental eyes. Belonging to the inner circle involved a similar if more benign form of scrutiny, in which one was both the shaper and the subject of the *donnée*. The horror in "The Eyes" lies in the "I." Culwin experiments with the youths he favors, and his patronizing friendship is a disintegrating influence. His role as experimenter-spectator-artist transforms him into a horrific old man who likes "'em juicy" ("Eyes," 116). On the other hand, he watches himself while watched by his recruits, who have the potential to make him at any moment see himself with their eyes. The story makes one wonder if Wharton questioned her own motives, if she intuited Lubbock's unflattering portrait of her in the memoir that bears her name.

The question of where fictional lives became lived and lived lives fictional must remain unanswered. In her letters to the happy few, Edith Wharton tried to deny the gap between language and meaning, self and other. She authored a world where history gave way to romance. But what she wrote for the inner circle, she unwrote in her memoir. Emphasizing individuals over the group and bio, the story of her life, over its emotional texture, she conforms to a tradition usually attributed to male autobiographers.[46] There fiction gives way to history, the collective to the individual. Somewhere perhaps in the division between fiction and history lies the source of exile. Like her heroines, Wharton leaves this region, the result of an imperfect world, unarticulated.

When members of the inner circle spent weeks together living like family, they allowed one another the dignity of silence, the right to their own interior lives. "What is the significance of English silence, and to what does it correspond?" asks Bernard Berenson. "Certain circles specifically create the cult of 'disposition,' proclaiming the rule which forbids doing anything to which one is not 'disposed,' so when you don't feel like talking you don't talk."[47] Percy Lubbock was an initiate of this club, as were Robert Norton and Gaillard Lapsley. "I must tell you about my fellow cavaliers," Nicky Mariano wrote Berenson,

> Lapsley yesterday did not utter one word. He morosely munched or read or meditated. Norton was scarcely better. He too spends most of his time when indoors reading by himself. Last night both men fell upon the two last numbers of *The Times* that had just arrived while Edith whirled through *Punch, The Times Literary Supplement* and the illustrated papers.[48]

Among themselves, the happy few possessed the ability—some might say the genius—to occupy their own secret gardens. In her heart of hearts, Wharton believed that at crucial moments the same veil of unreality would always fall between herself and the soul nearest her, that "the creator of imaginary beings must always feel alone among the real ones" (*HRB*, 536). Yet the hushed turning of the pages testifies to the depth of the inner circle's intimacy, their faith in "that solitary spark of understanding burning in another mind like a little light in an isolated house" (*HRB*, 482).

A Meditation on Place

*We live in our own souls as in an unmapped region, a few
acres of which we have cleared for our habitation; while of
the nature of those nearest us we know but the boundaries
that march with ours.*
EDITH WHARTON, *THE TOUCHSTONE*

*America is my country and Paris is my home town . . . and I
have lived half my life in Paris, not the half that made me
but the half in which I made what I made.*
GERTRUDE STEIN, "AN AMERICAN AND FRANCE"

WHATEVER HOMES OR COUNTRIES we have are deep down in us.
Identity and place may not be synonymous, but in some ways they seem
inseparable. The corners we hid in as children or the wallpaper covered
with cabbages in an aunt's front hall mark the stages of our evolving consciousness as tangibly as first teeth or school diplomas. The meanings associated with and generated by place help to determine cultural as well as
personal identity. Home is "the form of the dream," Larry Levis writes,
"and not the dream" itself.[1] Certainly this proved true of the inner circle
and its expatriate members, who fleeing the constrictions of one environment rooted themselves in another. Walter Berry returned to Paris, the
place of his birth, and Gaillard Lapsley became, like T. S. Eliot, more
British than the British. When Henry James—to use his own phrase—
"took possession" of London in 1876, he little realized how his adopted
country would gradually possess him. Renouncing his American citizenship in 1915, James ceased being a stranger: he paid literally with his person.
In her tireless efforts for the Belgium refugees during the First World War,
Edith Wharton did the same. "Exquisite stranger as she was," Madame
Saint-René Taillandier testifies, she "went deep into our French life, to our
people and the ministrants of our faith."[2]

The inner circle appreciated places rich in history, both remote and immediate. For Wharton especially, the past so informed the present that

they sometimes existed contemporaneously. Robert Norton tells us that she could not approach the Mediterranean without imagining Xerxes on his throne watching the battle of Salamis, nor could she look at the coastline without conjuring Barbary pirates. Almost painfully sensitive to space, itself transformed into place as it acquires definition and meaning,[3] she advised parents to direct their children's tastes by decorating their rooms with large photographs of old Flemish and Italian prints—Bellini's baby angels, for example—rather than Christmas cards, newspaper chromos, and storybook pictures, "put together without any attempt at color-harmony or composition."[4] Written to educate the wives of Midwest millionaires invading old New York, Wharton's *The Decoration of Houses* (1897) argues—as does James's *The Portrait of a Lady* (1881) and Howard Sturgis's *Belchamber* (1904)—that place not only reflects but also shapes an interior domain. Bernard Berenson echoed James's Madame Merle and confusedly incorporated Wharton's metaphor of the innermost room when he observed that a house has "a social and even political importance beyond one's clothes even, for these are seen by fewer people: acquaintances, friends who can penetrate under one's outer garments and some one or two who get so far as to see one naked and unashamed."[5]

The symbolic value of place was not lost on a group whose very name, "the inner circle," situated it. *Earlham* (1922) and *Shades of Eton* (1929) show Percy Lubbock intent on defining places he internalized, while his memoir of Wharton dispassionately addresses what he perceived to be the detrimental effect of cultural displacement on her fiction. Gaillard Lapsley saw the intrinsic qualities of place contributing to the formation of Great Britain's constitution, its policies, and its persona. Bernard Berenson felt that he had the Renaissance in his blood. John Hugh Smith, a member of an old English family and himself the recipient of the advantages of a class associated with specific places such as Eton, wondered whether his "place" and its attendant responsibilities were not strangling his soul.

In Robert Norton's watercolor landscapes, which tacitly extend Wharton's argument about the interdependence of place and self in *The Decoration of Houses*, the former assumes another, more ephemeral dimension, becoming something we create, not something that exists in and of itself.[6] The flickering light reflected in his large canvases, the shimmering, almost palpitating colors that allowed him to dispense with outline, force the viewer to piece together each brush stroke, to join it with component parts, until the scene coalesces into what Elizabeth Bishop in "The Fish" calls "rainbow, rainbow, rainbow!" Empty of people, Norton's emotionally charged landscapes seem to ask the viewer to imagine the lives that are or are not lived in them, the lives that could be.

Following a tradition of expatriation as old as the beginning of their nation, the American members of the inner circle had a vision of manifest destiny that took them east, not west. Where they differed from a group like Bloomsbury, which also had ties to France, and many of their compatriots—including Benjamin Franklin, James Fenimore Cooper, Stephen Crane, Ernest Hemingway, Gertrude Stein, and F. Scott Fitzgerald—was in their allegiance to their chosen places of exile. For James, Sturgis, Berry, and Wharton, place and self slowly intertwined. For Lapsley, the two never wholly grafted: dividing his time between Cambridge and Connecticut, he found himself exiled from one home or another. Norton's concern with the effect of color and light on perception aligns him with a painter like Vanessa Bell, whose interiors are often independent of the people they reflect.[7] His thinking about the self-constructed quality of place locates Norton alongside those writers in the twenties who followed James to Europe and settled, like Wharton, in Paris. "If you are lucky enough to have lived in Paris as a young man," Hemingway wrote a friend, "then wherever you go for the rest of your life, it stays with you."[8] Memory and place seem to grant, as Hemingway suggests, a sense of a continuous self.[9] The causal relationship between place and self reflects the dream of the American Adam: if, as *A Moveable Feast* (1964) asserts, "there is never any ending to Paris" (*MF*, 208–209), there may not be any limit to oneself. Place retains its integrity or constancy through memory, which allows one to recover for an instant a previous incarnation.

The concreteness of place, especially in Fitzgerald's mannered portraits of the jazz age, highlighted the Lost Generation's sense of alienation or homelessness, which itself afforded a kind of liberation. In his thinking about place, Fitzgerald was closer to the inner circle than his contemporaries. He may have acted as though the world existed for his own pleasure, but he knew that those pleasures were illusory. To the inner circle, those avid readers of Ruskin, place exerted a sacred influence. "It is Ruskin," James writes in *Italian Hours* (1909) "who beyond anyone helps us to enjoy."[10] Ruskin taught them that civilization allows the artist to appreciate the beauty of nature,[11] whose significance comes from human endurance, valor, and virtue. Wharton especially appreciated landscapes she thought "sophisticated," those "where the face of nature seems moulded by the passions and imaginings of men."[12]

The next generation was more pragmatic. Gertrude Stein—who shared with Wharton a childhood spent partly abroad, a liking for the Berensons, and a love of dogs, motorcars, and contained spaces—simply sought a place that did not take anything away. The wish, itself a critique of the country left behind, suggests a fluid relationship, which Stein sought to circumvent, between self and place.[13] Like Wharton, she created a Land of Letters. By living in France and refusing to read French, she made English hers in a way that it could not be in the United States. Here she could preserve and dismantle the language in a private laboratory of self. Because she was the authority, no one could (or, as legend goes, dared) take any-thing away. Stein barricaded herself with words, and they sealed her in a double envelope, wrapping the signature of self (what Wharton called the "irreducible core") in its own self-narrative. The strategy isolated Stein as much as it maintained the writer's integrity. Arguing that there is little distinction between "space," "time," and "self," she states that "a space of time is a natural thing for an American to always have inside them as something in which they are continuously moving."[14]

In contrast to Stein, Wharton chose Paris for what it gave. No one could live there without literature: "the fact that I was a professional writer, instead of frightening my fashionable friends, interested them."[15] To her, French culture had an eminently social quality missing in the Anglo-Saxon countries. Place could emanate from self: "wherever two or three educated French people are gathered together, a *salon* immediately comes into be-ing" (*ABG*, 262). Wharton did her best to master the intricate protocol of dinners in the Faubourg: "an Academician takes precedence of every one but a Duke or an Ambassador . . . a foreigner of no rank whatever takes precedence of every rank but that of an Academician, a Cardinal or an Ambassador" (*ABG*, 261). Percy Lubbock observes that "she had a closer intimacy with France than it is often granted to an alien—with France of the French, the old and the traditional, which has never easily opened to a stranger's knock" (*Portrait*, 171).

Although Wharton and Stein really experienced two different countries, France welcomed them both. Paris, to Stein's mind, was the only place—because of its unassailable sense of its own identity—for artists interested in shaping the future. She and Wharton each located the city's allure in its past and people: for the French, Stein writes: "life is tradition and human nature."[16] Despite their differences, Stein, James, and Whar-ton luxuriated in the freedom, not the angst, of exile, which Ezra Pound often found in the place selected rather than the one deserted. One must beat out exile, he writes in "The Rest."

Wharton may have come more as a supplicant to the French aristocrats and academicians on the Right Bank and Stein as a pasha to the American artists and collectors on the Left, but the salon gave them both a stage. It was a place that simultaneously could be singular and shared, private and public. The talk that Wharton found in the salon of Rosa de Fitz-James suited her for two reasons: it centered on ideas and it regulated relation-ships. Stein observed that "humanly speaking, Frenchwomen nor French-men do not really interest themselves in intimacy, intimacy is something essentially uncivilized. . . ." (*PF*, 39). The structure of the salon, which demanded that one listen as well as converse, secured individual privacy and restricted involvement to the free meeting of like minds. It particularly appealed to Stein and Wharton, who complained about the openness and the promiscuity of American homes.

Unlike other women, whose "absorbed and intelligent attention . . . makes a perfect background for the talk of men" (*ABG*, 274), Wharton and Stein were equal competitors, bringing, as Wharton writes, their best "for barter" (*ABG*, 273). To compete a woman had to have "a man's sense of fair play" (*ABG*, 277). The great female conversationalists claimed the power associated with men without diminishing their power as women: after all, they were the spectacle. Ford Madox Ford sensed this about Stein in another context when he described her "trundling" through the streets in her high-wheeled American car, being a spectacle and being herself at the same time. Katherine Anne Porter saw Stein belonging to "the company of Amazons,"

> which nineteenth-century America produced among its prodigies: not-men, not-women, answerable to no function in either sex, whose careers were carried on, and how successfully, in whatever field they chose: they were educators, writers, editors, politicians, artists, world travelers, and international hostesses, who lived in public and by the public and played out their self-assumed, self-created rôles in such masterly freedom as only a few medieval queens had equaled.[17]

Minus Porter's obvious bias against Stein's lesbianism, the description could also fit Wharton, whose humorous characterization of herself as a self-made man called attention to her "feminine" charms and her "masculine" intelligence. Wharton envied men their "closer connection to reality" (defined in terms of "civilization" rather than "nature") and their wider audience, which the "sheltered life" denied women: "It is because American women are each other's only audience," she writes in *French Ways and Their Meaning* (1919), "and to a great extent each other's only companions, that they seem, compared to women who play an intellectual and social part in the lives of men, like children in a baby-school."[18]

Stein's salon at rue de Fleurus—"a kind of cultural halfway house between the European vanguard [including Roger Fry, Wyndham Lewis, and Clive Bell] and the nearest beginnings of the *avant-garde* in the United States"—mirrored her place in the Paris literary community.[19] Amid the crowd, she liked the feel of her own isolation or self-containment. In a sense, she was a room of her own. As Shari Benstock writes, "she had separated herself from the world of women [by respectably encasing herself in middle-class domesticity] and she [a self-proclaimed genius and the mother of the twentieth century] was a powerful threat to the community of men."[20] If Stein was her own standpoint in a collective universe, this stance perhaps made possible—or at least mitigated the consequences of—the intentional separation of language from meaning. Unlike Wharton, Stein welcomed comparisons to James. She particularly admired his ability to detach the whole paragraph "from what it said what it did" and "what it was from what it held": "over it all something floated not floated away but just floated, floated up there" (*LA*, 53). Acknowledging a debt to America, the place that first made her, she implies that places, in which she made what she made, exist archetypally in oneself. They are self-perpetuated and perpetuating in the sense that one births and imprints them. In this, she differs from Virginia Woolf, who, surrendering her own agency, thought that the whole world was a work of art and that we are parts of it.[21]

Despite Woolf's belief that "a writer's country is a territory within his own brain,"[22] Bloomsbury also sought in France a model for art and a way of living. Vanessa Bell, Duncan Grant, and Roger Fry exhibited there. Because of the positive response to his work, Fry felt especially at home: "I do feel now that I've got somewhere where no one else in England has, but I don't think that that'll help me in England."[23] Bell and Grant set up housekeeping at La Bergère in Cassis, a small fishing village between Marseille and Toulon.[24] Woolf saw her sister creating a kind of artists' utopia, a place where love and work fed one another. At La Bergère, Bell had a salon comparable to the ones Wharton and Stein enjoyed. The members of Bloomsbury, who could tolerate a rootless life no more than those of the inner circle, almost immediately arrived on her doorstep. Unlike the inner circle, however, Bloomsbury replicated England in France. La Bergère was an extension of their English home, Charleston, itself reminiscent of the Stephens's summer house at St. Ives. Bell tried to lead an antisocial life in France, and this made it possible for her to re-create Charleston's oasis of culture, independent of place. Charleston and La Bergère combined architecture and painting in a way that Wharton would have appreciated in principle, if not in execution. Over the years, their walls, furniture, and contents "came to bear the distinctive palette of lilac, gray and yellow, pale salmon and unripe apple-green, and the voluptuous shapes of nymphs and gods, bowls of flowers and fruit, circles and bars."[25] This created a sense of continuity and security, reinforced by the household pattern of reserving (as did the inner circle) mornings for work and afternoons for play.

Esteemers of habit, James and Wharton anchored themselves in their chosen places of exile. Wharton had only disdain for Riviera drifters, portrayed as parasites in *The Mother's Recompense* (1925) and *The Gods Arrive* (1932), and James advised tourists to reexamine their own perspectives. He liked and repeated the observation, "What you call dirt, I call color."[26] If one can lie at ease "in the bosom of the past," he writes in *Italian Hours*, one practices an intimacy "so much greater than the mere accidental and ostensible" (*IH*, 505). As *Italian Hours* and James's other travel writing illustrate, that intimacy, which involves a heightened awareness of passing thoughts and sensations, is with oneself, possibly with another. The motor-flight that James and Wharton took through France, for instance, sealed their friendship. The voyeuristic delight they experienced in "taking a town unawares, stealing on it by back ways and unchronicled paths, and surprising in it some intimate aspect of past time,"[27] served as a paradigm for their developing relationship.

In truth, France was, for all the expatriates it homed, an abstraction, an imagined "other" country to one's own—a kind of wonderland where values and assumptions were turned upside down. Fitzgerald's *Tender is the Night* (1934) perhaps best captures the dark side of the looking glass. For Wharton and the inner circle, Wordsworth's formula was always at one's disposal, "and emotion recollected in tranquility could be made to live again."[28] "When I now return to Earlham and wander through my thought of the house and garden," Percy Lubbock writes, "it is always to-day and to-day only: there is no budding morrow, bringing on the unknown."[29] Memory is "safe" for Lubbock because it keeps the past intact. James argues much the same in *The American Scene* (1907): "there was no escape from the ubiquitous alien into the future, or even into the present; there was an escape but into the past."[30] Despite this assertion, the book itself shows how (unlike James's hero in *The Sense of the Past*) one cannot step into an earlier time or an earlier self. Even if our perceptions of place did not change as we changed, our perceptions of ourselves would. Wharton plays with the concurrent evolution of place and self most in her ghost stories. "Kerfol," for example, contains a manor house that is a repository of ever-accumulating histories, of present lives lived in the context of consuming past ones.[31] Memory may be finally, as Hadley Hemingway said, a kind of hunger (*ME*, 56).

Binding all the lives we lead, place becomes, in a sense, memory's, even the self's, objective correlative. The inner circle longed to realize all the meanings found in "place"—a sense of identity, a feeling of belonging, a connection to the past, a page in history. Yet they remained, like all sensitive minds, as Ellen Glasgow writes, exiles on earth.[32] In what place then can we see a group which saw itself nowhere and everywhere? How do we place a group primarily defined by its geographical, cultural, and sexual displacement? Of the inner circle, Bloomsbury, and the next generation of American expatriates, one might wonder if their true lives were here or there, "here in this ancient order, fabric of centuries, or there in the other world, the world still in the making," communed with in books (*Portrait*, 172). Percy Lubbock answers for Wharton: "It was neither here nor there, it was securely in herself . . . she couldn't be less than herself, or more either, whatever her surroundings" (*Portrait*, 172). The same is true for all these leaders of double lives, actual and dreamed, in places tangible and intangible. Although their spirits must finally be found in lands of their own making, they can also be found, as Wharton's *The Touchstone* (1900) reminds us, in that unmapped region of the heart, along the border where you imagine another marches.

Notes

PREFACE

1. Edith Wharton, *A Backward Glance*, 169.

2. Letter of Henry James to Edith Wharton, February 8, 1910, *Henry James and Edith Wharton, Letters: 1900–1915*, ed. Lyall H. Powers, 146–147.

3. Margaret Chanler, memoir of Edith Wharton, Percy Lubbock Papers, Beinecke Library, p. 2.

4. Edith Wharton, *The Custom of the Country*, 45.

5. Letter of Edith Wharton to Bernard Berenson, February 17, 1917, *The Letters of Edith Wharton*, ed. R. W. B. Lewis and Nancy Lewis, 392–393.

6. R. G. Collingwood, *The Idea of History*, 246.

7. Virginia Woolf, "Sketch of the Past," in *Moments of Being*, ed. Jeanne Schulkind, 72.

8. Bernard Berenson, *The Bernard Berenson Treasury*, ed. Hanna Kiel, 138 (hereafter cited as *BBT*).

9. Alain Besançon, "Vers une histoire psychanalytique," in *Histoire et expérience du moi*, 66.

10. Ernest Hemingway, Preface to *A Moveable Feast*.

INTRODUCTION. EDITH WHARTON'S INNER CIRCLE

1. Percy Lubbock, *Portrait of Edith Wharton*, 3 (hereafter cited as *Portrait*). I have taken liberty with my description in using details from the May 1906 gathering at Qu'Acre, which John Hugh Smith did not attend.

2. See Edith Wharton, *A Backward Glance*, 367 (hereafter cited as *ABG*). James supposedly uttered the phrase before he died.

3. Edith Wharton, "The Fullness of Life," in *The Collected Short Stories of Edith Wharton*, ed. R. W. B. Lewis, 1: 16–17 (hereafter cited as "Life").

4. Edith Wharton, *The House of Mirth*, 108.

5. Letter of Henry James to Edith Wharton, August 17, 1902, *Henry James and Edith Wharton, Letters: 1900–1915*, ed. Lyall H. Powers, 33–35.

6. Desmond MacCarthy, "Henry James," in *Portraits*, 149–150.

7. Letter of Edith Wharton to Gaillard Lapsley, April 12, 1913, Beinecke Library.

8. Letter of Percy Lubbock to Gaillard Lapsley, April 7, 1913, Beinecke Library.

9. Letter of Percy Lubbock to Gaillard Lapsley, April 16, 1913, Beinecke Library. For additonal information about the birthday gift to James, see Fred Kaplan, *Henry James: The Imagination of Genius*, 547–548.

10. Gerard Hopkins, Introduction to *Belchamber*, by Howard Sturgis, ix (hereafter cited as Hopkins).

11. Percy Lubbock, *Mary Cholmondeley: A Sketch from Memory*, 59, 60.

12. Harry Crosby, *Shadows of the Sun: The Diaries of Harry Crosby*, ed. Edward Germain, 62.

13. The 1956 date for the end of Bloomsbury is based on the last meeting of the Memoir Club and not on Virginia Woolf's death in 1941.

14. Patricia O'Toole, *The Five of Hearts: An Intimate Portrait of Henry Adams and His Friends, 1880–1918*, xii.

15. Letter of Henry James to Howard Sturgis, February 22, 1912, by permission of Houghton Library, bMS Am 1094 (1245). See Kaplan, *Henry James*, 512. Kaplan states that Wharton told James about her affair with Fullerton in early 1908.

16. Letter of Henry James to Gaillard Lapsley, January 12, 1912, in Millicent Bell, *Edith Wharton and Henry James: The Story of Their Friendship*, 178.

17. Letter of Henry James to Gaillard Lapsley, February 13 [1912], in M. Bell, *Edith Wharton and Henry James*, 179.

18. Letter of Henry James to Howard Sturgis, February 20, 1912, in M. Bell, *Edith Wharton and Henry James*, 179.

19. Letter of Henry James to Howard Sturgis, February 20, 1912, in M. Bell, *Edith Wharton and Henry James*, 179.

20. Letter of Edith Wharton to Gaillard Lapsley, September 21 [1908], Beinecke Library.

21. Letter of Edith Wharton to John Hugh Smith, April 30 [1909], *The Letters of Edith Wharton*, ed. R. W. B. Lewis and Nancy Lewis, 177–178.

22. Letter of Edith Wharton to Bernard Berenson, February 12, 1934, *Letters of Edith Wharton*, 574–576.

23. Letter of Edith Wharton to Gaillard Lapsley, May 27 [1917], Beinecke Library.

24. In *Hudson River Bracketed* (1929), Vance Weston criticizes the "me-novelists" who write disguised autobiography. See Margaret B. McDowell, "*Hudson River Bracketed* and *The Gods Arrive*," in *Edith Wharton*, ed. Harold Bloom, 53–56 esp.

25. Edith Wharton, "Henry James in His Letters," *Quarterly Review* 234 (1920): 194.

26. See George Santayana, *Persons and Places*, 52.

27. See Colin Simpson, *Artful Partners: Bernard Berenson and Joseph Duveen*.

28. Leon Edel, *Henry James: A Life*, 38–55.

29. Letter of Edith Wharton to Sara Norton, June 5, 1903, *Letters of Edith Wharton*, 84–85.

30. Henry James, *Notes of a Son and Brother*, in *Henry James: Autobiography*, ed. Frederick W. Dupee, 277 (hereafter cited as *Notes*).

31. William Dean Howells, *Literature and Life*, 202.

32. Letter of Henry James to Thomas Sargeant Perry, September 1867, Edel, *Henry James: A Life*, 87.

33. George W. Stocking, Jr., *Victorian Anthropology*, 29.

34. Letter of Edith Wharton to Gaillard Lapsley, April 13, 1927, Beinecke Li-

brary. Wharton is repeating a remark to Lapsley that she originally made to Walter Berry.

35. Charles Eliot Norton, *Notes of Travel and Study in Italy*, 1–2, quoted in T. J. Jackson Lears, *No Place of Grace: Antimodernism and the Transformation of American Culture, 1880–1920*, 244.

36. Letter of Henry James to Thomas Sargeant Perry, September 1867, Edel, *Henry James: A Life*, 87.

37. The expatriate members of the inner circle established identities by defining themselves, like the American Adam, "happily bereft of ancestry." See R. W. B. Lewis, *The American Adam: Innocence, Tragedy, and Tradition in the Nineteenth Century*, 5.

38. See Ruth Bernard Yeazell, *The Death and Letters of Alice James*, 21; also see Tom Lutz, *American Nervousness, 1903: An Anecdotal History*, 248.

39. See Edith Wharton, "The Valley of Childish Things, and Other Emblems," in *Collected Short Stories*, 1: 58–64. The heroine travels as an equal with a male companion, but when they return home she finds that he now prefers less independent women.

40. Respectively, letter of Percy Lubbock to Gaillard Lapsley, August 5, 1913, Beinecke Library; letter of Edith Wharton to Gaillard Lapsley, August 30 [1913], Beinecke Library.

41. Edith Wharton, *French Ways and Their Meaning*, 110 (hereafter cited as *FW*).

42. Letter of Edith Wharton to Gaillard Lapsley, February 18 [1913], Beinecke Library.

43. See Shari Benstock, "Expatriate Modernism," in *Women's Writing in Exile*, ed. Mary Lynn Broe and Angela Ingram, 19–40. Benstock argues that *matria* must always be ex*patria*ted (25).

44. Martha Banta, *Imaging American Women: Ideas and Ideals in Cultural History*, 6, 46–47, 254, 258 esp.

45. Theodore Roosevelt, *The Strenuous Life*, 18–19.

46. Henry James, *The American Scene*, 350.

47. See Santayana, *Persons and Places*, 357–360.

48. Percy Lubbock, *Mary Cholmondeley: A Sketch from Memory*, 61.

49. Letter of Geoffrey Scott to Vita Sackville-West, September 13, 1924. I am indebted to Richard Dunn for the reference and Nigel Nicolson for permission to use the quotation.

50. Letter of Edith Wharton to Bernard Berenson, September 4, 1917, *Letters of Edith Wharton*, 398–399.

51. Letter of Edith Wharton to Gaillard Lapsley, February 25 [1914], Beinecke Library.

52. Edith Wharton, *The Reef*, 124.

53. See Barbara Belford, *Violet: The Story of the Irrepressible Violet Hunt and Her Circle of Lovers and Friends—Ford Madox Ford, H. G. Wells, Somerset Maugham, and Henry James*, 162–165 esp. Also see Robert Secor, "Henry James and Violet Hunt, the 'Improper Person of Babylon,'" *Journal of Modern Literature* 13 (March 1986): 3–36.

54. Letter of Henry James to Edith Wharton, Oct. 9, 1913, *Henry James and Edith Wharton*, 269.

55. See Katherine Joslin-Jeske, "What Lubbock Didn't Say," *Edith Wharton Newsletter* 1.1 (Spring 1984): 2–4.

56. Letter of Howard Sturgis to Edith Wharton, Sunday, Sept. 16, 1917, Beinecke Library.

57. Leon Edel, "Walter Berry and the Novelists: Proust, James, and Edith Wharton," *Nineteenth-Century Fiction* 38 (March 1984): 528.

58. See Elizabeth Ammons, *Conflicting Stories: American Women Writers at the Turn into the Twentieth Century*, 158–159 esp.

59. Edith Wharton, "All Souls'," in *Collected Short Stories*, 2: 880 (hereafter cited as "AS").

60. See Annette Zilversmit, "Edith Wharton's Last Ghosts," *College Literature* 14 (Fall 1987): 296–304. Zilversmit isolates the source of Sara Clayburn's loneliness within herself. Also see Allan Gardner Smith, "Edith Wharton and the Ghost Story," in *Gender and Literary Voice*, ed. Janet Todd. Smith sees Wharton addressing the "unease of women in male roles, mistrust between women and the distortions of the master/servant, employer/employee situations" (92).

61. See Ross Posnick, *Henry James and the Problem of Robert Browning*, 10.

62. Gertrude Stein, *Paris France*, 2.

63. Letter of Henry James to Grace Norton, July 28 [1883], *The Letters of Henry James*, ed. Percy Lubbock, 1: 100–102.

1. THE LAND OF LETTERS

1. Percy Lubbock, *Portrait of Edith Wharton*, 28 (hereafter cited as *Portrait*).

2. See Elmer Borkland, "Howard Sturgis, Henry James, and *Belchamber*," *Modern Philology* 58 (May 1961): 255–269.

3. Edith Wharton, *A Backward Glance*, 192 (hereafter cited as *ABG*).

4. Letter of Howard Sturgis to Edith Wharton, December 3, 1904, Beinecke Library. For a description of the houseparty, see Fred Kaplan, *Henry James: The Imagination of Genius*, 482.

5. Edith Wharton, "Life and I," Beinecke Library, p. 24.

6. Nicky Mariano, *Forty Years with Berenson*, 162. See Gaillard Lapsley, "E. W.," Beinecke Library, p. 2 (hereafter cited as GL). The manuscript is part of the Percy Lubbock Papers, for his memoir of Wharton. Lubbock renumbered Lapsley's pages beginning at 106. Lapsley described seeing Wharton in her bedroom this way: "A three quarter modern wooden bed painted in some light shade, and flanked by night tables charged with telephone, travelling clock, reading light and such like. The room in half darkness and a log smouldering on the little hearth and Edith herself sitting up in bed with the light falling over her right shoulder gave you the chiaroscuro of a Vermeer interior without the slightest effect of calculation except that of convenience."

7. Letter of Edith Wharton to John Hugh Smith, October 15, 1927, *The Letters of Edith Wharton*, ed. R. W. B. Lewis and Nancy Lewis, 504–505.

8. G. C. R. Eley, "G. T. Lapsley: Sketch from a Pupil's Angle," Trinity College Library, 6 (hereafter cited as Eley). For information on Lapsley's relationship with James, see Kaplan, *Henry James*, 453–456.

9. Bernard Berenson, *Sunset and Twilight: From the Diaries of 1947–1958*, ed. Nicky Mariano, 285 (hereafter cited as *S & T*).

10. *The Diary of Arthur Christopher Benson*, ed. Percy Lubbock, 139.

11. See Charles Sanders Peirce, *Values in a Universe of Chance: Selected Writings of Charles S. Peirce*, ed. Phillip P. Wiener. Also see Vincent G. Potter, *Charles S. Peirce: On Norms and Ideals*.

12. Letter of Edith Wharton to John Hugh Smith, March 21, 1925, Beinecke Library.

13. Letter of John Hugh Smith to Percy Lubbock, February 17, 1938, Beinecke Library.

14. Letter of Edith Wharton to John Hugh Smith, November 25 [1912], *Letters of Edith Wharton*, 284–285.

15. Letter of Edith Wharton to John Hugh Smith, May 21 [1909], *Letters of Edith Wharton*, 187–188.

16. Letter of Edith Wharton to John Hugh Smith, April 30 [1909], *Letters of Edith Wharton*, 177–178.

17. Letter of Edith Wharton to Morton Fullerton [February 1909], *Letters of Edith Wharton*, 176.

18. For a discussion of the similarities between *The Reef* and Wharton's letters to Fullerton, see Susan Goodman, *Edith Wharton's Women: Friends and Rivals*, 87–89 esp. Also see Clare Colquitt, "Unpacking Her Treasures: Edith Wharton's 'Mysterious Correspondence' with Morton Fullerton," *Library Chronicle of the University of Texas* 31 (1985): 73–107; and Alan Gribben's introduction to the volume, which he edited, 7–18.

19. Letter of Edith Wharton to Bernard Berenson, July 10, 1933, *Letters of Edith Wharton*, 562–563.

20. Letter of Edith Wharton to John Hugh Smith, February 14, 1919, Beinecke Library.

21. Robert Norton, "Memoir," Beinecke Library, p. 13 (hereafter cited as RN).

22. Bernard Berenson, *Sketch for a Self-Portrait*, 52.

23. Ernest Samuels, with Jayne Newcomer Samuels, *Bernard Berenson: The Making of a Legend*, 468.

24. Meryle Secrest, *Being Bernard Berenson: A Biography*, 331.

25. Bernard Berenson, *Rumor and Reflection*, 204.

26. R. W. B. Lewis, *Edith Wharton: A Biography*, 148, 137.

27. Maurice Beebe, *Ivory Towers and Sacred Founts: The Artist as Hero in Fiction from Goethe to Joyce*.

28. Sandra M. Gilbert and Susan Gubar, *No Man's Land: The Place of the Woman Writer in the Twentieth Century*, 278.

29. Cynthia Griffin Wolff, *A Feast of Words: The Triumph of Edith Wharton*, 1–54 esp.

30. Sandra M. Gilbert and Susan Gubar, *The Madwoman in the Attic: The Woman Writer and the Nineteenth-Century Literary Imagination*, 73–74.

31. Letter of Howard Sturgis to Edith Wharton, February 10, 1913, Beinecke Library.

32. Letter of Percy Lubbock to Gaillard Lapsley, July 24, 1912, Beinecke Library.

33. Letter of Percy Lubbock to Gaillard Lapsley, February 23, 1926, Beinecke Library.

34. Letter of Henry James to Howard Sturgis, February 1, 1910, by permission of Houghton Library, bMS Am 1094 (1269).

35. Letter of Henry James to Morton Fullerton, February 25, 1897, *Henry James Letters*, ed. Leon Edel, vol. 4 (1895–1916), 41–42.

36. See Judith Sensibar, "Edith Wharton Reads the Bachelor Type: Her Critique of Modernism's Representative Man," *American Literature* 60 (December 1988): 575–590. Sensibar describes Wharton's heroes as having a Prufrockian sensibility. Also see Carol J. Singley, "Gothic Borrowings and Innovations in Edith Wharton's 'A Bottle of Perrier,'" in *Edith Wharton: New Critical Essays*, ed. Alfred Bendixen and Annette Zilversmit, 271–290, 278 esp. Singley argues that Wharton underwrites "the male homoerotic with the story of the female mother" (287) and presents homosexual relationships as another critique of patriarchal power.

37. See Barbara White, *Edith Wharton: A Study of the Short Fiction*; Gloria Erlich, *The Sexual Education of Edith Wharton*; David Holbrook, *Edith Wharton and the Unsatisfactory Man*; and Tom Lutz, *American Nervousness, 1903: An Anecdotal History*, 312n.20.

38. See Alfred Habegger, *Henry James and the "Woman Business,"* 1–2.

39. Letter of Edith Wharton to Bernard Berenson, August 14, 1935, *Letters of Edith Wharton*, 588–589.

40. Sara Norton, "Notes about E. W.'s early life—things she has told me," Beinecke Library.

41. Berenson, *Sunset and Twilight*, 219.

42. I am indebted for my information on Geoffrey Scott to Richard Dunn, who is currently working on Scott's biography. Scott later wrote *The Architecture of Humanism* (1914) and *The Portrait of Zélide* (1925). At the time of his death from pneumonia in 1929, he was editing Boswell's papers. Scott's marriage to Cutting was further complicated by the fact that Mary Berenson was in love with him, and he had been and still was in love with Berenson's secretary, Nicky Mariano. Scott had met Mariano in 1913. At the outbreak of the war, she left Florence and did not return for five years. In the meantime, Scott had married Sybil. See Mariano, *Forty Years with Berenson*, 14–16 esp.

43. Letter of Edith Wharton to John Hugh Smith, September 6, 1927, *Letters of Edith Wharton*, 501–502.

44. Paul Bourget, *Outre-Mer: Impressions of America*, 93. Wharton's thesis was grounded in her own experience. One newspaper reported that her engagement to Harry Stevens ended for two reasons: "a preponderance of intellect on the part of the intended bride . . . and it is said that, in the eyes of Mr. Stevens, ambition is a grievous fault" (Lewis, *Edith Wharton*, 45).

45. Letter of Edith Wharton to Gaillard Lapsley, April 6, 1927, Beinecke Library.

46. The relationship between Wharton and Lubbock, which cast him as the courtly admirer of the "dear & great & dear lady," who always "instantly understood" and "clarified and made all large & fine & beautiful" (Letter of Lubbock to Wharton, Jan. 7, 1913, Percy Lubbock Papers, Beinecke Library), had been strained for some time. He did not wholeheartedly approve of her or her fiction and she

did not take him entirely seriously. "Percy has totally forsaken me," she wrote Lapsley in 1920. "I'm glad that laying a book doesn't complicate life so much for me. If it *had*, I should be on Stylites perch by this time! But this is flippant, like my literature, & Percy is labouring with something far more than Little Fictions" (Letter of Sept. 24, 1920, Beinecke Library). By 1922, Wharton had scant patience with him. Asking Lapsley if Lubbock had said anything about his stay at Hyères, she explained: "It was one of the most trying experiences I have ever undergone. His gloom was unrelieved, & as he has simplified social life to the point of totally eliminating the feelings of others from his mind, he treated me & my other guests to some six weeks of a morose & unbroken silence. . . . When he and I were alone it was no better, & so often, when one came into the room suddenly, and he lifted that terrible *some one else's* face of which you once spoke, the sight of it gave me a cold chill" (Letter of May 13, 1922, *Letters of Edith Wharton*, 451–453).

47. Letter of Percy Lubbock to Gaillard Lapsley, March 19, 1933, Beinecke Library.

48. See Catharine R. Stimpson, "The Androgyne and the Homosexual," in *Where the Meanings Are*, 57 esp.; and Eve Kosofsky Sedgwick, "The Beast in the Closet: James and the Writing of Homosexual Panic," in *Speaking of Gender*, ed. Elaine Showalter, 243–268.

49. Letter of Edith Wharton to Gaillard Lapsley, March 16, 1916, Beinecke Library.

50. The short story "Copy," in which two former lovers and now famous writers spar over their letters, shows that the topic of private papers being made public troubled Wharton as early as 1901.

51. Copy of letter of Edith Wharton to Edmund Gosse, April 16, 1916, *Letters of Edith Wharton*, 375–377.

52. Letter of Henry James to Walter Berry, February 8, 1912, *The Letters of Henry James*, ed. Percy Lubbock, 2: 219.

53. Sturgis's "Birdlife" is not dated, but James tells Sturgis that he was amused by it in a July 16, 1909 letter. The manuscript is in the Edith Wharton Collection, Beinecke Library.

54. Copy of letter of Edith Wharton to Margaret James, June 1916, *Letters of Edith Wharton*, 377–378.

55. Letter of Edith Wharton to Howard Sturgis, June 17, 1916, *Letters of Edith Wharton*, 380–381.

56. Letter of Edith Wharton to Howard Sturgis, June 17, 1916, *Letters of Edith Wharton*, 380–381.

57. Edel, Introduction to *Henry James Letters*, vol. 1 (1843–1875), xvii.

58. Letter of Percy Lubbock to Gaillard Lapsley, June 12, 1916, Beinecke Library.

59. Letter of Howard Sturgis to Edith Wharton, September 16, 1917, Beinecke Library.

60. Lubbock, Introduction to *Letters of Henry James,* vol. 1, xvii.

61. Letter of Percy Lubbock to Edith Wharton, January 28, 1914, Beinecke Library.

62. Harry Crosby, *Shadows of the Sun: The Diaries of Harry Crosby*, ed. Edward B. Germain, 126.

63. Edith Wharton, "The Vice of Reading," *North American Review* 177 (October 1903): 521.

64. Letter of Edith Wharton to Gaillard Lapsley, January 24, 1932, Beinecke Library. The second line of the elegy reads: "Death doesn't bring an end of everything."

65. Letter of Edith Wharton to Gaillard Lapsley, July 15, 1930, *Letters of Edith Wharton*, 526—527.

66. Letter of Howard Sturgis to Edith Wharton, December 5, 1905, Beinecke Library.

67. Letter of Howard Sturgis to Edith Wharton, the last day of September 1917, Beinecke Library. For Wharton's treatment of the seduced-and-abandoned plot, see Barbara White, "Edith Wharton's *Summer* and Women's Fiction," *Essays in Literature* 11.2 (Fall 1984): 223—235.

68. Letter of Edith Wharton to Gaillard Lapsley, March 17, 1932, Beinecke Library.

69. Gaillard Lapsley Collection, Trinity College, Box A, 139.

70. Patricia Meyer Spacks, *Gossip*, 3—5 (hereafter cited as Spacks).

71. Bernard Berenson, *The Bernard Berenson Treasury*, ed. Hanna Keil, 67.

72. See Lewis, *Edith Wharton*, 517.

73. Letter of Edith Wharton to Bernard Berenson, April 9, 1937, *Letters of Edith Wharton*, 602—605.

2. THE INNER CIRCLE AND BLOOMSBURY

1. Leon Edel, *Bloomsbury: A House of Lions*, 59.

2. Desmond MacCarthy, "Henry James," in *Portraits*, 154 (hereafter cited as "HJ").

3. E. M. Forster, "Bloomsbury, An Early Note (February 1929)," in *The Bloomsbury Group*, ed. S. P. Rosenbaum, 25.

4. Clive Bell, "Old Friends," in *Civilization and Old Friends*, 137.

5. Maynard Keynes, *Two Memoirs*, 86—87.

6. Letter of Virginia Woolf to Gwen Ravert, 1st May [1925], *A Change of Perspective: The Letters of Virginia Woolf*, ed. Nigel Nicolson and Joanne Trautman, 3: 181.

7. Noel Annan, "The Intellectual Aristocracy," in *Studies in Social History*, ed. J. H. Plumb, 244.

8. Leonard Woolf, *Sowing: An Autobiography of the Years 1880 to 1904*, 202—203 (hereafter cited as *Sowing*). For the fallacies in Woolf's description, see Raymond Williams, "The Significance of 'Bloomsbury' as a Social and Cultural Group," in *Keynes and the Bloomsbury Group*, ed. Derek Crabtree and A. P. Thirlwall, 57—60 esp.

9. Virginia Woolf, *Moments of Being: Unpublished Autobiographical Writings*, ed. Jeanne Schulkind, 153.

10. Nigel Nicolson, "Bloomsbury: The Myth and the Reality," in *Virginia Woolf and Bloomsbury*, ed. Jane Marcus, 18. Also see Edel, *Bloomsbury*, 257—266.

11. Edith Wharton, *A Backward Glance*, 5 (hereafter cited as *ABG*).

12. Letter of Virginia Woolf to Vita Sackville-West [January 15, 1926], *A Change of Perspective*, 3: 228–229.

13. Bernard Berenson, *Sunset and Twilight: From the Diaries of 1947–1958*, ed. Nicky Mariano, 455 (hereafter cited as *S & T*).

14. Ernest Samuels, with Jayne Newcomer Samuels, *Bernard Berenson: The Making of a Legend*, 154, 274.

15. Edith Sitwell, *Taken Care of: The Autobiography of Edith Sitwell*, 88–89.

16. See Derek Crabtree, "Cambridge Intellectual Currents of 1900," in Crabtree and Thirlwall, *Keynes and the Bloomsbury Group*, 12.

17. Letter of Henry James to Grace Norton, July 28 [1883], *The Letters of Henry James*, ed. Percy Lubbock, 1: 100–101.

18. Letter of Edith Wharton to Gaillard Lapsley, Oct. 11, 1922, Beinecke Library. Wharton included a copy of the solicitation.

19. Gaillard Lapsley, "Tradition at Harvard," *University of California Magazine*, November 1902, 359.

20. See Henry James, *Notes of a Son and Brother*, in *Henry James: Autobiography*, ed. Frederick W. Dupee, 391. Norton's household may have provided a model for Qu'Acre: "the University circle consciously accepted, for its better satisfaction, or in other words just from a sense of what was, within its range, in the highest degree interesting, the social predominance of Shady Hill and the master there, and the ladies of the master's family."

21. Millicent Bell, *Edith Wharton and Henry James: The Story of Their Friendship*, 83. Like Berenson and Fry, Norton served on the board of *Burlington Magazine*.

22. Robert Norton, "Memoir," Beinecke Library, p. 2.

23. M. Bell, *Edith Wharton and Henry James*, 86.

24. Letter of Edith Wharton to Gaillard Lapsley, August 3, 1925, Beinecke Library.

25. See Edith Wharton, "Henry James in His Letters," *Quarterly Review* 234 (1920): 199.

26. See Johann Wolfgang von Goethe, *Essays on Art and Literature*, ed. John Gearey, trans. Ellen von Nardroff and Ernest H. von Nardroff; also see Johann Wolfgang von Goethe, *Goethe on Art*, ed. John Gage.

27. Maitland was the Downing Professor of the Laws of England. For a discussion of his influence on Lapsley, see the introduction by Helen M. Cam and Geoffrey Barraclough to G. Lapsley, *Crown, Community, and Parliament in the Later Middle Ages*, ed. Helen M. Cam and Geoffrey Barraclough, vii esp.

28. E. M. Forster, "Roger Fry: An Obituary Note," in *Abinger Harvest*, 38.

29. Letter of Henry James to Edith Wharton, 21 September 1914, *Henry James and Edith Wharton: Letters 1900–1915*, ed. Lyall H. Powers, 302.

30. Bernard Berenson, *Sketch for a Self-Portrait*, 72 (hereafter cited as *Sketch*).

31. Letter of Howard Sturgis to Edith Wharton, May 8, 1912, Beinecke Library.

32. Virginia Woolf, *The Diary of Virginia Woolf*, ed. Anne Oliver Bell, 2: 136.

33. Wharton expresses her anti-Semitism several times in letters to Gaillard Lapsley. John Hugh Smith seems to have been the most unabashedly prejudiced of the inner circle. In his memoir of Wharton, he says that the "American middle class was poisoned by a plague of Jews." Letter of John Hugh Smith to Percy Lubbock, February 17, 1938, Beinecke Library, p. 3.

34. See Noel Annan, "The Best of Bloomsbury," in *New York Review of Books*, May 29, 1990, 28 esp.

35. R. L. Chambers, *The Novels of Virginia Woolf*, 457.

36. Stephen Spender, *World within World*, 144 (hereafter cited as *WWW*).

37. Letter of Henry James to Lady Ritchie, December 21, 1906, *Henry James Letters*, ed. Leon Edel, vol. 4 (1895–1916), 433–434.

38. Letter of Henry James to Sara Norton Darwin, September 11, 1907, *Henry James Letters*, vol. 4 (1895–1916), 504n.1.

39. Letter of Leonard Woolf to Lytton Strachey, July 23, 1905, Quentin Bell, *Virginia Woolf: A Biography*, 1: 177.

40. Leon Edel, *Henry James: A Life*, 648.

41. Letter of Edith Wharton to Gaillard Lapsley, August 17, 1925, Beinecke Library. Woolf did not disparage all of Wharton's work; for example, she wrote an appreciative review of *The House of Mirth*. See Virginia Woolf, "*The House of Mirth*," *Guardian*, November 15, 1905, 1940.

42. Edith Wharton, *The Gods Arrive*, 116.

43. R. W. B. Lewis, *Edith Wharton: A Biography*, 483.

44. See Edith Wharton, *The Writing of Fiction*, 120 esp.

45. See letter of Edith Wharton to John Hugh Smith, May 25, 1925, *The Letters of Edith Wharton*, ed. R. W. B. Lewis and Nancy Lewis, 479–480.

46. Percy Lubbock, *Portrait of Edith Wharton*, 79 (hereafter cited as *Portrait*).

47. Letter of Virginia Woolf to Ethel Smyth [21 May 1934], *A Change of Perspective*, 5: 305.

48. Letter of Edith Wharton to Gaillard Lapsley, June 26, 1928, Beinecke Library.

49. Letter of Edith Wharton to Bernard Berenson, September 30 [1914], *Letters of Edith Wharton*, 341.

50. Letter of Edith Wharton to Bernard Berenson, January 23, 1932, *Letters of Edith Wharton*, 544–545.

51. Virginia Woolf, *A Writer's Diary: Being Extracts from the Diary of Virginia Woolf*, ed. Leonard Woolf, 239.

52. Howard Sturgis, "Anne Isabella Thackeray (Lady Ritchie)," *Cornhill Magazine*, November 1919, 461, 468. For more information on Anne Thackeray Ritchie, see Katherine C. Hill-Miller, "'The Skies and the Trees of the Past': Anne Thackeray Ritchie and William Makepeace Thackeray," in *Fathers and Daughters*, ed. Lynda E. Boose and Betty S. Flowers, 361–383.

53. Letter of Virginia Woolf to V. Sackville-West, 16th March 1926, *A Change of Perspective*, 3: 246–249.

54. Letter of Virginia Woolf to Lady Ottoline Morrell, Nov. 30 [1922], *A Change of Perspective*, 2: 589.

55. Letter of Virginia Woolf to R. C. Trevelyan, Dec. 29th 1922, *A Change of Perspective*, 2: 601.

56. See Daniel R. Schwarz, *The Humanistic Heritage: Critical Theories of the English Novel from James to Hillis Miller*, 48. Also see E. M. Forster, *Aspects of the Novel*, 56.

57. David Fogel, *Covert Relations: James Joyce, Virginia Woolf, and Henry James*, 103. Fogel writes that, while Woolf primarily disagreed with Lubbock's elevation

of form over emotion, her notes reveal "that she was being instructed by Lub-bock." Also see Carol Dole, "Oppression, Obsession: Virginia Woolf and Henry James," *Southern Review* 24 (1988): 253–271; and Vijay Lakshmi, "Mr. James and Mrs. Woolf," in *The Magic Circle of Henry James: Essays in Honor of Darshan Singh Maini*, ed. Amritjit Singh and K. Ayyappa Paniker, 285–293. Lakshmi demon-strates how "certain echoes of Jamesian aesthetics keep breaking through" Woolf's criticism (289).

58. Letter of Virginia Woolf to E. M. Forster, 16th Nov. [1927], *A Change of Perspective*, 3: 438.

59. Q. Bell, *Virginia Woolf*, 1: 366.

60. Virginia Woolf, "The Method of Henry James," in *The Essays of Virginia Woolf*, vol. 2 (1912–1918), ed. Andrew McNeillie, 348.

61. David Garnett, *Great Friends: Portraits of Seventeen Writers*, 125 (hereafter cited as *GF*).

62. Virginia Woolf, "Phases of Fiction" (typescript), Monk's House Papers B.6, University of Sussex, quoted in Fogel, *Covert Relations*, 114.

63. V. Woolf, *Moments of Being*, 136.

64. Virginia Woolf, "Women and Fiction," in *Collected Essays*, ed. Leonard Woolf, 2: 146. One trend in Wharton criticism, which sees *The House of Mirth* and *The Reef*, for example, as responses to *The Portrait of a Lady* and *The Golden Bowl*, illustrates Woolf's point. See Carolyn Karcher, "Male Vision and Female Revision in James's *The Wings of the Dove* and Wharton's *The House of Mirth*," *Women's Studies* 10.3 (1984): 227–244.

65. See Lyall H. Powers, *Henry James and the Naturalist Movement*; also see H. Peter Stowell, *Literary Impressionism, James and Chekhov*.

66. Sandra M. Gilbert, "Life's Empty Pack: Notes toward a Literary Daughter-onomy," *Critical Inquiry* 11 (March 1985): 357. Gilbert argues that writers such as George Eliot, Emily Dickinson, Wharton, and Woolf parodoxically proclaim an allegiance to the law or standards or traditions which they themselves appear to have violated. Also see Bradford K. Mudge, "Exiled as Exiler: Sara Coleridge, Virginia Woolf, and the Politics of Literary Revision," in *Women's Writing in Exile*, ed. Mary Lynn Broe and Angela Ingram. Mudge writes that Woolf's "desire for historical revision warred against the unchallengeable supremacy of 'Art' and its accompanying (and unavoidable) dependence on hierarchy" (204).

67. Virginia Woolf, "Modern Fiction," in *Collected Essays*, 2: 106.

68. See Harvena Richter, *Virginia Woolf: The Inward Voyage*, 30. Also see Pe-nelope Vita-Finzi, *Edith Wharton and the Art of Fiction*.

69. Jane Dunn, *A Very Close Conspiracy: Vanessa Bell and Virginia Woolf*, 85.

70. Letter of Virginia Woolf to Ethel Smyth, 22 June [1930], *A Change of Per-spective*, 4: 179–180.

71. Virginia Woolf, "Mr. Bennett and Mrs. Brown," in *Collected Essays*, 1: 320.

72. Edith Wharton, "Visibility in Fiction," *Yale Review* (March 1929): 480–488, 482 esp.

73. Henry James, "Preface to *The Portrait of a Lady*," in *The Art of the Novel: Critical Prefaces by Henry James*, ed. Richard P. Blackmur, 45.

74. Virginia Woolf, "Mr. Henry James's Last Novel," *Guardian*, February 22, 1905, 339; Wharton, *A Backward Glance*, 191. Also see Umberto Morra, *Conversa-*

tions with Berenson, 221. Berenson said that James constructed "a style of absolutely artificial arabesques." Wharton might have thought the same of Woolf.

75. Virginia Woolf, "Women Novelists," in *The Essays of Virginia Woolf*, vol. 2, (1912–1918), 315.

76. Virginia Woolf, *A Room of One's Own*, 108. See Carolyn G. Heilbrun, "The Bloomsbury Group," in *Toward a Recognition of Androgyny*, 115–167.

77. Nicky Mariano, *Forty Years with Berenson*, 164.

78. E. M. Forster, "Good Society," *New Statesman and Nation*, June 1934, 951–952.

79. T. S. Eliot, "Virginia Woolf," *Horizon* (June 1941): 315.

3. EDITH WHARTON AND HENRY JAMES: SECRET SHARERS

1. The quotation is from a letter of Henry James to Edith Wharton, October 4, 1907, in *Henry James and Edith Wharton: Letters, 1900–1915*, ed. Lyall H. Powers, 74–76.

2. I am paraphrasing from a letter of Henry James to Edith Wharton, August 11 [and 12], 1907, in *Henry James and Edith Wharton*, 68–72.

3. Edith Wharton, *A Backward Glance*, 173 (hereafter cited as *ABG*).

4. Letter of Henry James to Edith Wharton, May 9, 1909, *Henry James and Edith Wharton*, 112–113.

5. Letter of Henry James to Edith Wharton, February 2, 1912, *Henry James and Edith Wharton*, 211.

6. Letter of Henry James to Edith Wharton, September 7, 1911, *Henry James and Edith Wharton*, 186–187.

7. Letter of Henry James to Edith Wharton, August 17, 1902, *Henry James and Edith Wharton*, 33–35. For information on the professional relationship between James and Wharton, see Millicent Bell, *Edith Wharton and Henry James: The Story of Their Friendship*.

8. See letter of Henry James to Edith Wharton, July 2, 1906, *Henry James and Edith Wharton*, 65.

9. Letter of Henry James to Edith Wharton, Nov. 24, 1907, *Henry James and Edith Wharton*, 77–78.

10. Letter of Henry James to Edith Wharton, October 25, 1911, *Henry James and Edith Wharton*, 194–195.

11. Letter of Henry James to Edith Wharton, September 10, 1913, *Henry James and Edith Wharton*, 265–266.

12. The expression is from a letter of Edith Wharton to Gaillard Lapsley, February 25 [1914], Beinecke Library. Wharton's desire to have James publicly acknowledge her work can be inferred perhaps from her sending the Nortons a copy of the August 17, 1902, letter in which he praised *The Valley of Decision* and begged her to "do New York."

13. Letter of Edith Wharton to Gaillard Lapsley, February 23 [1913], Beinecke Library.

14. W. C. Brownwell, *American Prose Masters*, 359–361. For a further discussion of Wharton and James's "literary rough-and-tumbles," see Jean Frantz Blackall,

"Henry and Edith: 'The Velvet Glove' as an 'In' Joke," *Henry James Review* 7 (Fall 1985): 21–25.

15. Letter of Edith Wharton to Gaillard Lapsley, March 1 [1916], *The Letters of Edith Wharton*, ed. R. W. B. Lewis and Nancy Lewis, 370.

16. Edith Wharton, "Henry James in His Letters," *Quarterly Review* 234 (1920): 191.

17. Letter of Henry James to Edith Wharton, May 2, 1913, *Henry James and Edith Wharton*, 251–253.

18. Letter of Henry James to Edith Wharton, September 6, 1913, *Henry James and Edith Wharton*, 263–265.

19. See George Santayana, *Persons and Places*, 357–361, 358 esp. Objecting to his cousin's liberal politics, cultivation of feeling over intellect, and his obsessive attachment to his mother's memory, Santayana called Howard Sturgis "a perfect young lady of the Victorian type." In contrast, the memoirs of Lubbock and Wharton affectionately recall him "occupied with knitting-needles or embroidery silks, a sturdily-built handsome man with brilliantly white wavy hair, a girlishly clear complexion, and tender mocking eyes" (*ABG*, 225). Also see Leland S. Person, Jr., "Henry James, George Sand, and the Suspense of Masculinity," *PMLA* 106 (May 1991): 515–529. Person argues that James expanded his notion of masculinity, influenced by Balzac, to accommodate his response to George Sand. Sand inscribed herself on James through his reading and writing about her, and it affected him in some of the same ways as his correspondence with Wharton.

20. Percy Lubbock, *Portrait of Edith Wharton*, 11 (hereafter cited as *Portrait*).

21. Letter of Edith Wharton to Morton Fullerton, Saturday Night [Late summer 1909], *Letters of Edith Wharton*, 189–190.

22. Fred Kaplan, *Henry James: The Imagination of Genius*, 406.

23. Letter of Henry James to Edith Wharton, January 16, 1905, *Henry James and Edith Wharton*, 44–46.

24. Letter of Henry James to Edith Wharton, December 16, 1908, *Henry James and Edith Wharton*, 104.

25. Letter of Henry James to Edith Wharton, Oct. 4, 1907, *Henry James and Edith Wharton*, 74–76. For a description of the Comtesse de Fitz-James's salon, see Wharton, *A Backward Glance*, 264–282.

26. See Kaplan, *Henry James*, 406–407. Kaplan suggests that James assumed a similar role in Fullerton's previous affair with Margaret Brooke.

27. Letter of Henry James to Howard Sturgis, February 27, 1907, by permission of Houghton Library, bMS Am 1094 (1245).

28. Leon Edel, *Henry James: A Life*, 654. See Barbara Belford, *Violet: The Story of the Irrepressible Violet Hunt and Her Circle of Lovers and Friends—Ford Madox Ford, H. G. Wells, Somerset Maugham, and Henry James*, 162–165 esp. Also see Robert Secor, "Henry James and Violet Hunt, the 'Improper Person of Babylon,'" *Journal of Modern Literature* 13 (March 1986): 3–36.

29. See R. W. B. Lewis, *Edith Wharton: A Biography*, 259–260 (hereafter cited as Lewis).

30. Letter of Henry James to Edith Wharton, January 7, 1908, *Henry James and Edith Wharton*, 87–88. This letter contains the *donnée* for Wharton's story "The Pretext."

31. Letter of Henry James to Edith Wharton, December 30, 1909, *Henry James and Edith Wharton*, 135–137.

32. Letter of Henry James to Edith Wharton, October 13, 1908, *Henry James and Edith Wharton*, 101–102.

33. Lynne T. Hanley, "The Eagle and the Hen: Edith Wharton and Henry James," *Research Studies* 49 (September 1981): 143–153.

34. Edel, *Henry James: A Life*, 7.

35. See Shuli Barzilai, "Borders of Language: Kristeva's Critique of Lacan," *PMLA* 106 (March 1991): 295. Also see Julia Kristeva, *Powers of Horror: An Essay on Abjection*, trans. Leon S. Roudiez, 2.

36. Letter of Henry James to Edith Wharton, January 11, 1909, *Henry James and Edith Wharton*, 105–107.

37. Letter of Henry James to Morton Fullerton, October 2, 1900, *Henry James Letters*, ed. Leon Edel, vol. 4 (1895–1916), 168–170. For more information about the homoerotic nature of James and Fullerton's relationship, see Kaplan, *Henry James*, 406–408; 511–513 esp.

38. Letter of Henry James to Morton Fullerton, January 4, 1906, *Henry James Letters*, vol. 4 (1895–1916), 389–390.

39. Letter of Henry James to Morton Fullerton, November 14, 1907, *Henry James Letters*, vol. 4 (1895–1916), 472–477.

40. Letter of Henry James to Edith Wharton, April 19, 1909, *Henry James and Edith Wharton*, 110–112.

41. Letter of Henry James to Edith Wharton, Christmas Eve, 1909, *Henry James and Edith Wharton*, 131–134. For a discussion of the James-Fullerton-Wharton triangle, see Gloria Erlich, *The Sexual Education of Edith Wharton*, 86–92, 124.

42. For information about Wharton's relationship with her mother, Lucretia Jones, see Cynthia Griffin Wolff, *A Feast of Words: The Triumph of Edith Wharton*, 38–47 esp. Also see Edith Wharton, "Life and I," Beinecke Library, p. 36. In this first and more candid draft of her autobiography, Wharton paradoxically recalls that, although she had "more will" and "more strength" than her childhood friends, she did not care to use it or know to what use to put it because she did not want to dominate—she wanted to be adored. Despite recent critics like Barbara White and David Holbrook arguing or assuming that Wharton was an incest survivor, there remains no way of moving the discussion beyond speculation without more concrete evidence.

43. See Lewis, *Edith Wharton*, 263–264.

44. See letter of Henry James to Edith Wharton, July 26, 1909, *Henry James and Edith Wharton*, 114–115.

45. Letter of Henry James to Edith Wharton, August 3, 1909, *Henry James and Edith Wharton*, 117–118.

46. Letter of Henry James to Morton Fullerton, November 14, 1907, *Henry James Letters*, vol. 4 (1895–1916), 472–474.

47. Letter of Henry James to Edith Wharton, August 3, 1909, *Henry James and Edith Wharton*, 117–118.

48. Letter of Henry James to Edith Wharton, August 15, 1909, *Henry James and Edith Wharton*, 118–119.

49. Letter of Henry James to Edith Wharton, December 30, 1909, *Henry James and Edith Wharton*, 135–137.

50. Letter of Henry James to Edith Wharton, October 29, 1909, *Henry James and Edith Wharton*, 125–126.

51. Letter of Henry James to Morton Fullerton, November 26, 1907, *Henry James Letters*, vol. 4 (1895–1916), 477–480.

52. Letter of Henry James to Edith Wharton, February 5, 1910, *Henry James and Edith Wharton*, 145–146.

53. Letter of Henry James to Edith Wharton, June 29, 1912, *Henry James and Edith Wharton*, 224–226. In a letter of July 30, 1913, James is particularly cutting when he suggests that Fullerton could get "a tip" from the cousin he was engaged to during the time of his affair with Wharton, Katherine Fullerton Gerould, "a real & natural magazinist." See *Henry James and Edith Wharton*, 261–262.

54. Henry James, "The Jolly Corner," in *The Complete Tales of Henry James*, ed. Leon Edel, 12: 209.

55. Eve Kosofsky Sedgwick, "The Beast in the Closet: James and the Writing of Homosexual Panic," in *Speaking of Gender*, ed. Elaine Showalter, 243–268.

56. Edith Wharton, "The Pretext," in *The Collected Short Stories of Edith Wharton*, ed. R. W. B. Lewis, 1: 649 (hereafter cited as "Pretext").

57. Edith Wharton, "The Letters," in *Collected Short Stories*, 2: 202 (hereafter cited as "Letters").

58. See C. Wolff, *A Feast of Words*, 206–207, 203–204.

59. Letter of Henry James to Edith Wharton, May 2, 1913, *Henry James and Edith Wharton*, 251–253.

60. Letter of Henry James to Edith Wharton, February 16, 1914, *Henry James and Edith Wharton*, 275–277. James literally tried to entice Wharton home when he offered her the loan of five hundred pounds to buy an English estate, Coopersale, and settle permanently near him.

61. Edith Wharton, *French Ways and Their Meaning*, 18.

62. Leon Edel, "Walter Berry and the Novelists: Proust, James, and Edith Wharton," *Nineteenth-Century Fiction* 38 (March 1984): 518. Marcel Proust dedicated *Pastiches et mélanges* to Walter Berry, "Avocat et lettré, qui, depuis le premier jour de la guerre, devant l'Amerique encore indécise, a plaidé, avec une énergie et un talent incomparable, la cause de la France, et l'a gagnée."

63. Bernard Berenson, *Rumor and Reflection*, 49.

64. See C. Wolff, *A Feast of Words*, 267–268 esp. Also see Alan Price, "Writing Home from the Front: Edith Wharton and Dorothy Canfield Fisher Present Wartime France to the United States: 1917–1919," *Edith Wharton Newsletter* 5 (Fall 1988), 1–5, 8. During the war, Wharton also wrote *The Marne* (1918).

65. See Leonard Woolf, *Downhill All the Way: An Autobiography of the Years 1919–1939*, 195.

66. Letter of Henry James to Edith Wharton, May 23, 1915, *Henry James and Edith Wharton*, 341–343.

67. Letter of Henry James to Edith Wharton, September 3, 1914, *Henry James and Edith Wharton*, 298–300.

68. Lewis, *Edith Wharton*, 371.

69. Letter of Henry James to Edith Wharton, May 23, 1915, *Henry James and Edith Wharton*, 341–343. See Alan Price, "Edith Wharton at War with the American Red Cross: The End of *Noblesse Oblige*," *Women's Studies* 20 (December 1991): 121–132.

70. Letter of Henry James to Edith Wharton, March 23–24, 1915, *Henry James and Edith Wharton*, 330–334.

71. Letter of Henry James to Edith Wharton, September 22, 1915, *Henry James and Edith Wharton*, 354–355.

72. Edel, *Henry James: A Life*, 663. See Michael Anesko, *"Friction with the Market": Henry James and the Profession of Authorship*, 141–162. Also see R. W. B. Lewis, *The Jameses: A Family Narrative*, 574–580. Lewis states that James ostensibly began work on the edition in the summer of 1904 when his agent, James Pinker, began negotiating with publishers.

73. Letter of Roger Fry to Helen Fry, March 16, 1906, *Letters of Roger Fry*, ed. Denys Sutton, 1: 258.

74. William James, *"Pragmatism" and Four Essays from "The Meaning of Truth,"* 133.

75. See Alan Holder, *Three Voyagers in Search of Europe: A Study of Henry James, Ezra Pound, and T. S. Eliot*, 84–131, 128 esp. Holder argues that James's international theme seems indebted to his father's vision of a denationalized humanity, "a universal form which, being animated by God's own infinite spirit, the spirit of human fellowship, will quickly shed all the soils it has contracted in the past."

76. Henry James, Preface to "Lady Barbarina," in *The Novels and Tales*, 14: ix–x.

77. Leon Edel, *Henry James: The Conquest of London, 1870–1881*, vol. 2 of *The Life of Henry James*, 33.

78. For more on Romney Marsh, see Iain Finlayson, *The Sixth Continent: A Literary History of Romney Marsh*. Also see Miranda Seymour, *A Ring of Conspirators: Henry James and His Literary Circle, 1895–1915*.

79. Henry James, "Madame de Mauves," in *The Novels and Tales*, 13: 247.

80. Henry James, *Hawthorne*, 122.

81. Henry James, *The Portrait of a Lady*, 53 (hereafter cited as *PL*).

82. Quoted by Nobushige Amenomori in "Lafcadio Hearn, the Man," *Atlantic Monthly* 96 (October 1905): 520.

83. Henry James, "A Roman Holiday," *Atlantic Monthly*, July 1873, 9.

84. Henry James, *The Ambassadors*, 196 (hereafter cited as *Amb.*).

85. James, *The Golden Bowl*, in *The Novels and Tales*, 24: 349 (hereafter cited as *GB*). *The Golden Bowl* was originally published as two volumes, of which the first is volume 23 and the second is volume 24 of *The Novels and Tales*.

86. Letter of Henry James to Morton Fullerton, October 2, 1900, *Henry James Letters*, vol. 4 (1895–1916), 168–170.

87. Virginia Woolf, "Henry James," in *Collected Essays*, ed. Leonard Woolf, 1: 282.

88. Letter of Henry James to Morton Fullerton, October 2, 1900, *Henry James Letters*, vol. 4 (1895–1916), 168–170.

89. See Alwyn Berland, *Culture and Conduct in the Novels of Henry James*, 62 esp. Berland notes that "James presents us with the essential incommunicability of identity."

90. Henry James, "Preface to *The Spoils of Poynton*," in *The Art of the Novel: Critical Prefaces by Henry James*, ed. R. P. Blackmur, 129–130.

91. See Jerry Loving's essay "The Death of Romance: Lily Bart and the 1908 *Portrait of a Lady*" in *The Other Romance*, ed. Donald Pease and Jeffrey Ruben-Dorsky (forthcoming).

92. Henry James, *The Turn of the Screw*, ed. Robert Kinbrough, 16, 52.

93. Letter of Edith Wharton to Gaillard Lapsley, February 18 [1913], Beinecke Library.

94. Edith Wharton, "The Muse's Tragedy," in *Collected Short Stories*, 1: 75.

95. "Les Derniers Mots" (notes taken by Elisina Tyler during Wharton's last days), Beinecke Library.

96. Letter of Edith Wharton to Gaillard Lapsley, March 3, 1923, Beinecke Library.

97. Robert Norton, "Memoir," Percy Lubbock Papers, Beinecke Library, p. 39 (hereafter cited as RN).

98. *Ladies' Companion*, January 1838, 147.

99. See Marianne Hirsch, "*The Golden Bowl*: 'That Strange Accepted Finality of Relation,'" in *Beyond the Single Vision: Henry James, Michel Butor, Uwe Johnson*, 57–81. Hirsch argues that *The Golden Bowl* represents "James's determination to supersede his other international works, to redress all errors, to eliminate all imperfections, reconcile all irreconcilables" (60). Also see Paula Marantz Cohen, "*The Golden Bowl*: The 'True' Marriage Realized," in *Portraits of Marriage in Literature*, ed. Anne C. Hargrove and Maurine Magliocco, 87–95.

100. Edith Wharton, "Summer Afternoon," *Scribner's Magazine*, March 1911, 278.

4. HOWARD STURGIS, PERCY LUBBOCK, AND BERNARD BERENSON

1. Percy Lubbock, *Mary Cholmondeley: A Sketch from Memory*, 62 (hereafter cited as *MC*). For biographical information on Howard Sturgis, see Miranda Seymour, *A Ring of Conspirators: Henry James and His Literary Circle, 1895–1915*, 228–234 esp.

2. Bernard Berenson, *Sunset and Twilight: From the Diaries of 1947–1958*, ed. Nicky Mariano, 41.

3. *The Selected Letters of Bernard Berenson*, ed. A. K. McComb, xiii, xiv.

4. Peter Watson, "Hard Times at Harvard's Tuscan Outpost," *New York Times*, September 6, 1992, 25.

5. Bernard Berenson, *Sketch for a Self-Portrait*, 151.

6. Letter of Howard Sturgis to Edith Wharton, September 16, 1917, Beinecke Library.

7. Percy Lubbock, *Earlham*, 73 (hereafter cited as *Earlham*).

8. See letter of Percy Lubbock to Edith Wharton, January 7, 1913, Beinecke Library.

9. Howard Sturgis, "Birdlife," 1909, Edith Wharton Collection, Beinecke Library.

10. E. M. Forster, *Abinger Harvest*, 122.

11. Sandra M. Gilbert and Susan Gubar, *No Man's Land: The Place of the Woman Writer in the Twentieth Century.*

12. See *Letters of Sarah Orne Jewett*, ed. Annie Fields, 246–247.

13. Letter of Howard Sturgis to Edith Wharton, December 3, 1904, Beinecke Library.

14. Letter of Henry James to Howard Sturgis, November 23, 1903, *Henry James Letters*, ed. Leon Edel, vol. 4 (1895–1916), 294.

15. Letter of Henry James to Howard Sturgis, December 2, 1903, *Henry James Letters*, vol. 4 (1895–1916), 295.

16. Letter of Howard Sturgis to Edith Wharton, December 5, 1905, Beinecke Library.

17. Letter of Henry James to Edith Wharton, August 11 [and 12], 1907, *Henry James and Edith Wharton, Letters: 1900–1915*, ed. Lyall H. Powers, 68–72, 72 esp.

18. Elmer Borklund, "Howard Sturgis, Henry James, and *Belchamber*," *Modern Philology* 58 (May 1961): 268 (hereafter cited as Borklund). "China Pot" is part of Borklund's Ph.D. dissertation, "Howard Overing Sturgis" hereafter cited as "CP").

19. Howard Sturgis, *All That Was Possible: Being the Record of a Summer in the Life of Mrs. Sybil Crofts, Comedian*, 9 (hereafter cited as *ATWP*).

20. See Ida M. Tarbell, *The Business of Being a Woman.*

21. Edith Wharton, "Mr. Sturgis's *Belchamber*," *Bookman* 21 (May 1905): 308 (hereafter cited as *Bookman*). Sturgis makes the same point about the traditional hero of fiction in "The China Pot": "The idea that the dull man is bound to be a good fellow runs like a coarse thread through the whole web of our insular fiction" (314).

22. R. W. B. Lewis, *Edith Wharton: A Biography*, 155.

23. Edith Wharton, *A Backward Glance*, 235, 234 (hereafter cited as *ABG*).

24. Letter of Edith Wharton to Gaillard Lapsley, March 31, 1928, Beinecke Library.

25. Percy Lubbock, *The Craft of Fiction*, 251 (hereafter cited as *CF*).

26. Letter of Edith Wharton to Gaillard Lapsley, August 19 [1912], *The Letters of Edith Wharton*, ed. R. W. B. Lewis and Nancy Lewis, 276–277.

27. Letter of Edith Wharton to Gaillard Lapsley, December 17, 1923, Beinecke Library.

28. Percy Lubbock, *Roman Pictures*, 19.

29. Percy Lubbock, Introduction to *The Letters of Henry James*, 1: xiv.

30. Percy Lubbock, *Elizabeth Barrett Browning in Her Letters*, 35 (hereafter cited as *EBB*).

31. Percy Lubbock, *Portrait of Edith Wharton*, 10 (hereafter cited as *Portrait*). See Bell Gale Chevigny, "Daughters Writing: Toward a Theory of Women's Biography," in *Between Women: Biographers, Novelists, Critics, and Artists Write about Their Work on Women*, ed. Carol Ascher, Louise DeSalvo, and Sara Ruddick, 356–379. Chevigny addresses the relationship of the biographer and her subject and shows how their identities intertwine.

32. For a discussion of *Red Pottage* as a New Woman Novel, see Ann L. Ardis, "Mary Cholmondeley's *Red Pottage*," in *Writing the Woman Artist: Essays on Poetics, Politics, and Portraiture*, ed. Suzanne W. Jones, 333–352.

33. Letter of Edith Wharton to Gaillard Lapsley, August 13, 1928, *Letters of Edith Wharton*, 516–517.

34. Percy Lubbock, *George Calderon: A Sketch from Memory*, 106.

35. Letter of Percy Lubbock to Gaillard Lapsley, January 4, 1912, Beinecke Library.

36. Letter of Percy Lubbock to Gaillard Lapsley, March 10, 1909, Beinecke Library.

37. Henry James, *The Art of the Novel: Critical Prefaces by Henry James*, ed. Richard P. Blackmur, 286 (hereafter cited as *AN*).

38. Virginia Woolf, *A Writer's Diary: Being Extracts from the Diary of Virginia Woolf*, ed. Leonard Woolf, 60.

39. William Dean Howells, *Literature and Life*, 202.

40. Letter of Edith Wharton to Gaillard Lapsley, October 30, 1925, *Letters of Edith Wharton*, 486–487.

41. Percy Lubbock, *The Region Cloud*, 285 (hereafter cited as *RC*).

42. Lubbock, *Letters of Henry James*, 1: xxix–xxx.

43. Henry James, "The Lesson of the Master," in *The Complete Tales of Henry James*, ed. Leon Edel, 7: 265 (hereafter cited as "LM").

44. Edith Wharton, "The Potboiler," in *The Collected Short Stories of Edith Wharton*, ed. R. W. B. Lewis, 1: 684.

45. Letter of Bernard Berenson to Carlo Plaggi, July 14, 1896, *The Selected Letters of Bernard Berenson*, ed. A. K. McComb, 50–51.

46. See Colin Simpson, *Artful Partners: Bernard Berenson and Joseph Duveen*, 79–85 (hereafter cited as *AP*); also see Ernest Samuels, *Bernard Berenson: The Making of a Legend*, 39–40, 133–134, 146–147, 316–317.

47. Letter of Roger Fry to Henry Rutgers Marshall, July 24, 1909, *Letters of Roger Fry*, ed. Denys Sutton, 1: 323.

48. Edith Wharton, *Italian Backgrounds*, 173–174.

49. Ernest Samuels, *Bernard Berenson: The Making of a Connoisseur*, 371 (hereafter cited as Samuels).

50. Letter of Bernard Berenson to Judge Learned Hand, December 13, 1933, *Selected Letters of Bernard Berenson*, 122–123.

51. Letter of Edith Wharton to Bernard Berenson, April 19 [1913], *Letters of Edith Wharton*, 296–297.

52. Letter of Edith Wharton to Bernard Berenson, August 6 [1911], *Letters of Edith Wharton*, 251–252.

53. Letter of Edith Wharton to Bernard Berenson, January 27, 1919, *Letters of Edith Wharton*, 421–422.

54. Edith Wharton, *The Decoration of Houses*, 9 (hereafter cited as *DH*).

55. Bernard Berenson, *The Bernard Berenson Treasury*, ed. Hanna Kiel, 59–60 (hereafter cited as *BBT*).

56. Edith Wharton, *The Writing of Fiction*, 28 (hereafter cited as *WF*). For a discussion of Wharton's aesthetics, see Penelope Vita-Finzi, *Edith Wharton and the Art of Fiction*, 24–46 esp.

57. Letter of Roger Fry to Helen Anrep, August 7, 1927, *Letters of Roger Fry*, 2: 604.

58. Letter of Edith Wharton to Sara Norton, September 30, 1905, Beinecke Library. For a discussion of Wharton's relationship with Sara Norton, see Susan Goodman, *Edith Wharton's Women: Friends and Rivals*, 29–47.

59. Edith Wharton, *A Motor-Flight through France*, 178.

60. Edith Wharton, "The Criticism of Fiction," *Times Literary Supplement*, May 14, 1916, 229–230.

61. Letter of Edith Wharton to Bernard Berenson, January 29, 1917, *Letters of Edith Wharton*, 388–389.

62. Nicky Mariano, memoir of Edith Wharton, Percy Lubbock Papers, Beinecke Library, p. viii.

63. Edith Wharton, *The Age of Innocence*, 4.

64. Edith Wharton, "The Daunt Diana," in *Collected Short Stories*, 2: 52 (hereafter cited as "DD").

65. Bernard Berenson, *The Central Italian Painters of the Renaissance*, 33, 98.

5. LOVE AND EXILE: EDITH WHARTON'S FICTIONAL SELVES

1. Robert Norton, "Memoir," Percy Lubbock Papers, Beinecke Library, p. 29 (hereafter cited as RN).

2. See Judith Fryer, *Felicitous Space: The Imaginative Structures of Edith Wharton and Willa Cather*, 69, 73–74 esp.

3. Edith Wharton, *A Backward Glance*, 159 (hereafter cited as *ABG*).

4. Edith Wharton, *The Gods Arrive*, 77 (hereafter cited as *GA*).

5. Edith Wharton, *Hudson River Bracketed*, 272 (hereafter cited as *HRB*). For a discussion of the evolution of the representation of this space, see Susan Goodman, *Edith Wharton's Women: Friends and Rivals*, 27.

6. Louis Auchincloss, Introduction to *The Reef*, by Edith Wharton, xiii–xiv.

7. Letter of Betty McCagg to Susan Goodman, September 27, 1991.

8. Nicky Mariano, *Forty Years with Berenson*, 164.

9. See D. W. Winnicott, "The Capacity to Be Alone," in *The Maturational Processes and the Facilitating Environment*, 29, 36 esp.

10. See Anthony Storr, *Solitude: A Return to the Self*.

11. Edith Wharton, *The House of Mirth*, 249 (hereafter cited as *HM*).

12. Edith Wharton, *The Fruit of the Tree*, 624.

13. Nancy K. Miller, *The Heroine's Text: Readings in the French and English Novel, 1722–1782*, xi, 151, 157; and Rachel Blau DuPlessis, *Writing beyond the Ending: Narrative Strategies of Twentieth-Century Women Writers*, 4–7.

14. For a similar discussion on Henry James, see Alfred Habeggar, *Henry James and the "Woman Business,"* 17.

15. Nina Baym, *Women's Fiction: A Guide to Novels by and about Women in America, 1820–1870*, 11.

16. Edith Wharton, *Summer*, 123.

17. For a discussion of Julia Kristeva, language, and motherhood, see Susan Rubin Suleiman, "Writing and Motherhood," in *The (M)other Tongue: Essays in Feminist Psychoanalytic Interpretation*, ed. Shirley Nelson Garner, Claire Kahane, and Madelon Sprengnether, 352–377.

18. See Walter Benn Michaels, *The Gold Standard and the Logic of Naturalism:*

American Literature at the Turn of the Century, 230, 241. Michaels sees Lily's death as a statement about becoming a woman writer.

19. See Elaine Showalter, "The Death of a Lady (Novelist): Wharton's *House of Mirth*," *Representations* 9 (1985): 133–149.

20. Henry James, *The Portrait of a Lady*, 175.

21. See Cynthia Griffin Wolff, "Lily Bart and the Beautiful Death," *American Literature* 46 (1974): 16–40.

22. See Jennifer Radden, "Defining Self-Deception," *Dialogue* 23 (March 1984): 103–120.

23. For readings that emphasize the economic exchanges in *The House of Mirth*, see Wai-Chee Dimock, "Debasing Exchange: Edith Wharton's *The House of Mirth*," *PMLA* 100 (1985): 783–792; and Michaels, *Gold Standard*, 225–244.

24. See Marianne Hirsch, "Spiritual Bildung: The Beautiful Soul as Paradigm," in *The Voyage In: Fictions of Female Development*, ed. Elizabeth Abel, Marianne Hirsch, and Elizabeth Langland, 23–48.

25. See Susan Gubar, "The 'Blank Page' and Female Creativity," in *Writing and Sexual Difference*, ed. Elizabeth Abel, 73–94. Gubar observes that Lily's lifeless form allows Selden to author a fiction of their imaginative union.

The same transformation occurs in Wharton's next novel, *The Fruit of the Tree*. Reading the past reconstructively, John Amherst translates his deceased wife's plans for a private gymnasium into a Utopian blueprint for the betterment of the Westmore employees. His interpretation holds his second wife, Justine Brent, hostage to a falsely manufactured memory. Bessy's death has repaired the fantasy that her marriage to Amherst exposed, just as Lily's death again makes her the "wonderful spectacle" (*HM*, 105) Selden first perceived her to be. The opposite happens in *Ethan Frome* (1911), where Mattie's crippled presence makes a mockery of the past.

26. Letter of Edith Wharton to Morton Fullerton, Sunday [May 1908], *The Letters of Edith Wharton*, ed. R. W. B. Lewis and Nancy Lewis, 145.

27. Edith Wharton, *The Custom of the Country*, 213 (hereafter cited as *CC*).

28. For discussion of female plots, see Mary P. Ryan, *The Empire of the Mother: American Writing about Domesticity, 1830–1860*, 120–124. Also see Annis Pratt, with Barbara White, Andrea Loewenstein, and Mary Wyer, *Archetypal Patterns in Women's Fiction*; and Rachel Brownstein, *Becoming a Heroine: Reading about Women in Novels*.

29. For an excellent discussion of Undine as a representative of an American literary tradition and Ralph Marvell as an artist, see Candace Waid's Introduction to Wharton, *Custom of the Country*, v–xxvii.

30. Edith Wharton, *The Reef*, 331–332 (hereafter cited as *Reef*).

31. Henry James, *The Golden Bowl*, in *The Novels and Tales*, 23: 235.

32. Edith Wharton, *Ethan Frome*, 130.

33. For a discussion of this process, see Goodman, *Edith Wharton's Women*, 89–95.

34. Edith Wharton, *The Age of Innocence*, 339 (hereafter cited as *Age*).

35. Adeline Tintner, "Mothers, Daughters, and Incest in the Late Novels of Edith Wharton," in *The Lost Tradition: Mothers and Daughters in Literature*, ed. Cathy N. Davidson and E. M. Broner, 147–156.

36. Gaillard Lapsley, "E. W.," Beinecke Library, p. 45.

37. See Julie Olin-Ammentorp, "Edith Wharton's Challenge to Feminist Criticism," *Studies in American Fiction* 16 (Autumn 1988): 237–244. Also see James Tuttleton, "The Feminist Takeover of Edith Wharton," *New Criterion* 7 (March 1989): 6–14.

38. Letter of Edith Wharton to Bernard Berenson, February 9, 1917, *Letters of Edith Wharton*, 391–392.

39. Henry James, *The Ambassadors*, 172 (hereafter cited as *Amb.*).

40. Julia Kristeva, *Tales of Love*, trans. Leon S. Roudiez, 29.

41. Edith Wharton, *Twilight Sleep*, 285.

42. See Joanna Russ, "What Can a Heroine Do? Or Why Women Can't Write," in *Images of Women in Fiction: Feminist Perspectives*, ed. Susan Koppelman Cornillon, 3–20.

43. For a discussion of the freedom from action embodied in Wharton's concept of the "Republic of the Spirit," see Michaels, *Gold Standard*, 230–233 esp.

44. Edith Wharton, "The Eyes," in *The Collected Short Stories of Edith Wharton*, ed. R. W. B. Lewis, 2: 120 (hereafter cited as "Eyes").

45. Edith Wharton, Preface to *Ghosts*, in *Collected Short Stories*, 2: 878.

46. See Susan Goodman, "Competing Visions of Freud in the Memoirs of Ellen Glasgow and Edith Wharton," *Colby Library Quarterly* 25.4 (1989): 218–226.

47. Umberto Morra, *Conversations with Berenson*, 84–85.

48. Mariano, *Forty Years with Berenson*, 169.

CONCLUSION. A MEDITATION ON PLACE

1. Larry Levis, "Our Sister of Perfect Solitude," in *The Widening Spell of the Leaves*, 40.

2. Percy Lubbock, *Portrait of Edith Wharton*, 173 (hereafter cited as *Portrait*).

3. Yi-Fu Tuan, *Space and Place: The Perspective of Experience*, 136.

4. Edith Wharton, *The Decoration of Houses*, 182–183.

5. Bernard Berenson, *Sketch for a Self-Portrait*, 164.

6. One of Robert Norton's paintings, not in a private collection, can be seen at The Mount, Lenox, Massachusetts. It is of the garden at Hyères. Norton exhibited fifty-seven watercolors of landscapes and coastal scenes at the Fine Arts Society in 1928. The show was called "Wanderings from the Channel to North Africa." From the titles of his paintings—*Entrance to the Great Mosque, Kairouan* or *Cloister of Cugat del Vallés, near Barcelona*, for example—he seems to have shared Wharton's interest in architecture.

7. Diane Filby Gillespie, *The Sisters' Arts: The Writing and Painting of Virginia Woolf and Vanessa Bell*, 267.

8. Ernest Hemingway, Epigraph to *A Moveable Feast* (hereafter cited as *MF*).

9. See J. Gerald Kennedy, "Place, Self, and Writing," *Southern Review* 26 (Summer 1990): 496–516.

10. Henry James, *Italian Hours*, 4 (hereafter cited as *IH*).

11. For a discussion of Ruskin, see Carl Dawson, *Victorian Noon: English Literature in 1850*, 125.

12. Edith Wharton, *Italian Backgrounds*, 3.

13. The following discussion of Stein touches on topics that J. Gerald Kennedy examines more fully in his superb book (which appeared after my own was completed) *Imagining Paris: Exile, Writing, and American Identity*, 38–78.

14. Gertrude Stein, *Lectures in America*, 161 (hereafter cited as *LA*).

15. Edith Wharton, *A Backward Glance*, 261 (hereafter cited as *ABG*).

16. Gertrude Stein, *Paris France*, 8 (hereafter cited as *PF*).

17. Katherine Anne Porter, "Gertrude Stein: A Self-Portrait," *Harper's*, December 1947, 522.

18. Edith Wharton, *French Ways and Their Meaning*, 102.

19. James R. Mellow, *Charmed Circle*, 13. I am indebted to Mellow for general information on Stein.

20. Shari Benstock, *Women of the Left Bank: Paris, 1900–1940*, 189.

21. Virginia Woolf, "A Sketch of the Past," in *Moments of Being: Unpublished Autobiographical Writings*, ed. Jeanne Schulkind, 72.

22. Virginia Woolf, *Books and Portraits: Some Further Selections from the Literary and Biographical Writings of Virginia Woolf*, ed. Mary Lyon, 161.

23. Letter of Roger Fry to Margery Fry, November 1, 1921, *Letters of Roger Fry*, ed. Denys Sutton, 2: 516. Also see Mary Ann Caws, *Women of Bloomsbury: Virginia, Vanessa, and Carrington*, 188.

24. See Leonard Woolf, *Downhill All the Way: An Autobiography of the Years 1919–1939*, 178–185.

25. Jane Dunn, *A Very Close Conspiracy: Vanessa Bell and Virginia Woolf*, 269.

26. Henry James, "A Roman Holiday," *Atlantic Monthly*, July 1873, 9.

27. Edith Wharton, *A Motor-Flight through France*, 1.

28. Gaillard Lapsley, "E.W.," Percy Lubbock Papers, Beinecke Library.

29. Percy Lubbock, *Earlham*, 172.

30. Henry James, *The American Scene: Together with Three Essays from "Portraits and Places,"* 87.

31. See Edith Wharton, "Kerfol," *The Ghost Stories of Edith Wharton*, ed. Alfred Bendixen, 81.

32. Ellen Glasgow, *The Woman Within*, 271.

Bibliography

Amenomori, Nobushige. "Lafcadio Hearn, the Man." *Atlantic Monthly*, October 1905, 510–525.

Ammons, Elizabeth. *Conflicting Stories: American Women Writers at the Turn into the Twentieth Century*. New York: Oxford University Press, 1991.

———. *Edith Wharton's Argument with America*. Athens: University of Georgia Press, 1980.

Anesko, Michael. *"Friction with the Market": Henry James and the Profession of Authorship*. New York: Oxford University Press, 1986.

Annan, Noel. "The Best of Bloomsbury." *New York Review of Books*, May 29, 1990, 28–30.

———. "The Intellectual Aristocracy." In *Studies in Social History*, edited by J. H. Plumb, 243–287. London and New York: Longmans, Green, 1955.

Auchincloss, Louis. Introduction to *The Reef*, by Edith Wharton, v–xiv. New York: Macmillan, 1987.

Banta, Martha. *Imaging American Women: Ideas and Ideals in Cultural History*. New York: Columbia University Press, 1987.

Barzilai, Shuli. "Borders of Language: Kristeva's Critique of Lacan." *PMLA* 106 (March 1991): 295–305.

Baym, Nina. *Women's Fiction: A Guide to Novels by and about Women in America, 1820–1870*. Ithaca: Cornell University Press, 1978.

Beebe, Maurice. *Ivory Towers and Sacred Founts: The Artist as Hero in Fiction from Goethe to Joyce*. New York: New York University Press, 1964.

Belford, Barbara. *Violet: The Story of the Irrepressible Violet Hunt and Her Circle of Lovers and Friends—Ford Madox Ford, H. G. Wells, Somerset Maugham, and Henry James*. New York: Simon and Schuster, 1990.

Bell, Clive. *Civilization and Old Friends*. London and Chicago: University of Chicago Press, 1973.

Bell, Millicent. *Edith Wharton and Henry James: The Story of Their Friendship*. New York: George Braziller, 1965.

Bell, Quentin. *Bloomsbury*. New York: Basic Books, 1969.

———. *Virginia Woolf: A Biography*. 2 vols. New York: Harcourt Brace Jovanovich, 1972.

Benson, Arthur Christopher. *The Diary of Arthur Christopher Benson*. Edited by Percy Lubbock. London: Hutchinson, 1926.

———. *Edwardian Excursions: From the Diaries of A. C. Benson, 1898–1904*. Edited by David Newsome. London: John Murrary, 1981.

Benstock, Shari. "Expatriate Modernism." In *Women's Writing in Exile*, edited by

Mary Lynn Broe and Angela Ingram, 19–40. Chapel Hill and London: University of North Carolina Press, 1989.

———. *Women of the Left Bank: Paris, 1900–1940*. Austin: University of Texas Press, 1986.

Berenson, Bernard. *The Bernard Berenson Treasury*. Edited by Hanna Kiel. New York: Simon and Schuster, 1962.

———. *The Central Italian Painters of the Renaissance*. London: Putnam, 1897.

———. *Rumor and Reflection*. New York: Simon and Schuster, 1952.

———. *The Selected Letters of Bernard Berenson*. Edited by A. K. McComb. Boston: Houghton Mifflin, 1964.

———. *Sketch for a Self-Portrait*. Bloomington: Indiana University Press, 1959.

———. *Sunset and Twilight: From the Diaries of 1947–1958*. Edited by Nicky Mariano. New York: Harcourt, Brace & World, 1963.

Berland, Alwyn. *Culture and Conduct in the Novels of Henry James*. Cambridge: Cambridge University Press, 1981.

Besançon, Alain. "Vers une histoire psychanalytique." *Histoire et expérience du moi*. Paris: Flammarion, 1971.

Blackall, Jean Frantz. "Henry and Edith: 'The Velvet Glove' as an 'In' Joke." *Henry James Review* 7 (Fall 1985): 21–25.

Borklund, Elmer. "Howard Overing Sturgis: An Account of His Life and Writings Together with His Unpublished Works." Ph.D. diss., University of Chicago, 1959.

———. "Howard Sturgis, Henry James, and *Belchamber*." *Modern Philology* 58 (May 1961): 255–269.

Bourget, Paul. *Outre-Mer: Impressions of America*. New York: 1895.

Brownstein, Rachel M. *Becoming a Heroine: Reading about Women in Novels*. New York: Viking, 1982.

Brownell, W. C. *American Prose Masters*. New York: Charles Scribner's Sons, 1923.

Caws, Mary Ann. *Women of Bloomsbury: Virginia, Vanessa, and Carrington*. New York and London: Routledge, 1990.

Chambers, R. L. *The Novels of Virginia Woolf*. London: Oliver and Bond, 1947.

Chevigny, Bell Gale. "Daughters Writing: Toward a Theory of Women's Biography." In *Between Women: Biographers, Novelists, Critics, and Artists Write about Their Work on Women*, edited by Carol Ascher, Louise DeSalvo, and Sara Ruddick, 356–379. Boston: Beacon Press, 1984.

Cohen, Paula Marantz. "*The Golden Bowl*: The 'True' Marriage Realized." In *Portraits of Marriage in Literature*, edited by Anne C. Hargrove and Maurine Magliocco. Macomb, Ill.: Western Illinois University, 1984.

Collingwood, R. G. *The Idea of History*. New York: Oxford, 1946.

Colquitt, Clare. "Unpacking Her Treasures: Edith Wharton's 'Mysterious Correspondence' with Morton Fullerton." *Library Chronicle of the University of Texas* 31 (1985): 73–107.

Crabtree, Derek, and A. P. Thirlwall, eds. *Keynes and the Bloomsbury Group*. London: Macmillan, 1980.

Crosby, Harry. *Shadows of the Sun: The Diaries of Harry Crosby*. Edited by Edward B. Germain. Santa Barbara: Blue Sparrow Press, 1977.

Dawson, Carl. *Victorian Noon: English Literature in 1850*. Baltimore and London: Johns Hopkins Press, 1979.

Delbanco, Nicholas. *Group Portrait: Joseph Conrad, Stephen Crane, Ford Madox Ford, Henry James, and H. G. Wells*. New York: William Morrow, 1982.

Dimock, Wai-Chee. "Debasing Exchange: Edith Wharton's *The House of Mirth*." *PMLA* 100 (1985): 783–792.

Dole, Carol. "Oppression, Obsession: Virginia Woolf and Henry James." *Southern Review* 24 (1988): 253–271.

Dunn, Jane. *A Very Close Conspiracy: Vanessa Bell and Virginia Woolf*. Boston: Little, Brown, 1990.

DuPlessis, Rachel Blau. *Writing beyond the Ending: Narrative Strategies of Twentieth-Century Women Writers*. Bloomington: Indiana University Press, 1985.

Edel, Leon. *Bloomsbury: A House of Lions*. Philadelphia and New York: J. B. Lippincott, 1979.

———. *Henry James: A Life*. New York: Harper & Row, 1985.

———. *The Life of Henry James*. 5 vols. Philadelphia and New York: J. B. Lippincott, 1953–1973.

———. "Walter Berry and the Novelists: Proust, James, and Edith Wharton." *Nineteenth-Century Fiction* 38 (March 1984): 514–528.

Eliot, T. S. "Virginia Woolf." *Horizon*, June 1941, 315.

Erlich, Gloria. *The Sexual Education of Edith Wharton*. Berkeley: University of California Press, 1992.

Finlayson, Iain. *The Sixth Continent: A Literary History of Romney Marsh*. New York: Atheneum, 1986.

Fogel, David. *Covert Relations: James Joyce, Virginia Woolf, and Henry James*. Charlottesville: University Press of Virginia, 1990.

Forster, E. M. *Abinger Harvest*. New York: Harcourt, Brace, 1936.

———. *Aspects of the Novel*. New York: Harcourt, Brace & World, 1954.

———. "Good Society." *New Statesman and Nation*, June 1934, 951–952.

Fry, Roger. *Last Lectures, ix–xxix*. New York and Cambridge: Cambridge University Press, 1939.

———. *Letters of Roger Fry*. Edited by Denys Sutton. 2 vols. New York: Random House, 1972.

Fryer, Judith. *Felicitous Space: The Imaginative Structures of Edith Wharton and Willa Cather*. Chapel Hill: University of North Carolina Press, 1986.

Garnett, David. *Great Friends: Portraits of Seventeen Writers*. London: Macmillan, 1979.

Gilbert, Sandra M. "Life's Empty Pack: Notes toward a Literary Daughteronomy." *Critical Inquiry* 11 (March 1985): 355–384.

Gilbert, Sandra M., and Susan Gubar. *The Madwoman in the Attic: The Woman Writer and the Nineteenth-Century Literary Imagination*. New Haven: Yale University Press, 1979.

———. *No Man's Land: The Place of the Woman Writer in the Twentieth Century*. New Haven: Yale University Press, 1988.

Gillespie, Diane Filby. *The Sisters' Arts: The Writing and Painting of Virginia Woolf and Vanessa Bell*. Syracuse: Syracuse University Press, 1988.

Glasgow, Ellen. *The Woman Within*. New York: Harcourt Brace, 1954.

Goethe, Johann Wolfgang von. *Essays on Art and Literature*. Edited by John Gearey. Translated by Ellen von Nardroff and Ernest von Nardroff. New York: Suhrkamp, 1986.

―――. *Goethe on Art*. Edited by John Gage. Berkeley and Los Angeles: University of California Press, 1980.

Goodman, Susan. "Competing Visions of Freud in the Memoirs of Ellen Glasgow and Edith Wharton." *Colby Library Quarterly* 25.4 (1989): 218–226.

―――. *Edith Wharton's Women: Friends and Rivals*. Hanover and London: University Press of New England, 1990.

Goodwyn, Janet. *Edith Wharton: Traveller in the Land of Letters*. London: Macmillan, 1990.

Gossman, Lionel. *Between History and Literature*. Cambridge: Harvard University Press, 1990.

Gribben, Alan. "'The Heart Is Insatiable': A Selection from Edith Wharton's Letters to Morton Fullerton." *Library Chronicle of the University of Texas* 31 (1985): 7–18.

Gubar, Susan. "The 'Blank Page' and Female Creativity." In *Writing and Sexual Difference*, edited by Elizabeth Abel, 73–94. Chicago: University of Chicago Press, 1982.

Habeggar, Alfred. *Henry James and the "Woman Business."* Cambridge: Cambridge University Press, 1989.

Hanley, Lynne T. "The Eagle and the Hen: Edith Wharton and Henry James." *Research Studies* 49 (September 1981): 143–153.

Heilbrun, Carolyn G. *Toward a Recognition of Androgyny*. New York: Knopf, 1973.

Hemingway, Ernest. *A Moveable Feast*. New York: Bantam, 1964.

Hill-Miller, Katherine C. "'The Skies and the Trees of the Past': Anne Thackeray Ritchie and William Makepeace Thackeray." In *Fathers and Daughters*, edited by Lynda E. Boose and Betty S. Flowers. Baltimore and London: Johns Hopkins Press, 1989.

Hirsch, Marianne. *Beyond the Single Vision: Henry James, Michel Butor, Uwe Johnson*. York, S.C.: French Literature Publications, 1981.

―――. "Spiritual Bildung: The Beautiful Soul as Paradigm." In *The Voyage In: Fictions of Female Development*, edited by Elizabeth Abel, Marianne Hirsch, and Elizabeth Langland, 23–48. Hanover and London: University Press of New England, 1983.

Holbrook, David. *Edith Wharton and the Unsatisfactory Man*. New York: St. Martin's, 1991.

Holder, Alan. *Three Voyagers in Search of Europe: A Study of Henry James, Ezra Pound, and T. S. Eliot*. Philadelphia: University of Pennsylvania Press, 1966.

Hopkins, Gerard. Introduction to *Belchamber*, by Howard Sturgis. London: World's Classics, 1935.

Howells, William Dean. *Literature and Life*. New York: Harper, 1902.

James, Henry. *The Ambassadors*. New York: W. W. Norton, 1964.

―――. *The American Scene: Together with Three Essays from "Portraits and Places."* New York: Charles Scribner's Sons, 1948.

―――. *The Art of the Novel: Critical Prefaces by Henry James*. Edited by Richard P. Blackmur. New York: Charles Scribner's Sons, 1934.

————. *The Complete Notebooks of Henry James.* Edited by Leon Edel and Lyall H. Powers. New York: Oxford University Press, 1987.

————. *The Complete Tales of Henry James.* Edited by Leon Edel. 12 vols. Philadelphia and New York: J. B. Lippincott, 1962–1965.

————. *The Golden Bowl.* Vols. 23 and 24 of *The Novels and Tales.* New York: Charles Scribner's Sons, 1909.

————. *Hawthorne.* Ithaca, New York: Cornell University Press, 1975.

————. *Henry James and Edith Wharton, Letters: 1900–1915.* Edited by Lyall H. Powers. New York: Charles Scribner's Sons, 1990.

————. *Henry James: Autobiography.* Edited by Frederick W. Dupee. New York: Criterion Books, 1956.

————. *Henry James Letters.* Edited by Leon Edel. 4 vols. Cambridge: Harvard University Press, 1974–1984.

————. *Italian Hours.* New York: Horizon Press, 1968.

————. *The Letters of Henry James.* Edited by Percy Lubbock. 2 vols. New York: Charles Scribner's Sons, 1920.

————. *Letters of Henry James to Walter Berry.* Edited by Walter Berry. Paris, 1928.

————. "Madame de Mauves." Vol. 13 of *The Novels and Tales,* 215–331. New York: Charles Scribner's Sons, 1908.

————. *The Portrait of a Lady.* New York: W. W. Norton, 1976.

————. Preface to "Lady Barbarina." Vol. 14 of *The Novels and Tales,* v–xxi. New York: Charles Scribner's Sons, 1908.

————. "A Roman Holiday." *Atlantic Monthly,* July 1873, 1–11.

————. *A Small Boy & Others.* New York: Charles Scribner's Sons, 1913.

————. *The Turn of the Screw.* Edited by Robert Kinbrough. New York: W. W. Norton, 1966.

James, William. *"Pragmatism" and Four Essays from "The Meaning of Truth."* New York: Meridian Books, 1955.

Jewett, Sarah Orne. *Letters of Sarah Orne Jewett.* Edited by Annie Fields. Boston: Houghton Mifflin, 1911.

Johnstone, J. K. *A Study of E. M. Forster, Lytton Strachey, Virginia Woolf, and Their Circle.* New York: Octagon Books, 1978.

Jones, Suzanne W., ed. *Writing the Woman Artist: Essays on Poetics, Politics, and Portraiture.* Philadelphia: University of Pennsylvania Press, 1991.

Joslin-Jeske, Katherine. "What Lubbock Didn't Say." *Edith Wharton Newsletter* 1.1 (Spring 1984): 2–4.

Kaplan, Fred. *Henry James: The Imagination of Genius.* New York: William Morrow, 1992.

Karcher, Carolyn. "Male Vision and Female Revision in James's *The Wings of the Dove* and Wharton's *The House of Mirth." Women's Studies* 10.3 (1984): 227–244.

Kennedy, J. Gerald. *Imagining Paris: Exile, Writing, and American Identity.* New Haven and London: Yale University Press, 1993.

————. "Place, Self, and Writing." *Southern Review* 26 (Summer 1990): 496–516.

Keynes, Geoffrey. *Henry James in Cambridge.* Cambridge: W. Heffer & Sons, 1967.

Keynes, Maynard. *Two Memoirs.* London: Rupert Hart-Davis, 1949.

Kristeva, Julia. *Powers of Horror: An Essay on Abjection.* Translated by Leon S. Roudiez. New York: Columbia University Press, 1982.

————. *Tales of Love*. Translated by Leon S. Roudiez. New York: Columbia University Press, 1987.

Lakshmi, Vijay. "Mr. James and Mrs. Woolf." In *The Magic Circle of Henry James: Essays in Honor of Darshan Singh Maini*, edited by Amritjit Singh and K. Ayyappa Paniker, 285–293. New York: Envoy Press, 1989.

Lapsley, Gaillard. *The Country Palatine of Durham: A Study in Constitutional History*. Cambridge: Harvard University Press, 1924.

————. *Crown, Community, and Parliament in the Later Middle Ages: Studies in English Constitutional History*. Edited by Helen M. Cam and Geoffrey Barraclough. Studies in Mediaeval History, vol. 6. Oxford: Blackwell, 1951.

————. "Tradition at Harvard." *University of California Magazine*, November 1902, 357–365.

————, ed. *An Essay on the House of Commons by D. Pasquet*. Translated by R. G. D. Laffan. With preface and notes by Gaillard Lapsley. Cambridge, England: University Press, 1925.

————, ed. With H. D. Hazeltime and P. H. Winfield. *Frederic William Maitland: Selected Essays*. Freeport, N.Y.: Books for Libraries Press, 1968.

Lears, T. J. Jackson. *No Place of Grace: Antimodernism and the Transformation of American Culture, 1880–1920*. New York: Pantheon, 1981.

Levis, Larry. "Our Sister of Perfect Solitude." *The Widening Spell of the Leaves*. 39–43. Ithaca: Cornell University Press, 1991.

Lewis, R. W. B. *The American Adam: Innocence, Tragedy, and Tradition in the Nineteenth Century*. Chicago: Chicago University Press, 1955.

————. *Edith Wharton: A Biography*. New York: Fromm International Publishing, 1985.

————. *The Jameses: A Family Narrative*. New York: Farrar, Straus, and Giroux, 1991.

Loving, Jerome. "The Death of Romance: Lily Bart and the 1908 *Portrait of a Lady*." In *The Other Romance*, edited by Donald Pease and Jeffrey Ruben-Dorsky. Forthcoming.

Lubbock, Percy. *The Craft of Fiction*. New York: Peter Smith, 1947.

————. *Earlham*. London: Lowe and Brydone, 1922; Jonathan Cape, 1963.

————. *Elizabeth Barrett Browning in Her Letters*. London: Smith, Elder, 1906.

————. *George Calderon: A Sketch from Memory*. London: Grant Richard, 1921.

————. *Mary Cholmondeley: A Sketch from Memory*. London: Jonathan Cape, 1928.

————. *Portrait of Edith Wharton*. New York and London: Appleton-Century-Crofts, 1947.

————. *The Region Cloud*. New York: Charles Scribner's Sons, 1925.

————. *Roman Pictures*. New York: Charles Scribner's Sons, 1923.

————. *Shades of Eton*. London: Jonathan Cape, 1929.

Lubbock, Lady Sybil. *The Child in the Crystal*. London: Jonathan Cape, 1939.

————. *On Ancient Ways: A Winter Journey*. London: Jonathan Cape, 1928.

————. With the Earl of Desart. *A Page from the Past*. London: Jonathan Cape, 1936.

Lutz, Tom. *American Nervousness, 1903: An Anecdotal History*. Ithaca: Cornell University Press, 1991.

MacCarthy, Desmond. *Portraits*. London: Douglas Saunders with MacGibbon & Kee, 1955.

Marcus, Jane, ed. *Virginia Woolf and Bloomsbury*. Bloomington: Indiana University Press, 1987.

Mariano, Nicky. *Forty Years with Berenson*. London: Hamish Hamilton, 1966.

McDowell, Margaret B. "*Hudson River Bracketed* and *The Gods Arrive*." In *Edith Wharton*, edited by Harold Bloom, 51–63. New York: Chelsea House, 1986.

Mellow, James. *Charmed Circle*. New York: Praeger Publishers, 1974.

Michaels, Walter Benn. *The Gold Standard and the Logic of Naturalism: American Literature at the Turn of the Century*. Berkeley: University of California Press, 1987.

Miller, Nancy K. *The Heroine's Text: Readings in the French and English Novel, 1722–1782*. New York: Columbia University Press, 1980.

Morra, Umberto. *Conversations with Berenson*. Boston: Houghton Mifflin, 1965.

Mudge, Bradford K. "Exiled as Exiler: Sara Coleridge, Virginia Woolf, and the Politics of Literary Revision." In *Women's Writing in Exile*, edited by Mary Lynn Broe and Angela Ingram, 199–224. Chapel Hill and London: University of North Carolina Press, 1989.

Nicolson, Nigel. "Bloomsbury: The Myth and the Reality." In *Virginia Woolf and Bloomsbury*, edited by Jane Marcus. Bloomington: Indiana University Press, 1987.

Norton, Charles Eliot. *Notes of Travel and Study in Italy*. Boston, 1859.

Olin-Ammentorp, Julie. "Edith Wharton's Challenge to Feminist Criticism." *Studies in American Fiction* 16 (Autumn 1988): 237–244.

O'Toole, Patricia. *The Five of Hearts: An Intimate Portrait of Henry Adams and His Friends, 1880–1918*. New York: Clarkson Potter, 1990.

Peirce, Charles Sanders. *Values in a Universe of Chance: Selected Writings of Charles S. Peirce*. Edited by Phillip P. Wiener. New York: Dover, 1966.

Person, Leland S. "Henry James, George Sand, and the Suspense of Masculinity." *PMLA* 106 (May 1991): 515–529.

Porter, Katherine Anne. "Gertrude Stein: A Self-Portrait." *Harper's*, December 1947, 519–527.

Posnick, Ross. *Henry James and the Problem of Robert Browning*. Athens: University of Georgia Press, 1985.

Potter, Vincent G. *Charles S. Peirce: On Norms and Ideals*. Worcester: University of Massachusetts Press, 1967.

Powers, Lyall H. *Henry James and the Naturalist Movement*. Lansing: Michigan State University Press, 1971.

Pratt, Annis. With Barbara White, Andrea Lowenstein, and Mary Wyer. *Archetypal Patterns in Women's Fiction*. Bloomington: Indiana University Press, 1981.

Price, Alan. "Edith Wharton at War with the American Red Cross: The End of *Noblesse Oblige*." *Women's Studies* 20 (December 1991): 121–132.

———. "Writing Home from the Front: Edith Wharton and Dorothy Canfield Fisher Present Wartime France to the United States: 1917–1919." *Edith Wharton Newsletter* 5 (Fall 1988): 1–5, 8.

Radden, Jennifer. "Defining Self-Deception." *Dialogue* 23 (March 1984): 103–120.

Richter, Harvena. *Virginia Woolf: The Inward Voyage*. Princeton: Princeton University Press, 1970.

Roosevelt, Theodore. *The Strenuous Life*. London: Putnam, 1902.

Rosenbaum, S. P., ed. *The Bloomsbury Group: A Collection of Memories, Commentary and Criticism*. Toronto and Buffalo: University of Toronto Press, 1975.

Russ, Joanna. "What Can a Heroine Do? Or Why Women Can't Write." In *Images of Women in Fiction: Feminist Perspectives*, edited by Susan Koppelman Cornillon, 3–20. Bowling Green: Bowling Green University Popular Press, 1972; rev. ed. 1973.

Ryan, Mary P. *The Empire of the Mother: American Writing about Domesticity, 1830–1860*. New York and London: Harrington Park Press, 1985.

Samuels, Ernest. *Bernard Berenson: The Making of a Connoisseur*. Cambridge: Harvard University Press, Belknap Press, 1979.

———. With Jayne Newcomer Samuels. *Bernard Berenson: The Making of a Legend*. Cambridge: Harvard University Press, Belknap Press, 1987.

Santayana, George. *Persons and Places: Fragments of Autobiography*. Edited by W. G. Holzberger and H. J. Saatkamp, Jr. The Works of George Santayana, vol. 1. Cambridge, MA: MIT Press, 1986.

Schwarz, Daniel R. *The Humanistic Heritage: Critical Theories of the English Novel from James to Hillis Miller*. Philadelphia: University of Pennsylvania Press, 1986.

Secor, Robert. "Henry James and Violet Hunt, the 'Improper Person of Babylon.'" *Journal of Modern Literature* 13 (March 1986): 3–36.

Secrest, Meryle. *Being Bernard Berenson: A Biography*. New York: Holt, Rinehart & Winston, 1979.

Sedgwick, Eve Kosofsky. "The Beast in the Closet: James and the Writing of Homosexual Panic." In *Speaking of Gender*, edited by Elaine Showalter, 243–268. New York and London: Routledge, 1989.

———. *Between Men: English Literature and Male Homosocial Desire*. New York: Columbia University Press, 1985.

Sensibar, Judith. "Edith Wharton Reads the Bachelor Type: Her Critique of Modernism's Representative Man." *American Literature* 60 (December 1988): 575–590.

Seymour, Miranda. *A Ring of Conspirators: Henry James and His Literary Circle, 1895–1915*. Boston: Houghton Mifflin, 1989.

Showalter, Elaine. "The Death of a Lady (Novelist): Wharton's *House of Mirth*." *Representations* 9 (1985): 133–149.

Silve, Claude. *Benediction*. Translated by Robert Norton. New York and London: D. Appleton-Century, 1936.

Silver, Brenda R. *Virginia Woolf's Reading Notebooks*. Princeton: Princeton University Press, 1983.

Simpson, Colin. *Artful Partners: Bernard Berenson and Joseph Duveen*. New York: Macmillan, 1986.

Singley, Carol. "Gothic Borrowings and Innovations in Edith Wharton's 'A Bottle of Perrier.'" In *Edith Wharton: New Critical Essays*, edited by Alfred Bendixen and Annette Zilversmit. New York: Garland Publishing, 1992.

Sitwell, Edith. *Taken Care of: The Autobiography of Edith Sitwell*. New York: Atheneum, 1965.

Smith, Allan Gardiner. "Edith Wharton and the Ghost Story." In *Gender and Literary Voice*, edited by Janet Todd, 149–159. New York: Holmes & Meier, 1980.

Spacks, Patricia Meyer. *Gossip*. New York: Alfred A. Knopf, 1985.

Spender, Stephen. *World within World*. New York: Harcourt, Brace, 1951.

Stein, Gertrude. *Lectures in America*. New York: Random House, 1935.

———. *Paris France*. New York: Charles Scribner's, 1940.

Stimpson, Catharine R. *Where the Meanings Are*. New York and London: Methuen, 1989.

Stocking, George W., Jr. *Victorian Anthropology*. New York: Free Press, 1987.

Storr, Anthony. *Solitude: A Return to the Self*. New York: Free Press, 1988.

Stowell, H. Peter. *Literary Impressionism, James and Chekov*. Athens: University of Georgia Press, 1980.

Sturgis, Howard. *All That Was Possible: Being the Record of a Summer in the Life of Mrs. Sybil Crofts, Comedian*. New York and London: G. P. Putnam Sons, 1906.

———. "Anne Isabella Thackeray (Lady Ritchie)." *Cornhill Magazine* 47 (November 1919): 449–467.

———. *Belchamber*. New York: Howard Fetig, 1976.

———. "On the Pottlecombe Cornice." *Fortnightly Review* 89 (January–June 1908): 550–564.

———. *Tim*. London and New York: Macmillan, 1891.

Suleiman, Susan Rubin. "Writing and Motherhood." In *The (M)other Tongue: Essays in Feminist Pschoanalytic Interpretation*, edited by Shirley Nelson Garner, Clare Kahane, and Madelon Sprengnether, 352–377. Ithaca and London: Cornell University Press, 1985.

Tarbell, Ida M. *The Business of Being a Woman*. New York: Macmillan, 1912.

Tintner, Adeline. "Mothers, Daughters, and Incest in the Late Novels of Edith Wharton." In *The Lost Tradition: Mothers and Daughters in Literature*, edited by Cathy N. Davidson and E. M. Broner. New York: Frederick Unger, 1980.

Tuan, Yi-Fu. *Space and Place: The Perspective of Experience*. Minneapolis: University of Minnesota Press, 1977.

Tuttleton, James. "The Feminist Takeover of Edith Wharton." *New Criterion* 7 (March 1989): 6–14.

Veeser, H. Aram, ed. *The New Historicism*. New York and London: Routledge, 1989.

Vita-Finzi, Penelope. *Edith Wharton and the Art of Fiction*. New York: St. Martin's Press, 1990.

Waid, Candace. "Introduction." In *The Custom of the Country*, by Edith Wharton. New York: Signet, 1989.

———. *Edith Wharton's Letters from the Underworld*. Chapel Hill and London: University of North Carolina Press, 1991.

Watson, Peter. "Hard Times at Harvard's Tuscan Outpost." *New York Times*, September 6, 1992, 25.

Wharton, Edith. *The Age of Innocence*. New York: Macmillan, 1987.

———. *A Backward Glance*. New York: Charles Scribner's Sons, 1985.

———. *The Collected Short Stories of Edith Wharton*. Edited by R. W. B. Lewis. 2 vols. New York: Charles Scribner's Sons, 1968.

————. "The Criticism of Fiction." *Times Literary Supplement*, May 14, 1916, 229–230.

————. *The Custom of the Country*. New York: Penguin, 1987.

————. *Ethan Frome and Other Short Fiction by Edith Wharton*. New York: Macmillan, 1987.

————. *French Ways and Their Meaning*. New York: D. Appleton, 1919.

————. *The Fruit of the Tree*. New York: Charles Scribner's Sons, 1907.

————. *The Gods Arrive*. New York: Appleton-Century-Crofts, 1962.

————. "Henry James in His Letters." *Quarterly Review* 234 (1920): 188–202.

————. *The House of Mirth*. New York: Charles Scribner's Sons, 1905.

————. *Hudson River Bracketed*. New York: Charles Scribner's Sons, 1985.

————. *Italian Backgrounds*. New York: Charles Scribner's Sons, 1905.

————. "Kerfol." In Edith Wharton, *The Ghost Stories of Edith Wharton*, edited by Alfred Bendixen, 70–102. New York: Charles Scribner's Sons, 1990.

————. *The Letters of Edith Wharton*. Edited by R. W. B. Lewis and Nancy Lewis. New York: Charles Scribner's Sons, 1988.

————. *A Motor-Flight through France*. New York: Charles Scribner's Sons, 1908.

————. "Mr. Sturgis's *Belchamber*." *Bookman* 21 (May 1905): 309.

————. *The Reef*. New York: Charles Scribner's Sons, 1912.

————. *Summer*. New York: Macmillan, 1987.

————. "Summer Afternoon." *Scribner's Magazine*, March 1911, 278.

————. *Twilight Sleep*. New York and London: D. Appleton, 1927.

————. "The Vice of Reading." *North American Review* 177 (October 1903): 513–521.

————. "Visibility in Fiction." *Yale Review* (March 1929): 480–488.

————. *The Writing of Fiction*. New York: Charles Scribner's Sons, 1925.

————. With the collaboration of Ogden Codman. *The Decoration of Houses*. New York: Charles Scribner's Sons, 1897.

White, Barbara. *Edith Wharton: A Study of the Short Fiction*. New York: Twayne, 1991.

————. "Edith Wharton's *Summer* and Women's Fiction." *Essays in Literature* 11.2 (Fall 1984): 223–235.

Williams, Raymond. *Culture and Society*. London: Chatto & Windus, 1958.

————. *The Sociology of Culture*. New York: Schocken Books, 1982.

Winnicott, D. W. "The Capacity to Be Alone." In *The Maturational Processes and the Facilitating Environment*. London: Hogarth Press, 1965.

Wolff, Cynthia Griffin. *A Feast of Words: The Triumph of Edith Wharton*. New York: Oxford University Press, 1977.

————. "Lily Bart and the Beautiful Death." *American Literature* 46 (1974): 16–40.

Wolff, Geoffrey. *Black Sun: The Brief Transit and Violent Eclipse of Harry Crosby*. New York: Random House, 1976.

Woolf, Leonard. *Downhill All the Way: An Autobiography of the Years 1919–1939*. New York: Harcourt, Brace & World, 1967.

————. *Sowing: An Autobiography of the Years 1880 to 1904*. London: Hogarth Press, 1960.

Woolf, Virginia. "American Fiction." *Saturday Review of Literature* 2 (1925): 1–3.

————. *Books and Portraits: Some Further Selections from the Literary and Biographical Writings of Virginia Woolf.* Edited by Mary Lyon. New York: Harcourt Brace Jovanovich, 1977.

————. *A Change of Perspective: The Letters of Virginia Woolf.* Edited by Nigel Nicolson and Joanne Trautman. 6 vols. London: Hogarth Press, 1975–1980.

————. *Collected Essays.* Edited by Leonard Woolf. 4 vols. New York: Harcourt Brace Jovanovich, 1967.

————. *The Common Reader.* London: Hogarth Press, 1925.

————. *The Diary of Virginia Woolf.* Edited by Anne Oliver Bell. 5 vols. New York and London: Harcourt Brace Jovanovich, 1977–1984.

————. *The Essays of Virginia Woolf.* Edited by Andrew McNeillie. 3 vols. New York: Harcourt Brace Jovanovich, 1986–1989.

————. "*The House of Mirth.*" *Guardian*, November 15, 1905, 1940.

————. "The Method of Henry James." *Times Literary Supplement*, December 26, 1918, 655.

————. "Modern Novels." *Times Literary Supplement*, April 10, 1919, 189–190.

————. *Moments of Being: Unpublished Autobiographical Writings.* Edited by Jeanne Schulkind. Sussex: University Press, 1976; revised and rpt., Hogarth Press, 1985.

————. *Mr. Bennet and Mrs. Brown.* London: Hogarth Press, 1928.

————. "Mr. Henry James's Last Novel." *Guardian*, February 22, 1905, 339.

————. *A Room of One's Own.* New York and London: Harcourt Brace Jovanovich, 1957.

————. *A Writer's Diary: Being Extracts from the Diary of Virginia Woolf.* Edited by Leonard Woolf. New York: Harcourt, Brace, 1954.

Yeazell, Ruth Bernard. *The Death and Letters of Alice James.* Berkeley: University of California Press, 1981.

Zilversmit, Annette. "Edith Wharton's Last Ghosts." *College Literature* 4 (Fall 1987): 296–304.

MANUSCRIPT COLLECTIONS

Percy Lubbock Papers, Beinecke Rare Book and Manuscript Library, Yale University, New Haven, Connecticut.

Edith Wharton Collection, Beinecke Rare Book and Manuscript Library, Yale University, New Haven, Connecticut.

Henry James Collection, Houghton Library, Harvard University, Cambridge, Massachusetts.

Gaillard Lapsley Collection, Trinity College, Cambridge University, England.

Index